# CARS
## OF THE FASCINATING '40s

### A DECADE OF CHALLENGES AND CHANGES

Publications International, Ltd.

Louis Weber, CEO
Publications International, Ltd.
7373 North Cicero Avenue
Lincolnwood, Illinois 60712

Manufactured in China.

8 7 6 5 4 3 2 1

ISBN: 0-7853-6274-6

# Acknowledgements

Chapter Introduction Illustrations: Frank Peiler

**PHOTOGRAPHY**
*The editors gratefully acknowledge the cooperation of the following people who supplied photography to help make this book possible:*

**DaimlerChrysler Historical Collection**; Doug Mitchel; Chan Bush; Vince Manocchi; **Motor Vehicle Manufacturers Association**; **Ford Photographic**; Nicky Wright; Milton Kieft; Thomas Glatch; Sam Griffith; **GM Photographic**; David Temple; Richard Spiegelman; Bud Juneau; Dan Lyons; **Oldsmobile History Center**; Scott Brandt; W.C. Waymack; Fergus Hernandes; Gary Smith; Richard Quinn; David Gooley; Joseph H. Wherry; Jerry Heasley; Don Heiny; Terry Burton; Bert Johnson; Denis L. Tanney; Gary Cameron; Jim Thompson; Jay Peck; Jim Frenak; Tom Storm; Reed Hutchinson; Cassie Stone; Joe Bohovic; Jeff Johnson; Nina Padgett-Russin; **George C. Marshall Research Foundation**; Steve Johnson; **American Automobile Manufacturers Association**; Ed Goldberger; Richard Spiegelman; Alan Hewko de Christopher; Phil Toy; **Jack Thompson Oldsmobile, Inc.**; Steve Statham; Dick Sherer; **Zoom Photo**; Peggy Dyer; Scott Baxter; Rick Lenz; **Studebaker National Museum**; Roland Flessner; Hub Wilson; Tom Shaw; Bill Corby; Mike Mueller; Neil Nissing; Jeff Rose; David Newhardt; **Michigan State Police**; Tom Buchkoe; Morton Oppenheimer; **Richard M. Langworth Auto History Collection**; William A. Coby.

**OWNERS**
*Special thanks to the owners of the cars featured in this book for their enthusiastic cooperation. They are listed below:*

**1940:** Ray Pfeiffer; Monty G. Ostberg; Ralph Neubauer; Jim and Mary Shanahan; S. Ray Miller; Dick Colarossi; Thomas Venezia; Robert N. Seiple; Robert M. Jarrett; Thomas F. Lerch; Domino's Classic Cars; Val Price; Joe Consalvo; Richard Krist; Annette and Dan Darling; Rod Miller; Tom West; Shirley and Gene Heller; Basil Lewis; Ronald Ray Lipang; Terry Radey; Ray Menefee; Bobby Wiggins; Jim Miller; William Giembroniewicz; Tom Meleo; Mick Thrasher; Bob Briggs; Larry Lange; Alan Baumer; Eldon and Esta Hostetler; David Reidy; Francis Frisch; Robert V. Russell; David Holls; Steve Hipsak; Sam LaRove, Jr.; Les Ludwig; Bob and Phyllis Leach; Wesley Lantz; Gregg Smith.

**1941:** Gerald J. DePersio; Blackhawk Collection; Robert W. Paige; James K. Buffington; Robert Brelsford; Farnum Alston; Robert McAfee; Joe Moss; Donald E. Desing; Vito Ranks; Frank Donnelly; Harry A. DeMenge; Oceanside Police Officer's Association; Jerry Schlorff; Fred C. Fischer; Lloyd Duzell; Phil Wilder; Jewell Thomas; Dean Hammond; Phillip and Nancy Hoffman; Clay Nichols; David Holls; Jack Karleskind; Ed Rouge; Rene M. Hoenscheid; Rick and Joanne Scheffel; Jim Mueller; James H. Bowersox; Ben and Alice Oliver; Robert S. Montgomery; William Schwanbeck; Mike Kaminsky; Dick Pyle; E.R. Bufkin; Robert Sauenschell; Hannes Schachtner; Thomas B. Smiley; William Lockwood; Bill Goodsene; Dave Doud; Paul F. Miller; John Poochigan; Richard DeVecchi; Bob Briggs; Carlo Cola; Paul A. Jacobs; Terry Johnson; Lee Greer; Kyle J. Wood; Bernie Hackett; Mr. and Mrs. John Blackowski; Ross Helko; William D. Albright; Edward C. Brehm; Robert Loudon; Marvin E. Yount, Jr.; Ralph Geissler; John Shanahan; Paul Hem; John Kepich; Eugene T. Luning; Gene L. Kappel; Edward Bratton; Edward and Arlene Cobb; Wilbert Endres; Ed Barwick; Buzz and Fran Beckman; James P. Manak; Jim Chernock; Tom Hincz; John F. Hare; Ron and Debbie Ladley.

**1942:** Robert Brelsford; Art Astor; Joseph Leia Memorial Auto; Dr. R. Leia; Raymond J. Reis, Sr.; William H. Leonhardt; Robert Reeves; Dr. Irv Warren; Norman and Joyce Booth; Charlene Neyer; Harry Wynn; Al Wilkiewicz; Lewis Jenkins; Domino's Collection; Arnie Addison; Dr. Gerald M. Levitt; David A. Aiken; Chris Lapp;

Roger A. James; Fairway Chevrolet; Harold Sage; Glenn Eisenhamer; Bill Lauer; Ken Poynter; Terry Davies; Wilmer E. and Lila Walker; James R. Lauzon; George Augeston; Robert and Sandi Kostka; Thomas Barratt III.

**1943-1945:** Dick Tait; Michael Hall; Dale P. Allyward; Jay Koblenz.

**1946:** Lloyd and Martha Mayes; Ralph G. McQuoid; Vincent Daul; Suburban Motors; Wayne Kidd; Joe Abela; Chip Turtzo; Donald Passardi; Richard Kughn; Nick Alexander; Erik Akins; John Andreason; Joel Prescott; Fairway Chevrolet; Bill Wendelaar; Whitney and Diane Haist; Ralph M. Johnson; Jack Miller; Everett and Mona Shoemaker; Vern Ellis; Emily Tax and Roger Nichols; Arthur D. Gloss; Commander Marr; Paul Garrell; Peter Welch.

**1947:** Robert N. Carlson; Blaine Jenkins; Tony Yenne; David W. Truax; Carroll and Dawn Bramble; Tom Morgan; Blaine Jenkins; Tony Donna; Richard Wayne Durham; Bob Zarnowski; Herman W. Cox; Joe and Chris Jelinski; Leonard Shaw; Bill Schwanbeck; Phil Kuhn, Chicago Car Exchange; Chuck and Mark Vandervelde; Roy A. Schneider; Walter E. Herman; Harry Nicks; Elmer F. Brown; Harold D. Evans; Mark Sherman; Louis and Inez Nosse; Jim and Mary Ashworth; Larry and Jan Malone; Roger Kash; Charles Regnerus; Jack C. Miller; Jerry and Adell Laurin; National Automobile Museum; Harvey Hedgecock; Mike Moore; Ken Havekost; Rosemarie Hansen; Neil Torrence; Donald W. Curtis; Jerry Wuichet; Robert McAfee; Roger W. Lamm; Raymond E. Dade; Terry Silcoy; Tom Stackhouse; Bob Johnson; Gary Loomer; Jim Hull; Ronald and Sonya Halbauer; National Automobile Museum; Stanton P. Belland.

**1948:** Nicholas and Margaret LaCosta; Ed Gunther; Al Adams; Robert H. Miller; Garfield Button; Henry Smith; Robert Bradley; Gary L. Faulk; Jim Laverdiere; Richard O. Matson; Larry and Beverly Bowman; Dr. Roger Leir; Art Astor; Jack L. Kaylor; Paul J. Ravenna; Tom L. Carver; Suburban Motors; Ronald Szymanowski; Dick Pyle; George Ball; Unique Motor Cars; Jerry Windle; S. Ray Miller, Jr.; Richard Staley; Jack Bart; Thomas F. Lerch; Ron Bransky; Nick Alexander; Bud Juneau; Larry Klein; Dr. Steven Colsen; Blaine Jenkins; Tom Meleo; Bobby Wiggins; Willam and Joseph Schoenbeck; Dick McKean; Terry Knight; James E. Cafarelli; Gerald Quam; Donald Jensen; Bud Dutton; Angelo Finaldi; Peter M. Krakowski; Mike Callahan; Chris and Pete Jakubowski; Garry McGee; John Otto; Ed and Edna Brown; Jim Mueller; Arthur J. Sabin; Neil S. Black; Richard Brune; Ken Havekost; Jim Dworschack; Sharon Hielefeldt; Lloyd DeWester; Kenneth Koehler; Gordon Blixt; Ed Goldberger; William H. Lauer; Herb Rathman and Ted Davidson; Terri Gardner; Jeremy M. Janss; Erica Tenney; Burt Van Flue; Bev Ferreira; Melvin R. Mull; Dave Cammack; David Marshall; H. Robert and Kathryn Stamp; B.C. Pyle; Petersen Automotive Museum; Autoputer, Inc.; John H. Horning; Ben Rose.

**1949:** Russel A. Liechty; John Oliver; John G. Oliver III; John Spring, MD; Harry A. DeMenge; Robert Wagner; Larry Martin; Verl D. Mowery; Monty Ostberg; George Adams; Glenn Eisenhamer; Dean Skinner; Myron Davis; Tom Moon; Jack Buchanan; William Baumgartner; Benjamin R. Caskey; Dan and Audrey Kaiser; Richard L. Youngman; Don Morris; Ken Hutchinson; Bob Ward; Rader's Relics; Bob Getsfried; Bud Juneau; Bob Brelsford; Larry Martin; David Doyle; Suburban Motors, Inc.; Ed Gunther; Don Reel; Tenny Natkin; Myron Reichert; Raymond Silva, Jr.; Sam Turner; Bobby Wiggins; Bill Halliday; Joe Gergits; Ron Haulman; Glenn D. Kelly; Dr. John Joseph D'Attilio; Mrs. Penny Casteele; John A. Beekman; Anthony and Eloise Wells; Donald Sharp; Chevs 'n Vettes, Inc. of Scottsdale; Dick Choler; Press and Janet Kale; Bill Hill; W.E. Davis; John Segedy; Bill Hubert; Bill Reinhardt; Edward L. Hess; Thomas A. Hoffman; Ray Tomb; Charles Newton; Sonny and Mari Glasbrenner; David A. Baird; Donald and Phyllis Bueter; Eugene and Catherine Thomas; Ruben Polanco; Roland Olm; Woody World; Classic Showcase; Dr. Carlos E. Aviles; National Motor Museum; Duffy and Kelly Nopenz; Marty Chung; Danny L. Steine; David Hill.

# Table of Contents

As the war intensified in Europe, the Great Depression was starting to ease in the U.S. Car sales were picking up—too late for the automakers that had gone under in the '30s. Lincoln built the first Continental and Oldsmobile offered Hydra-Matic, the first factory automatic transmission.

High demand and government contracts brought profits to the U.S. auto industry. War was imminent, so automakers were gearing up for wartime production. America was drawn into the war after Japan attacked Pearl Harbor in December. Automakers still made cars, but not for long.

All U.S. automakers sold "blackout" specials after January 1, then halted automobile production completely by February 10. Automotive plants turned to the production of war materiel. World War II ended the Depression, but the early stages of the war didn't go well for the Allies.

Factories welcomed women to work as U.S. industry became the "arsenal of democracy," the automakers taking the lead. Only a few hundred cars were built during the war—all for military use. The Allies won the war in August 1945, and automakers scrambled to resume car production.

# 1946

GIs came home and started building their lives, sparking inflation and an auto sellers' market. The cars were warmed-over '42s, but they sold anyway. Not all was rosy for the automakers: GM was hit by a strike, Ford had financial troubles, and materials shortages plagued the industry.

# 1947

While cars from the Big Three changed very little, Studebaker and newcomer Kaiser-Frazer issued the first true postwar car designs. The sellers' market prompted imports to trickle in and other independents to sprout up, but most soon failed. The world mourned Henry Ford's death in April.

# 1948

Preston Tucker intended to take on the Big Three but was thwarted and convicted of fraud. Hudson introduced its "Step-Down" models, while Ford, Cadillac, and Olds offered new models midyear, Ford's as '49s. The slab-sided, envelope bodies, represented the latest step in automotive design.

# 1949

America was moving to suburbia as the sellers' market began to wane. All of the Big Three had new cars for '49, which hurt the independents. Cadillac and Olds introduced revolutionary V-8 engines, GM offered the first hardtops, and station wagons traded wood bodies for steel.

# Foreword

Imagine your life without the computer you use at work every day, the car you drive to get there, the television you watch every night, or the energy that powers all the gadgets around your home. All of these items were invented or significantly developed in a decade that also witnessed America play an important role in winning a world war, then emerge as a world superpower.

If you had to pinpoint a time period as the start of life as it's lived today, a strong case could be made for the 1940s. More than half a century removed from that seemingly distant decade, our lives are still shaped by its ideas and inventions.

For instance, what could be more essential to today's technological world than the computer? (The very words you're reading were composed on one.) The first electronic computer was created in 1946. The transistor, which would eventually make things like computers and televisions more efficient, was invented by Bell Laboratories in 1947. And what *of* television? After years of experimen-

tation, the first commercial stations in the U.S. were operating by 1941; the first "network season" as we know it began in 1948.

The desperation of warfare has always spurred innovation and the 1940s, riven by the most terrible war ever, saw the first practical applications of numerous technologies. The scientific legacy of World War II includes jet aircraft, radar, and nuclear energy.

Society, too, has links that trace back to the 1940s. To this day, countries attempt to resolve their differences in the United Nations. When that fails, though, the western democracies circle their wagons under the banner of the North Atlantic Treaty Organization. The stout walls that divided Americans of different races began to show cracks when two of the nation's most visible institutions—the armed services and Major League baseball—were integrated. The GI Bill of Rights extended education and housing assistance to American war veterans. Some headed off to college, swelling enrollments and making the pursuit of higher education a more-egalitarian ideal; others trooped out of the cities to homes in newly developed

suburbs, intent on raising families of—bless 'em or curse 'em—"baby boomers."

One reward to which Americans felt entitled after enduring economic deprivation in the 1930s and global war in the '40s was a new automobile. Cars were no more immune to innovation than anything else, and many of the breakthroughs made in the '40s have stood the test of time.

The quest for improved driving ease took a huge step forward when Oldsmobile introduced the fully automatic Hydra-Matic transmission in its 1940 models. Today, automatics are in the vast majority of vehicles sold in America. So, too, high-compression engines. Cadillac and Olds pioneered the type in 1949 with overhead-valve V-8s that put a new emphasis on horsepower. Even though many engines today have been cut back to four or six cylinders, they owe much to these designs.

Bold new styling directions after the war from Ford, General Motors, Studebaker, and newcomer Kaiser-Frazer redefined what a car should look like. "Envelope" bodies rendered separate fenders and running boards obsolete. Brighter, sealed-beam headlamps became standard; and large,

curved, one-piece windshields were beginning to be installed. Nash studied aerodynamic principles in the design of its '49 Airflyte models. Steel-bodied station wagons from Plymouth, General Motors, and Willys (the last related to the wartime 4×4 jeep) brought a whole new degree of utility within reach of more motorists without the high price and maintenance needs of old-style wood-bodied wagons.

Even the automotive culture changed in the 1940s in ways we still recognize. Consider that the National Association for Stock Car Auto Racing (NASCAR) started sanctioning races in 1948. New publications devoted to cars included *Road & Track* (1947), *Hot Rod* (1948), and *Motor Trend* (1949).

*Cars of the '40s: A Decade of Challenges and Changes* celebrates a remarkable era whose ideas, inventions, and, yes, automobiles, shape our lives today.

7

Prosperity wasn't quite around the corner just yet, but as 1940 emerged, the Great Depression was finally beginning to ease. A deep recession in 1937-38 had shot the economy down another notch. Little by little, though, more Americans were working and earning enough to buy products, including automobiles. America's gross national product (GNP) was 60 percent higher in '39 than it had been in '33, at the low point of the Depression. Translating that growth to dollars in the hands of ordinary workers was a slow process, but at last the economic future was looking positive.

Outside the U.S., on the other hand, the world was looking bleak. A few months earlier, in September 1939, Hitler's army had invaded Poland, inducing Britain and France to declare war on Germany. In spring 1940, Hitler spread his tentacles into additional Western European countries, including France. Italy, under Fascist dictator Benito Mussolini, joined with Germany to form the Axis powers. Hitler now controlled virtually all of Western Europe, with the exception of Britain.

America officially remained neutral, and isolationist sentiment was strong. A December 1939 poll had shown that two-thirds of Americans were opposed to taking sides in the European conflict.

Everyday life continued as before, for the most part, and those who had a few extra nickels to spend had plenty of possibilities. *Gone With the Wind*, based on Margaret Mitchell's popular Civil War novel, had premiered late in 1939. The epic tale entranced movie audiences throughout '40, centering on scheming Scarlett O'Hara (Vivien Leigh) and dashing Rhett Butler (Clark Gable).

Charlie Chaplin released *The Great Dictator*, featuring himself playing a parody version of Adolf Hitler named Adenoid Hynkel. Mickey Rooney ranked as Hollywood's most-popular movie star on a list that included the likes of Spencer Tracy, Clark Gable, Tyrone Power, James Cagney, and Judy Garland.

On the radio, Wee Bonnie Baker sang *Oh, Johnny! Oh!* in her little-girl voice, one of the top tunes of the 1940 "Hit Parade," along with *South of the Border, When You Wish Upon a Star*, and a curiosity called *The Woodpecker Song*. Young Americans, lured by big bands and swing music, jitterbugged their way around the nation's dance floors. Their parents might prefer the Lambeth Walk, a dance that had made its way to America from England. But "hepcats" of the time were leaning toward Benny Goodman, Gene Krupa, and Count Basie, or to the other serious jazz sounds that were brewing.

Families often gathered around the console radio in the evening to listen to such programs as *Gangbusters* or *Amos 'n Andy*, or to enjoy the antics of Charlie McCarthy and his ventriloquist friend, Edgar Bergen. Younger listeners might have preferred *Little Orphan Annie* or *Jack Armstrong, the All-American Boy*. Television had been exhibited at the 1939 New York World's Fair, but few consumers would be buying sets until another decade passed.

Women might find a pair of the new nylon stockings—with noticeable seams running up the back—at the local department store. Introduced by the DuPont company late in 1939, stockings were among the first applications of this miraculous new substance—the first totally man-made fiber.

Automobile production was growing, after several weak seasons during the 1930s. Americans had purchased barely more than 2 million new cars in 1938, but total output grew to nearly 3.7 million in 1940.

Following a series of difficult labor actions during the late 1930s, the United Auto Workers Union was stronger than ever. Labor unions, in general, were on an upward

swing, but additional battles had yet to be waged.

During the 1930s, independent automakers had faded out of the picture, one by one. Auburn, Cord, Duesenberg, Pierce-Arrow, Franklin, Marmon—all vanished into history. By 1939, the Big Three automakers accounted for 90 percent of sales and only a handful of significant independent car manufacturers remained.

This would be the last year for LaSalle—a less-costly cousin to Cadillac—and for the "sharknose" Graham. New 1940 models included the Graham Hollywood and similar Hupp (Hupmobile) Skylark, both of which used body dies from the defunct Cord. Neither would last through a complete second season.

Ford Motor Company launched the first Lincoln Continental in 1940, bringing a European look to the American automotive scene. Equipped with a V-12 engine, the Continental was based on a car that Edsel Ford, son of Henry and the president of the company, had ordered created for himself as a "Florida car." Friends were so impressed with the shapely two-door that Edsel had his executives look into production.

Cadillac offered its last V-16 engine in 1940. Near the opposite end of the size spectrum, the Crosley minicar was in its second season. So were Mercury—a cousin to Ford but aimed at a slightly more-affluent audience—and the low-budget Studebaker Champion.

Oldsmobile earned the technology prize for 1940 with its new Hydra-Matic transmission—the first fully automatic transmission offered on a regular-production model.

"Woody" station wagons, made of actual wood, were issued by several manufacturers. Convertible sedans were still around, but not for long.

Powered convertible tops were beginning to trickle into the market, having been introduced on 1939 Plymouths. Nearly all American cars now had steering-column-mounted gearshifts, with Ford being the last major automaker to make the change from a floor-mounted lever.

Unpopular or not, American involvement in the European war seemed inevitable. In his 1940 State of the Union address, President Franklin Delano Roosevelt asked Congress for $1.8 billion for a military buildup—the largest sum ever spent in peacetime. A poll taken in May 1940 revealed an easing of isolationist thought. Two-thirds of Americans now favored aid to Britain in its looming battle with German forces. FDR asked Congress for almost $5 billion more, and requested manufacturers to boost production of airplanes dramatically.

Although Jeeps and Willys are considered almost synonymous, partly because of Willys-Overland's emergence into civilian Jeep production after World War II, the original light military cars were actually produced by three companies. The American Bantam Car Company, Ford Motor Company, and Willys-Overland all won contracts to design the four-wheel-drive general purpose vehicle that would become known as the Jeep. American Bantam came closest to the mark the government had set, but Ford actually designed the trademark flat grille. American Bantam produced fewer than 3,000 of them before going under. Far more—eventually, some 650,000 in all—were built by Willys-Overland and Ford. Ford's versions differed from those made by Bantam and Willys, featuring curved front fenders and elliptical bodyside cutouts.

As global war loomed on the horizon, President Roosevelt was considering a run for an unprecedented third term. In July, FDR was renominated at the Democratic National Convention in Chicago. He would face a formidable opponent in Wendell Wilkie, but emerge victorious in November.

Meanwhile, incessant bombing of Britain erupted in August 1940. Americans who tuned in to Edward R. Murrow's nightly broadcasts from Britain heard the air-raid sirens and wondered if such frightful sounds might eventually be heard in America as well. In September, the first peacetime draft took effect, helping to set an ominous tone for the near future.

# Chrysler Corporation

In the 1940s, Chrysler's four badges were known for conservative styling, strong engineering, and sound construction.

Topping the price spectrum, Chrysler models earned a modernized look for 1940. Fluid Drive, using a viscous-coupled clutch, was a new option.

A pair of exciting Chrysler show cars debuted in 1940. The Newport dual-cowl phaeton, created by LeBaron, paced the Indianapolis 500 race. The following year, Chrysler's Thunderbolt was designed by Alex Tremulis.

Featuring prominent fenders and a low roofline, 1940 Dodges aimed at low- to midprice buyers. DeSoto aimed slightly higher in the marketplace than Dodge, but not quite into Chrysler territory. Both Dodge and DeSoto used six-cylinder engines, while Chrysler came with either a six or a straight-eight. Like the Chryslers, DeSotos were available with extended-length wheelbases, largely for commercial users who liked the back-seat legroom.

Plymouth, the budget make, was Chrysler's top-seller at third in the industry. Plymouths got a full body change for 1940, with new "speedline" fenders. Known for economy, six-cylinder Plymouths cost a bit more than comparable Fords.

## Chrysler

All-new bodies with longer wheelbases

Walter P. Chrysler dies on August 18

New body styles consist of three-window business coupe and Windsor Highlander club coupe

Traveler debuts as low-end eight-cylinder alternative

Model-year production up 30 percent to 92,419; good for 10th place in industry sales race

1

2

3

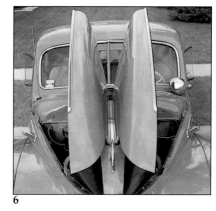

4

5

6

1. Chrysler was looking ahead in 1940, as a pair of concept cars would show a year later. Designer C. Hatfield Bills foresaw the lower, wider, integrated-fender look that would mark the postwar era in 1940 with this concept drawing for a '48 model.
2. The only exterior difference between the 1940 Royal four-door sedan (*shown*) and its Windsor counterpart was the nameplate below the Chrysler script up front. 3. The Highlander option, also known as "The Scottie," featured Scotch plaid and moleskin leather upholstery for Windsor or New Yorker.
4. Saratoga, with its 128.5-inch wheelbase, came only as a four-door sedan and was priced above New Yorker. 5. Royal (*shown*) and Windsor models rode a 122.5-inch wheelbase and had inline six-cylinder engines with horsepower ratings of 108 or 112 with an optional aluminum cylinder head. Inline eight-cylinder models produced 135 or 143 bhp. 6. The clamshell hood remained until 1942. 7. The Royal's dashboard made liberal use of plastic, the new wonder material. 8. Ads touted Chrysler's Fluid-Drive semiautomatic transmission (which debuted in '39) and unique interior options.

7

8

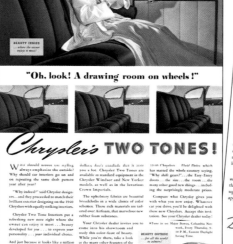

11

# DeSoto

All-new bodies with longer wheelbases

Engine and seats moved forward in chassis; creates better weight distribution

Early model-year production delayed by strike

Convertible coupe back in lineup after one-year absence; offered in Custom line

Sealed-beam headlights become standard industry-wide

All-Weather Air Control System made available to heat and ventilate all models

Prices fall $20 to $48 for "America's Family Car"

Model-year production up 20 percent to 65,467; good for 13th in industry

1

2

3

4

1. DeSotos came standard with a 228-cid inline six that made 100 bhp. An optional cylinder head boosted compression from 6.5:1 to 7:1 and output to 105 bhp. The new grille reflected a trend toward horizontal faces. 2. Two series were offered, DeLuxe and Custom. Here, a DeLuxe two-door sedan, priced at $905. 3. DeSoto's best-seller was the Custom four-door sedan at 25,221 units. A two-tone Sportsman (shown) joined the lineup midyear. 4. The DeLuxe two-door coupe cost the same as the two-door sedan, but the sedan outsold it 7072 to 2098. 5. DeSotos were fairly big cars, all with a 122.5-inch wheelbase. Here, the $1095 Custom convertible coupe. 6. Custom series cars had darker seats than DeLuxe models. Plastic was starting to appear, but in small amounts. 7. The DeSoto script was part one of the best-looking faces of its day. 8. The DeSoto goddess hood ornament lasted from 1932 until '49.

5

6

7

8

# Dodge

Revised sheetmetal on lengthened chassis

Dodge begins production of special Army vehicles

Early model-year production delayed by strike

Seven-passenger sedan and division-window limousine return to lineup

Sealed-beam headlights become standard industry-wide

Two-tone introduced midyear; body different color than hood and fenders

Running boards made optional

Rumble-seat coupe dropped from line

Safety-rim wheels introduced; industry first

Model-year production up 7 percent to 195,505, but Dodge falls from 5th to 6th in industry; passed by Pontiac

1

2

3

4

1. All-new sheetmetal on a longer wheelbase differentiated the 1940 Dodges from the redesigned '39s. The '40s also featured more chrome and a larger grille stretched across the prow. 2. Two Dodge series were offered, Special and DeLuxe. Here, the most popular model in the entry-level Special series, the $815 two-door sedan. 3. New instrument dials surrounded by more chrome trim marked the 1940 dashboard. This is a Special series interior; the DeLuxe series featured a full steering-wheel horn ring. High-quality, but hard, materials with lots of chrome marked interiors of the day. These traits were later found to be dangerous and distracting. 4. After a one-year hiatus, the convertible coupe returned to the lineup at a price of $1035. 5. Chrome strips along the beltline and running boards differentiated DeLuxe models from Specials. Running boards were made optional this year as the industry was moving away from including them. This DeLuxe Luxury Liner four-door sedan was Dodge's most-popular car, selling 84,976 units for the model year. 6. All Dodges were powered by a 218-cid L-head six that produced 87 bhp at 3600 rpm. The cars rode a 119.5-inch wheelbase chassis that was 2½ inches longer than the previous year. This DeLuxe Luxury Liner two-door sedan weighed in at 2990 pounds and cost $860.

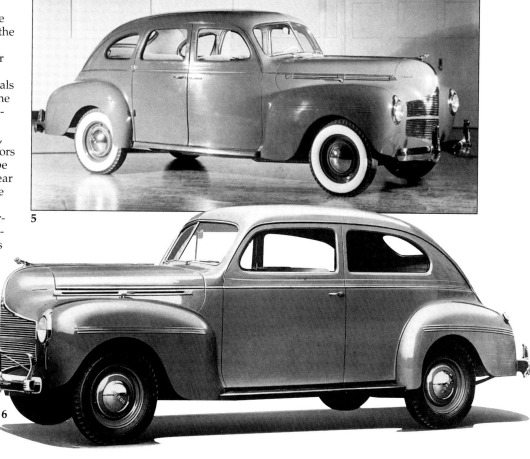

5

6

# Plymouth

Completely restyled bodies ride on 3-inch longer wheelbases

Cabins moved forward, creating more trunk space, better weight distribution, and better riding comfort

970 Roadking chassis shipped to customers without bodies

DeLuxe four-passenger coupe replaces rumble-seat coupe

Sealed-beam head-lights become the industry standard

DeLuxe four-door Touring sedan nabs best-seller status

Early model-year production delayed by strike

Woody DeLuxe station wagon moves from commercial line to passenger-car line

Model-year production up 1.3 percent to 423,155; good for 3rd in industry; closest Plymouth will ever get to overtaking Ford

1

2

1940 PLYMOUTH "Roadking"
THE LOW PRICED BEAUTY WITH THE *Luxury Ride*

1940 PLYMOUTH
Station Wagon
On the DeLuxe 117-inch Wheelbase Chassis

3

4

1940 DELUXE PLYMOUTH
Convertible Coupe
with Power Operated Top

5

**1.** Wheelbases grew three inches to 117. This DeLuxe Westchester station wagon sold for $970. **2.** The entry-level Roadking had a paint stripe rather than a chrome molding along the beltline, and lacked brightwork around the windshield. **3.** The second- and third-row seats could be removed from the maple- and ash-bodied station wagon. **4.** Standard features of the DeLuxe convertible coupe included a power top, chrome wheel trim rings, and whitewalls. **5.** With war approaching, a DeLuxe four-door sedan transported ordnance experts to Fort MacArthur to witness a U.S. defense demonstration. **6.** Priced at $950, 6986 DeLuxe convertible coupes were sold. **7.** Two-door sedans were offered in both Roadking (*shown*) and DeLuxe trim. **8.** The DeLuxe two-door coupe replaced the rumble-seat coupe of '39. **9.** At 173,351 cars, the DeLuxe four-door touring sedan was Plymouth's best-seller. **10.** Plymouth made taxicab options available for the Roadking and DeLuxe. The front-end guard on this car was not stock. **11.** While Fords were the popular choice, Plymouths of various body styles did serve as police cars. **12.** Tourists visiting Michigan were aided by courtesy cars equipped to provide travel information, road service, or first aid, all courtesy of the Michigan Auto Club. Here, club general manager Richard Harfst inspects the travel information.

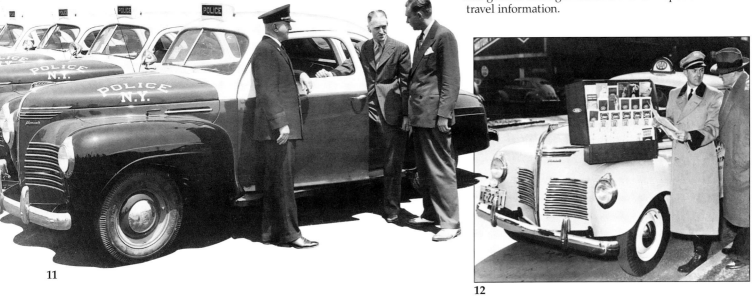

# Ford Motor Company

Luscious restyling made the 1940 Fords even prettier than the '39s—ensuring their collectibility later. Ford claimed 22 improvements, including a "fingertip" column shift and sealed-beam headlights. The unpopular, low-powered V-8/60 engine would be gone after 1940, leaving only the 85-bhp flathead V-8. This was only the second year for hydraulic brakes on Fords, which still used transverse springs.

One of the most striking automobiles of all time, created with a European flair, the shapely new Continental was based on a one-off design penned by E. T. "Bob" Gregorie for Edsel Ford,

the company president. An external spare tire at the rear, attached to a stubby squared-off trunk, added to the allure. Mechanical details, including the enlarged V-12 engine, were similar to the far cheaper Zephyr series. Production was very limited for the first-year Continental. Lincoln offered its massive K-Series for the last time in 1940, but the future belonged to the Zephyr.

Targeting the middle of the market—Dodge and Pontiac territory—Mercury was in its second year. Bigger and roomier than a Ford, sporting lushly curved fenders and a rounded body, Mercury used a larger flathead V-8 engine.

# Ford

New bodies are eight inches longer, but retain 112-inch wheelbase

Convertible sedan and rumble-seat convertible gone from line; DeLuxe convertible club coupe added

The final year for the tired little 136-cid, 60 bhp V-8/60

Model-year production up 11 percent to 541,896, but gap between 2nd-place Ford and 1st-place Chevy widens

1

2

3

4

5

6

7

1. Nearing mobilization for war, the Ford line ran at its usual pace. Here, three Tudor sedans approach completion. 2-3. Interiors were completely restyled for 1940. The Standard (*top*) differed from the DeLuxe (*bottom*) with its unique instrument cluster, dark dash-face color, and trimless glovebox door. 4. The 221-cid, 85-bhp V-8/85 was unchanged from the prior year. Ford touted its economy, performance, build quality, and smooth operation in period ads. 5. The DeLuxe convertible coupe, now with a hydraulic top, replaced the rumble-seat ragtop coupe and cost $61 more. 6. A new steering wheel and more plastic denoted '40 interiors. Note the DeLuxe's silver-beige lower dash panel. 7. A year after the 27 millionth Ford made the trek from San Francisco to the New York World's Fair and back, the 28 millionth Ford appeared at the Fair as part of its "International Good Will Tour." 8. DeLuxe models had a new horizontal-bat grille, while Standards carried the '39's vertical-bar grille. This DeLuxe woody station wagon started at $947.
9. Three engine choices were offered for the passenger-car style sedan delivery: the V-8/60, V-8/85, or the 95-bhp Mercury V-8.
10. The DeLuxe business coupe had two fold-down rear seats, and cost $20 more than the three-passenger, five-window coupe, which lacked rear seats.

8

9

10

19

# Lincoln

Birth of an American Classic: Continental debuts as part of Zephyr lineup; designed by E.T. "Bob" Gregorie under Edsel Ford's direction

Continental owners include Jackie Cooper, Randolph Scott, Mickey Rooney, and Frank Lloyd Wright

Minor trim changes to Continentals throughout the model year

Zephyr models get new sheetmetal, more-powerful V-12 engine

Zephyr coupe sedan replaced with five-window club coupe; convertible sedan discontinued

Brunn builds several semi-custom Town Cars based on Zephyr

Model K fades away; a few 1940 models may have been built unchanged from '39s

Model-year production up 3 percent to 21,765; good for 16th in industry

1

2

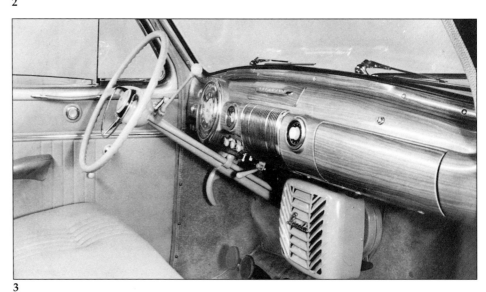

3

1. Maintaining a unibody design, the revamped Zephyr bodies were wider, taller, and slightly shorter than the previous year. The most popular Lincoln was the Zephyr four-door sedan. Total sales for this version, including those fitted with the optional $112 custom interior, were 15,764. Prices started at $1439. 2. At $1399, the three-passenger coupe was the least expensive of the Zephyrs. All Zephyrs got a V-12 with a larger bore that boosted horsepower from 110 to 120 and compression from 6.7:1 to 7.2:1. 3. Although they were in the same line, Continentals had different interiors than other Zephyrs. This is the Zephyr compartment. The Continental featured a twin-dial cluster, gold-finished speaker grille, translucent ruby plastic steering wheel, and metallic mahogany paint on the dashboard panel, steering column, parking-brake handle, shift lever, and linkage. All Ford products now featured a fingertip, column-mounted gearshift lever.

1

2

3

4

1. Lincoln division president Edsel Ford wanted a car with a "continental" look: long hood and a short rear deck sporting a rakishly mounted spare tire. In February 1939, he had his designers and engineers build a customized '39 Zephyr convertible. Feedback was so strong, it became a production car for '40. Two Continental body styles were offered as part of the Zephyr line: cabriolet and this club coupe. 2. Henry Ford gave this Continental to comedic actor Mickey Rooney as a gift. 3. Though it had full-frame doors and fixed vent windows, the way the club coupe's top was affixed to a convertible body makes it one of Detroit's first hard-top body designs. 4-5. Architect Frank Lloyd Wright bought a '40 Continental cabriolet and had it customized with a new roof. 6. Model-year production of Continentals was limited to 54 coupes and 350 cabriolets; prices were $2783 and $2916, respectively.

6

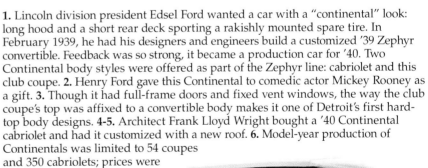

5

# 1940

# Mercury

New grilles highlight minor body changes

Mercury completes its second year of operations in lower-medium price field

Convertible sedan added to lineup; lasts just one year

Cars now badged "Mercury 8"

Engineering improvements include better hydraulic brakes, improved shocks, and a torsion-bar ride stabilizer

Sealed-beam headlamps become standard industry-wide

Model-year production up 8 percent to 81,128; good for 12th in industry

1

2

Our Derby Day favorite was the Mercury 8

Mercury 8

**3**

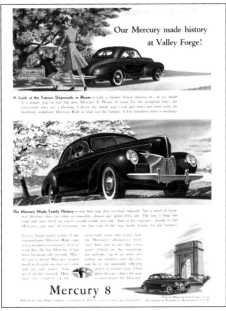

Our Mercury made history at Valley Forge!

Mercury 8

**4**

So we headed the MERCURY for Sun Valley!

Mercury 8

**5**

**6**

**7**

**1.** Mercurys were among the fastest cars of the day. The Mercury V-8 was a larger bore version of Ford's flathead. It displaced 239.4 cubic inches, 18.4 more than the largest Ford mill, and made 95 horsepower, trumping Ford by 10. **2.** Mercury made two styles of convertible for 1940: the club convertible (*shown*), which started at $1079, and a new convertible sedan. **3-5.** Period Mercury advertisements aimed at upper-middle-class buyers told stories of a day at the Derby, a family vacation to Valley Forge, and a ski trip. All noted Mercury's wide cabin, smooth ride, and fuel economy while making definite lifestyle statements. **6.** Club convertibles sported new vacuum-lift tops, available in either black with vermilion edging or tan-gray with tan edging. **7.** The five-passenger sedan coupes were Mercury's second-largest seller, garnering 16,189 orders in 1940. **8.** The dash was revised for 1940 models, but interior trim remained upmarket from Ford. A straight line speedometer replaced '39's rainbow-shaped unit. Like all Ford Motor Company products, 1940 Mercury's gained a finger-tip, column-mounted shift lever. **9-10.** The best-selling 1940 Mercury was the four-door town sedan at 42,806 units, almost half of the total production run. It weighed in at 2992 pounds and sold for $987.

**8**

**9**

**10**

# 1940

# General Motors

Three of the six GM makes ranked in the top five in volume in 1940, one more than in 1939. Chevrolet beat Ford again, turning out almost 765,000 cars against archrival Ford's 542,000.

Competing against Ford and Plymouth for budget-minded shoppers, Chevrolets sported new "Royal Clipper" styling. With a "Knee-Action" front suspension available, Chevrolets were considered a bit more modern than Fords.

Targeting loyal, largely upper-class buyers, Buicks came in six series, from low-priced Special to new Super and top-of-the-line Limited. With their straight-eight engines, Buicks scored high points for dependability.

Facelifting with plain-looking grilles didn't show Cadillacs to the best advantage. Even so, Cadillac had a firm grip on the luxury-car market.

For their final year in GM's lineup, LaSalles—cousin to Cadillac—came in two forms. Series 50 looked similar to 1939, but the new Series 52 displayed more modern "torpedo" styling.

Oldsmobile offered something completely different for 1940: a fully automatic transmission. Evolved from the semiautomatic that had been used in 1937-38 Oldsmobiles, Hydra-Matic Drive had four forward speeds and no clutch pedal.

Positioned just above Chevrolet, Pontiac issued four facelifted series for 1940.

# Buick

New grilles and fenders give new look to same basic design

Two new series: Super, which slots between Special and Century, and Roadmaster 70, which fits between Century and renamed Limited 80

Oil filters now standard on all engines

Super series includes Buick's first factory wagon

Model-year production up 34 percent to 278,784; good for 4th in industry in record sales year

1

2

3

4

5

6

7

1-2. The rarest of the Series 40 Specials was the sport phaeton. Priced at $1355, only 597 were built. All Specials and Centurys rode a 121-inch wheelbase. **3.** The most popular of the slow-selling 133-inch wheelbase Series 80 Limiteds was the $1550 four-door sedan; 3898 were built. **4.** Ivory Soap gave away 60 Special four-door sedans as contest prizes. Contestants were asked to finish the sentence: "I like Ivory soap because . . ." **5.** The best-seller among Buick's convertible coupes was the $1211 Series 50 Super. **6.** Buick's redesigned 1940 dashboard featured round gauges set into engine-turned metal panels surrounded by woodgrain. **7.** Convertible trunks housed a spare tire and enough room for a couple of suitcases or bags of golf clubs. **8.** The 126-inch wheelbase Centurys ran Buick's 320-cid, 141-bhp straight eight, making it one of the best performance car buys of the day. Lower-line models had the 248-cid, 107-bhp eight.

8

# Cadillac LaSalle

Cadillacs get minor facelift with restyled grilles

Final year for medium-priced LaSalle

LaSalle divided into Series 50 and higher-priced Series 52 Special

Cadillac Series 62 replaces Series 61 on a 3-inch-longer wheelbase

Cadillac Series 62 and LaSalle Series 52 share Fisher C-body

Cadillac adds Series 72 between Series 60 and 75; becomes one-year wonder

Final year for Cadillac Series 90 Sixteen

Final year for side-mounted spare tires

Running boards phasing out; no-cost delete option

LaSalle sales of 24,130, up 41 percent; beats Packard One-Twenty for the first time

Model-year production up 7 percent to 37,176, including 24,130 LaSalles

1

2

3

4          5

6

7

8

DRIVE A *LaSalle!*

FOR *Performance, Comfort and Economy*

9

10

11

12

1. Magazine ads laid out the complete Cadillac/LaSalle lineup for 1940. 2. Priced at $2090, the Series Sixty Special four-door sedan edged out its Series 62 counterpart as the most-popular 1940 Cadillac. 3-4. Affluent buyers could afford expensive one-off cars. Coachbuilding firm Bohman and Schwartz customized a pair of Series 62 coupes, turning them into dashing convertibles. 5. Series Sixty Special sedans could be ordered with a "Sunshine Turret-Top Roof," the precursor to today's sunroof. 6. Series 62 models rode a 129-inch wheelbase, three inches longer than the Series 61s they replaced. This four-door convertible sedan debuted midyear; only 75 were produced. 7. Series 52 LaSalles, like this four-door convertible sedan, shared Cadillac's sleek "torpedo" C-body. Series 50 models used the Buick B-body. 8. A total of 10,250 Series 52 Special four-door sedans were sold, making it the best-selling LaSalle. 9. Ads touted LaSalle's Cadillac power, smooth ride, and fuel economy. 10. That power came via a 322-cid, 130-bhp version of Cadillac's 346-cid, 135-bhp V-8. A slightly smaller bore made the difference. 11. LaSalle interiors reflected their Cadillac heritage with style and quality on a smaller scale. 12. LaSalle went out in style. Many feel the torpedo-bodied 52s were the best-looking LaSalles ever built.

# Chevrolet

New Royal Clipper styling has more flowing lines and Buick-like grilles

"Big" Bill Knudsen resigns as division president to serve on advisory commission to the Council on National Defense; C. E. Wilson takes over

25-millionth passenger car to roll of GM line is a Chevy Master DeLuxe town sedan

Top-of-the-line Special DeLuxe trim added; becomes most popular

First use of plastic parts and stainless-steel trim

Chevy signs first contract for U.S. Government weapons production in April

Juan Manual Fangio wins Gran Primo International Del Norte 6000-mile race in Chevy Master 85 business coupe

Model-year production up 38 percent to 775,073; good for 1st in industry—USA-1

1-2. Chevrolet ads said the Royal Clipper-style cars were bigger and better, noted engineering improvements, and boasted about the company's top industry position. 3. "Woody" station wagons were available in the Master 85 and Special DeLuxe series. This Special DeLuxe wagon cost $943, making it Chevy's most expensive car. 4. The most popular car was the Special DeLuxe two-door town sedan. Priced at $761, it sold 205,910 units. 5. A convertible returned for 1940 in the Special DeLuxe series. A power top and leather upholstery were standard, making it Chevy's heaviest car. 6. Chevy used the new wonder material, plastic, on its dashboards for the first time in 1940. 7. All Chevrolets were powered by a 217-cid, 85-bhp "stovebolt" six-cylinder engine. This Master DeLuxe business coupe had an open luggage area behind the front seat; sport coupes had a rear benchseat. 8. The Master 85 sedan delivery had its own new body. Knee-action front suspension was available for extra cost on commercial vehicles. 9. Sedan spare tires were mounted vertically against the front trunk wall; coupes mounted them horizontally on the trunk floor.

5

6

7

8

9

# Oldsmobile

Cars get facelift with new grilles, fenders

Hydra-Matic automatic transmission is introduced —an industry first

Hydra-Matic eliminates clutch pedal and is 10-15 percent more fuel efficient

General manager Charles L. McCuen steps down; replaced by Sherrod E. Skinner

Series 80 becomes Series 90 and wheelbase changes from 120 to 124 inches

Series 90 gets Oldsmobile's first convertible sedan, called phaeton

Sealed-beam headlights become standard industry-wide

Model-year production up 46 percent to 185,154; good for 7th in industry

1

2

3

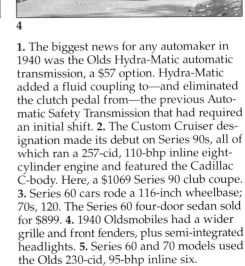

4

5

**1.** The biggest news for any automaker in 1940 was the Olds Hydra-Matic automatic transmission, a $57 option. Hydra-Matic added a fluid coupling to—and eliminated the clutch pedal from—the previous Automatic Safety Transmission that had required an initial shift. **2.** The Custom Cruiser designation made its debut on Series 90s, all of which ran a 257-cid, 110-bhp inline eight-cylinder engine and featured the Cadillac C-body. Here, a $1069 Series 90 club coupe. **3.** Series 60 cars rode a 116-inch wheelbase; 70s, 120. The Series 60 four-door sedan sold for $899. **4.** 1940 Oldsmobiles had a wider grille and front fenders, plus semi-integrated headlights. **5.** Series 60 and 70 models used the Olds 230-cid, 95-bhp inline six.

1. Like Chevrolet, bigger was better for Oldsmobile in 1940. 2. The one-millionth Oldsmobile under the watch of general manager C. L. McCuen and sales manager D. E. Ralston came off the line during the 1940 model year. 3. Seating could be added or removed for three-, five-, six-, or eight-passenger capacity in the Olds station wagon, which was offered only in Series 60 trim. 4. The best-selling 1940 Olds was the $1131 Series 90 four-door sedan. 5. Comprised of a white ash frame with walnut-finished birch panels, the woody body was built by the Hercules Body Co. All wagons offered special heavy-duty rear coil springs to carry heavy loads. 6. Available for the first time was a convertible sedan on the Series 90 platform. Like most automakers, Olds had a tough time selling its phaeton, with only 50 leaving the showroom floors.

31

# Pontiac

Cars get facelift with new grilles, semi-integrated headlights

Torpedo Eight debuts with Cadillac C-body as a sport coupe and sedan on 122-inch wheelbase

Special Six replaces Quality DeLuxe line at low end on 117-inch wheelbase

DeLuxe Six replaces DeLuxe 120

All engines boosted from 6.2:1 to 6.5:1 compression; raises horsepower slightly

Sealed-beam headlights become standard industry-wide

Extra-cost two-tone paint schemes offered for DeLuxe and Torpedo models

Model-year production up 50 percent to 217,001; Pontiac climbs to 5th in industry race in record sales year

1

2

1. Pontiac showcased most of its 1940 lineup in this two-page magazine spread. The corporate slogan announced Pontiac as "America's Finest Low-Priced Car." 2. The $25,000 Plexiglas Pontiac promotional car, a DeLuxe Six four-door sedan, showed "at a glance the hidden value built into Pontiac cars." 3. The gas filler cap location identifies this car as a DeLuxe Eight four-door sedan. 4. The Special Six woody station wagon sold for $1015 and came standard with a fender-mounted spare tire. Special and DeLuxe Six models used a 223-cid, 87-bhp inline six-cylinder engine. 5-6. All Pontiac interiors were trimmed with grained Continental Walnut. Note the metal signal stalk; the quality is a sign of the times. 7-8. The Special Six two-door touring sedan was based on the Chevrolet A-body and rode a 117-inch wheelbase. 9. All Torpedo Eights, like this four-door sedan, used Cadillac's C-body on a 122-inch wheelbase. 10-11. The Torpedo engine was a 103-bhp version of the DeLuxe Eight's 249 cid inline eight. Here, the $1016 sport coupe. 12. More than 35 percent of domestic cars were two-door sedans. This Special Six sold for $830.

3

4

5

6

7

8

9

10

11

12

# Hudson

Known both before and after World War II for swift performance, Hudsons invariably had a unique look about them, compared with their midlevel competition. The 1940 models were no exception. Rebodied and restyled, Hudsons exhibited a neat, lithe, and pleasing appearance, marred by little bodyside ornamentation.

Hudson had come to life in 1909, growing prosperous in the teens under president Roy D. Chapin, Sr. Several offshoots, including the fleet and frugal Terraplane, faded out during the 1930s.

The company liked to show off its cars' merits. In 1940, a Hudson ran more than 20,000 miles at an average of 70.5 mph, setting an American Automobile Association record.

This was not Hudson's finest economic hour, as the company lost $1.5 million. A broad lineup, with seven series on three wheelbases, accounted for 88,000 sales. Yet, Hudson ranked only 11th in production for the 1940 model year.

Hudsons are rebodied and facelifted

Economy-minded 113-inch wheelbase Traveler and DeLuxe lines debut; rest of lineup shuffles

First use of independent front suspension

Labor strike contributes to $1.5 million loss

Model-year production up 7 percent to 87,915, but Hudson falls from 11th to 9th place in industry

1

2

3

4

5

6

**1.** Hudson's brochure called the Six "the car to see with the 'Other Three,'" and boasted of "America's lowest priced Straight Eight." **2.** 1940's clamshell hoods opened in one motion and featured a locking mechanism on the dashboard. **3.** The three-passenger Six Traveler utility coupe had a 750-pound capacity pull-out pickup box that could be locked into three positions. **4-6.** All Hudson coupes and convertibles could be ordered with a version of the utility coupe's pull-out pickup box. This Six Traveler sold for $670. **7.** Priced at $1122, the Hudson Eight convertible sedan was powered by a 254-cid, 128-bhp inline eight-cylinder engine. Sixes had 92, 98, or 102 bhp. **8.** Six Travelers (*shown*) had sparse interiors, but Country Club models were known for luxury.

7

8

# Nash

Like Hudson and Studebaker, Nash was one of the foremost independent automakers remaining as the 1930s ended, catering to middle-income buyers. The company had taken shape in 1916 when Charles W. Nash—following a stint as president of General Motors—bought the Thomas B. Jeffery Company of Kenosha, Wisconsin. Two years later, Nash Motors issued its first cars.

Nash merged with the Kelvinator appliance company in 1937, with George Mason serving as president of the new organization. By 1940, Nash-Kelvinator was profitable, after some severe losses in 1938-39.

The last low-priced Nash Lafayette reached dealerships in 1940, though the idea of a budget-priced car would continue under another name. Nash's upper models came in Ambassador Six and upscale Ambassador Eight form, the latter powered by a straight-eight engine.

Cars cautiously facelifted after 1939 redesign

Final year for low-end LaFayette

Sleeper conversion available in all sedans

Weather-Eye conditioned air heating and ventilation system is among industry's best

Nash offers Packard-Darrin inspired limited-edition customized cabriolets

Sealed-beam headlights become standard industrywide

Model-year production down slightly to 62,131; good for 14th in industry

1

2

1. Universal Studios production manager Martin Murphy received an Ambassador Eight on his 25th anniversary with the company. 2. Eights derived power from a 261-cid, 115-bhp inline eight. The Eight rode a 125-inch wheelbase. Here, the $1195 four-door slipstream sedan. 3. Cabriolets were offered in every series. This Six cost $1085, $110 more than the LaFayette and $210 less than the Eight. Sixes had a 121-inch wheelbase; LaFayettes, 117. 4. Nash ads appealed to women, stating "We don't ask you to understand all of Nash's facts and figures—but your husband will." 5. Nash offered a limited run of factory-customized Eight cabriolets styled by Count Alexis de Sakhnoffsky. 6. A convertible bed was available for all sedans. The rear seats folded down and screens were provided for the windows, so drivers could sleep anywhere.

# Packard

Packard had long been known for prestigious motorcars, and the impressively quiet new 356-cid engine helped maintain that status. No more Packards came with V-12 engines, though, as they had through the 1930s. With sales coming increasingly from the lower end of the price spectrum, Packard's image was changing, as it would throughout the company's later years.

High-dollar automobiles simply weren't the big sellers anymore. Packard's volume leader, by far, was the more-modest One Ten series with a six-cylinder engine. Occupying the middle ground was Packard's One Twenty series, powered by a moderately strong straight-eight.

An extra dose of glamour was available in the limited-production Super Eight One-Eighty Victoria, styled by Howard "Dutch" Darrin with rakish cut-down doors. One of four Darrin-created models, it sold for $4593—more than twice the price of a comparable Packard sedan.

Packard's Eighteenth Series cars get minor facelift

Packard moving away from Cadillac toward midprice field

Three custom-bodied, Darrin-designed models in lineup, including a One Twenty Convertible Victoria

One Twenty Convertible Victoria body built by Auburn Central Mfg. Co., the last vestiges of Auburn-Cord-Duesenberg

Packard signs contract to produce Rolls-Royce Merlin aircraft engines for U.S. and British military

Rumble-seat models eliminated

Model-year production up 111 percent to 98,020; good for 9th in industry

1

2

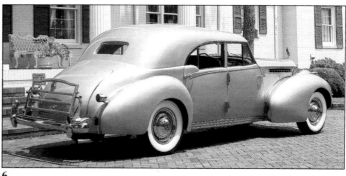

1. Internally, Packard referred to its 1940 models as its Eighteenth Series. By far the best-selling Packards were the six-cylinder One Tens, which competed in the midprice field. This convertible coupe sold for $1104, $32 more than a Buick 40 Special. With inboard headlights, Packard styling was falling behind. 2. The dashboard design was symmetrical, and like most cars by now, the gearshift had moved to the steering column. 3. The 282-cid straight eight in the One Twenty had a new head design, but horsepower remained at 120. This four-door touring sedan sold for $1166. 4. Ads for the One Twenty stressed eight-cylinder performance at a modest price. 5. Listed at $6332, the Packard-Darrin convertible sedan was Packard's most-expensive car. Based on the Custom Super Eight One Eighty, the long, low look was aided by a 138-inch wheelbase. 6. A few customers bought One Eighty chassis, then had them bodied by coachbuilders Rollson or Bohman and Schwartz using Darrin designs. This sport coupe is one such car. 7-9. Based on the 127-inch wheelbase Custom Super Eight One Eighty, the Packard-Darrin Convertible Victoria sold for $4593, almost four times as much as the One Twenty ragtop. Darrin modifications included the dip in the doors, the rakish top, and the lack of running boards. Note the padded dash and leather seats.

39

# Studebaker

With a heritage dating back to 1852, when it produced covered wagons—and to electric automobiles early in the 20th century—Studebaker had one of the longest histories in the industry.

Studebaker offered three series in 1940, but the Champion was taking over as the sales leader. Introduced in 1939, the low-budget Champion with its 78-bhp six-cylinder promised top fuel economy. Champs accounted for more than half of sales, and helped Studebaker hang onto its eighth-place ranking in annual production.

Midlevel Commanders—with stronger six-cylinder engines—and the posh straight-eight Presidents had a different front end than the Champion. Middle-class buyers leaned toward the bigger Studebakers, while the Champ competed against low-price Fords and Chevrolets.

Studebaker was the only automaker to offer a car-pickup, dubbed the coupe-delivery, with a short cargo bed in place of the trunk.

Commander and President models get slightly revised fenders, grilles

Champion, introduced mid-1939, continues with minor changes

Champion places first in AAA-sponsored Gilmore Economy Run, averaging 29.19 mpg

Steering-column hood look introduced

Model-year production up 25 percent to 107,185; good for 8th in industry

4

5

1. Studebaker ads said its 1940 cars made headlines, but the big news was the late '39 introduction of the Champion. A low-price leader, Champion helped Studebaker production more than double between 1938 and '40. 2. Presidents had '39's basic grille design, but the trend toward horizontal front ends was obvious. 3. Eight-cylinder-powered Presidents were outsold 10-1 by Champions. This is the $1095 four-door cruising sedan. 4. Champions had shorter wheelbases and weighed about 500 pounds less than low-end Chevys and Fords. 5. Ads pointed out Champion's fuel-cost savings—made possible by the 164-cid inline six—compared with the "other three." 6. Edwards Iron Works made a slide-in box to turn the Champ into a pickup. 7. Different color window frames made this President club sedan a Delux-Tone model. 8. Presidents varied little from Commanders externally. The major difference was a 122-inch wheelbase vs. 116.5. 9. A 226-cid, 90-horsepower inline six powered the Commander.

6

7

8

9

# Minor Makes

Introduced in 1936, the American Bantam minicar came in six body styles, including convertibles and a roadster, on a 75-inch wheelbase. Produced in Pennsylvania, Bantams competed against the newer Crosley, but were—and still are today—less well known. Only 800 Bantams were built in 1940. Bantam was one of three automakers—Ford and Willys-Overland were the others—to get government contracts to develop a general-purpose vehicle (later known as Jeep) for the United States military. Bantam's compact size gave it a competitive advantage in meeting the government's 2150 pound weight limit. Bantam submitted its design first and went on to build many Jeeps for the war effort. Eventually, aspects from all the proposals were used in the final Jeeps.

Crosley was in its second year, with five mini-sized body styles including a new station wagon. Powel Crosley, Jr. had been best known for radios, but launched his first car in April 1939. Early Crosleys had hand-operated windshield wipers and cable-actuated brakes. Priced between $299 and $450, with two-cylinder engines, they could reach 50 mph. These cars were frugal, as they could get more than 40 mpg, some claiming up to 50 mpg.

Graham issued its last "sharknose" models in 1940, with and without superchargers. Introduced in 1938 as the "Spirit of Motion" model with an undercut prow, the unique but controversial styling of these cars hurt sales. Graham had a brand-new car on tap, though. The firm had entered into an agreement with Hupmobile general manager Norman De Vaux to build cars based on the body dies for the stylish but defunct Cord 810/812 (De Vaux had purchased the dies). The resulting Graham Hollywood had rear-wheel drive rather than the Cord's front-wheel drive, exposed headlights, and a six-cylinder supercharged engine. A similar but unblown model, called the Skylark, was issued under the Hupmobile badge. Both were built in Graham's factory and sold only in 1940-41.

In addition to getting ready for entry into the military Jeep business, Willys-Overland produced a Series 440 passenger car with a four-cylinder engine. It was essentially a 1939 Overland, with sealed-beam headlights and a new name.

## American Bantam

Bantam submits first jeep prototype

Model-year sales plummet to 800; production ends June 30

1

2

3

**1.** Set upon a 75-inch wheelbase, the Custom Club roadster had dummy louvers on the front fenders. All 1940 American Bantams were powered by a 50-cid four-cylinder engine that put out 22 horsepower. A three main-bearing crankshaft replaced the previous two-bearing unit, improving highway reliability. **2-3.** Alex Tremulis designed the Hollywood convertible, and followed with the Riviera, a four-passenger convertible sedan. Priced at $549, the Riviera utilized the Speedster's rear body design. **4.** Speedsters had cut-down doors and four-passenger capacity. Note the headlight placement; they moved out to the fenders on 1940 models—aesthetically, a controversial move. **5.** In 1939, American Bantam introduced a woody wagon. The body was built by the Mifflinburg Body Company. It was the most-expensive model, selling for $565 in 1940. It weighed 1400 pounds. **6.** Tremulis designed the Hollywood convertible off the coupe. He cut the top off and built the prototype in ten days, upholstering it in leather and painting it desert sand. He drove the prototype from Los Angeles to Chicago, averaging 42.5 mpg.

4

5

6

# Crosley

Crosley enters its second year in automotive business

Crosleys can be purchased at hardware and appliance stores

Body styles expand, but production down to just 422 from 2017

**1.** Radio and refrigerator magnate Powel Crosley, Jr., entered the automotive business in 1939 with a two-passenger coupe and a four-passenger sedan, both convertibles. Five models were offered for 1940, including this two-door station wagon. At $450 and 1160 pounds, it was the heaviest and most-expensive model. **2-3.** Crosley's engine was a 35.3-cid, two-cylinder, four-cycle Waukesha that made 12 bhp. The cars weighed in the neighborhood of 1000 pounds, so 50 mph was possible and mileage was around 50 mpg.

# Graham

Failing "Spirit of Motion" styling for Supercharged and Standard gets minor facelift

Hollywood Custom Supers debut, utilize 1936-37 Cord 810/812 Beverly tooling

Model-year production of about 2000, good for 19th in industry

**1.** Graham's Supercharged and Standard models shared bodies. The difference was supercharged (120 bhp) and normally aspirated (93 bhp) versions of Graham's 217.8-cid inline six. DeLuxe and Custom trim levels were offered. **2.** Graham aimed to be America's style leader with an undercut, slanted face that came to be known, somewhat disparagingly, as the "sharknose." This style was introduced in 1938, and sales fell immediately.

# Hupmobile

Skylark debuts utilizing 1936-37 Cord 810/812 Beverly tooling

Skylarks are rear drive instead of Cord's front drive, and wheelbase is 115 inches, compared to Cord's 125

Model-year production of only 211

1

1. Hupmobile general manager Norman De Vaux had the bought body dies for the now-defunct Cord 810/812 Beverly. He struck a deal with Graham to build the bodies and added Hupmobile's 245-cid L-head six to produce the Hupmobile Skylark. The Skylark had its own nose and grille.

## Automotive product advertising

2-4. Auto product ads utilized a lot of illustration, but the copy didn't tell readers much about the technical aspects that made these staples help their cars run better and longer. As shown in the Champion Spark Plug advertisement, success at the Indianapolis 500 translated into prestige and, therefore, sales.

2    3    4

# International

Station wagons available as ½-ton model D2 and 1-ton model D15; both utilize truck chassis

Introduced in 1939, the International D2 station wagon had a 113-inch wheelbase ½-ton truck chassis, seating for seven, and a Willys-designed "Green Diamond" 213-cid, 78-bhp flat-head six-cylinder engine. The vehicle weighed 2300 pounds and sold for about $1000.

# Willys

Styling facelifted to be more orthodox

Models designated 440 for four cylinders, 1940; cars come in Speedway or DeLuxe trim

Willys submits design for first jeep

First station wagons appear

Joseph W. Frazer, former Chrysler vice-president, in second year as president and general manager

Model-year production of 26,698, good for 17th in industry

1

2

3

**1.** The undercut prow from 1939 was now gone as Willys attempted to join the design mainstream. Despite the front-end changes, 440s were essentially '39 Overlands with different faces. **2.** The Willys brochure touted the car as a leader in the low-price, full-size field. Management felt the cars were the right size and had adequate performance compared with the "oversized and over-built" cars offered by the Big Three. All Willys derived power from a 134-cid inline four-cylinder engine that made a modest 61 horsepower, just four horses less than Ford's small V-8. **3.** Willys' first station wagon rode the same 102-inch wheelbase as all 1940 model 440s. Weights ranged from 2124 to 2255 pounds. **4.** The reworked nose was rounding into the shape that would make the 1941 Willys a favorite of hot-rodders and drag racers in future years. **5.** Willys marketed a regional model called the Californian, which featured different chrome hood and side trim. **6.** Externally, Speedways lacked the chrome hood trim, dual wipers, and bumper guards of the DeLuxe models. This Speedway four-door sedan sold for $596; its DeLuxe counterpart cost $76 more. **7.** A three-year or 100,000-mile guarantee aided Willys sales in 1940.

4

5

6

7

Americans watched events in Europe—and the potential threat in the Pacific—with uncertainty, if not dread or suspicion. Preparations for war took place throughout the year, even if the details didn't always occupy the most prominent spot in the national news.

Although the Great Depression wasn't over yet, military production was already sending plenty of people back to work. Better yet, the new jobs tended to pay more than most of the spots available during the dark 1930s.

British Prime Minister Winston Churchill addressed a joint session of the U.S. Congress. Although concern about imminent war focused mainly on Europe, aggression by the Japanese army in Asia began to rival worries about Hitler's intentions. With that in mind, America "froze" the assets of Japan in the U.S., and enacted an embargo on strategic materials—including oil.

"America Firsters" and other isolationists were dismayed when President Roosevelt authorized the Lend-Lease bill, believing that it would be a first step toward American involvement in the conflict. Lend-Lease gave effective aid to the Allied forces, who paid for military products not in cash, but in goods and services.

Meanwhile, American life continued as normal, as the impact of the Depression eased and people had more money in their pockets. Serials and soap operas continued to emanate from console-size radios in the nation's living rooms. Movie palaces thrived. Orson Welles released what would later become one of the most revered movies of all time: *Citizen Kane*. On the lighter side, an animated elephant named *Dumbo* delighted younger audiences. Jazz and Big-Band music drew enthusiastic audiences.

Teenagers no longer led subdued lives in the shadow of their parents, but were coming to be more noticed—literally, in part, because of their often-distinctive apparel. A few zoot-suiters, nattily attired in "pegged" trousers, long coats, and flashy hats, could be spotted on urban streets. Most teens and 20-somethings were less-bold in the sartorial

department. Still, fashions in various flavors were gaining greater attention than they had during the Depression—a trend destined to become even more noteworthy after the war.

No one even envisioned the phenomenon of McDonald's, but American cities and towns had plenty of drive-in restaurants, many with smiling carhops to serve the burgers and malts. Drive-in movies had emerged in the mid-1930s, and continued to attract romance-minded teens as well as the family trade.

On the automotive front, many consider 1941 to be the finest year of the between-the-wars era in terms of design. Handsome, carefully-trimmed bodies were seen on such luxury models as the Cadillac Sixty Special (and other Cadillacs, for that matter), as well as the Lincoln Continental and the new Packard Clipper. But styling was nearly as striking on plenty of ordinary Chevrolets, Fords, Nashes, and Studebakers.

Running boards were mostly gone, though vestigial versions remained on Chrysler products, sticking only a short

way past the door—only enough room for a child's feet. Convertible sedans still existed, but were about to fade away. Only Lincoln offered a V-12 engine, and V-16s were history. Nearly every other make used an inline six- or eight-cylinder engine, or an L-head V-8.

1941 turned out to be the best automobile production year since 1929, with 3,779,682 cars built. Chevrolet again led the sales race, turning out more than a million vehicles in the model year against 691,455 for Ford.

No new makes were launched, but the final few Graham Hollywoods and Hupp Skylarks went to customers. The American Bantam was dying and Willys' fortunes would have been fading, but both companies got a boost as a result of military Jeep contracts. Willys renamed its passenger model the Americar. The 4-millionth Plymouth went to a dealership in 1941, and the 29-millionth Ford was produced.

Packard became the first manufacturer to offer optional air conditioning, but it was very expensive. Buick offered "Compound Carburetion," with a second carburetor that

kicked in when the gas pedal was tromped. DeSotos adopted the prominent grille "teeth" that would be their trademark until the make expired two decades later.

Hydra-Matic Drive could now be installed in Cadillacs as well as Oldsmobiles. Chrysler and DeSoto took another route to easier shifting, introducing a semiautomatic transmission. Packard stuck with a conventional three-speed, column-shifted gearbox, but came up with a semiautomatic Electromatic clutch.

After a turbulent period in the 1930s, labor made further inroads. Following a wildcat strike in 1941, Henry Ford permitted a union vote, which resulted in the first closed shop in the auto industry.

Suspicion that war wasn't far off might even be read into such performances as the Andrews Sisters' song *Boogie Woogie Bugle Boy*. Young men were registering at their local draft boards, wary of what the near-future might hold.

They soon found out. On Sunday morning, December 7, 1941, Japanese planes bombed Pearl Harbor, on the island of Oahu in Hawaii. More than 2400 American servicemen were killed, 347 planes were destroyed or severely damaged, and 18 ships were either sunk or irreparably disabled.

A possible attack on Pearl Harbor had been anticipated by military experts, but was surprising nonetheless when it actually happened. Any hope that America could remain out of the war evaporated in a hurry.

Referring to this "day of infamy" a day later, President Franklin Delano Roosevelt stated that a state of war had existed since the tragedy at Pearl Harbor, and asked Congress for authorization to officially declare war on Japan. Only one dissenting voice was heard. Outspoken isolationist thinking had nearly disappeared, as America geared up for a lengthy military conflict. Some 60 million Americans heard Roosevelt's comments on the radio.

By the end of 1941, 951 tanks had been sent to Britain from American manufacturing facilities. The U.S. was also shipping food, trucks, guns, and ammunition, and filling the U.S. arsenal at the same time. No one knew for sure at the time, but the age of free and easy auto travel was about to draw to a close for the duration.

# Chrysler Corporation

Despite a reputation for cars that were less than stylish, Chrysler came out with a stunner for 1941. Created by Dave Wallace, the Town & Country was Chrysler's first wagon, but it departed from tradition by displaying a clean, rounded shape. Distinctive "clamshell" rear doors opened at the center.

Chrysler and DeSoto made life a little easier for drivers, with new semiautomatic transmissions. The clutch had to be used only when actually changing gears. While moving forward, the car started off in Low range, then shifted into High when letting up on the gas.

Two-speed electric wipers were new, and power windows became an option for the Chrysler Crown Imperial. All Chrysler products wore new Safety Rim wheels.

DeSotos adopted what would become their "trademark" grille appearance, in the form of prominent "teeth." Bodies were longer, wider, and lower. Year-end sales totals sent DeSoto into its best spot ever: 10th in the industry.

Dodge models got a clean facelift, and model-year sales ranked seventh in the automotive production race. Plymouth, at the low-budget end of the Chrysler corporation spectrum, got a facelift of its own with a heart-shaped grille. Batteries moved under the hood. Powermatic Shift, a vacuum-operated transmission assist, was a new Plymouth option.

# Chrysler

Cars get facelift with fewer grille bars

Newport and Thunderbolt, custom-bodied concept cars, wow showgoers; Newport paces Indianapolis 500

Town & Country wood-sided wagon debuts

Traveler discontinued after one year

Semiautomatic "Vacamatic" transmission introduced

Model-year production leaps 75 percent to 161,704; Chrysler grabs 8th place in industry from Studebaker

1

2

1-3. Although the golden age of custom-bodied cars had long since past, coach-builder LeBaron built six Newport dual-cowl phaetons to be exhibited as Chrysler show vehicles. Using production chassis and running gear, they were hardly "all show and no go," and one paced the 1941 running of the Indianapolis 500, becoming the first custom-bodied car to do so. Some eventually made their way into private hands; actress Lana Turner reportedly owned a red one.

3

1

2

3

1-3. Preceding the Newport on the show circuit was the radical Thunderbolt, also built by LeBaron. Like the Newport, its aluminum body wore hidden headlights (foretelling the '42 DeSoto), but it also incorporated a grilleless nose and fully skirted front and rear fenders. Its claim to fame, however, was a retractable hardtop that hid beneath a rear decklid—both of which were electrically powered. Six were built, all eventually sold to well-heeled buyers. 4. More for the masses was the Windsor six-cylinder convertible, Chrysler's least-expensive ragtop at $1315. 5. A Windsor two-door brougham cost $1128. 6. Note the "suicide" rear-hinged back doors on Chrysler's most-popular model, the $1165 Windsor four-door sedan. 7. Windsor's standard trim included novel plastic dash pieces and button-tufted upholstery.

4

5

6

7

51

1

2

3

4

5

6

7

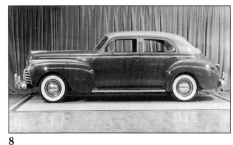

8

1-5. The first of the famous Town & Country wagons appeared for 1941. Bodywork aft of the cowl was made of mahogany-veneered panels outlined with white ash framing, all topped by a slope-back steel roof. The rear cargo area was accessed through unique "dutch doors," but since the window above them was fixed, the opening was too small to load bulky objects—a problem made worse by the obtrusive spare tire mounted against the wheel well. Town & Countrys were offered in six- and nine-passenger versions, the latter with a second-row auxiliary seat that folded forward for easier access to the rear. Town & Countrys were both heavy and pricey: At 3540 pounds, the six-passenger model weighed 240 pounds more than a comparable four-door sedan, and its $1412 sticker made it $247 more costly. Yet despite its heft—and up to nine-passenger capacity—it was offered only in the six-cylinder Windsor series. Fewer than 1000 were produced. 6. The least-expensive eight-cylinder Chrysler was the $1245 Saratoga business coupe. It only had a front bench seat, but the long trunk could hold the contents of a small apartment. 7. Less ungainly looking was the $1369 New Yorker club coupe. 8. Saratogas and New Yorkers—the latter represented by this $1399 town sedan—carried a 324-cid straight eight with 137 or 140 horsepower.

1

2

3

4

5

6

7

1. A New Yorker four-door sedan listed for $1389—$69 more than a comparable Saratoga. 2. A New Yorker dashboard is shown without the optional radio, normally mounted in the center; in its place is a fluted plastic filler panel. During this period, all Chrysler Corp. vehicles had symmetrically styled dashboards, but Chrysler's featured a taller, bolder design. 3. All four-door models except the new town sedan used "suicide" rear-hinged back doors. 4. The most-expensive Chrysler was the $1548 New Yorker convertible, of which only 1295 were sold. 5. An ad headlined "It's Smart to be Different!" courted buyers with the fact that Chryslers were available with "no less than twenty-three beautiful interior trim combinations . . . and fifteen outside color schemes." Indeed, the dark blue over Highland Plaid New Yorker convertible made for a striking illustration. 6. New for '41 was the town sedan body style, which combined blanked-out rear roof quarters with front-hinged back doors sporting a vent pane at the rear. It was offered in all four standard Chrysler trim levels, and also as a special Crown Imperial town sedan (*shown*), which was built on the standard New Yorker platform; as such, it was much smaller than other Crown Imperials, and at $1760, cost far less as well. 7. Topping the Chrysler line were the huge Crown Imperial sedans, which sat on a lengthy 145.5-inch wheelbase, 18 inches longer than the Saratoga/New Yorker. Crown Imperials used a one-piece curved windshield; other Chryslers had divided panes. Prices started at $2595. Note the trio of front bumper guards.

# DeSoto

Line is redesigned; wheelbase shrinks an inch, though new bodies are longer, lower, and wider

Curb weights rise by about 130 pounds

Town sedan body style with "blind" rear quarter windows returns after six-year hiatus

Revised styling incorporates vertical grille teeth that will become a DeSoto trademark

DeLuxe and Custom series remain

Standard—and only—engine is now the formerly optional 105-horsepower, 228-cid inline six

Like Chrysler, DeSoto introduces an optional semiautomatic transmission, here called "Simplimatic," in combination with "Fluid Drive"

Model-year production up 49 percent to 97,497; DeSoto moves up three places to 10th in industry sales race, its best showing to date

1

2

1. *Sketch Book of the 1941 DeSoto* depicted that year's new styling and engineering details. Artfully illustrated, the 11-page brochure contained color drawings of everything from steering wheels and door panels to the principles behind the Fluid Drive and Simplimatic transmissions. 2. The "long hood, long deck" look of a Custom business coupe could be yours for $982. 3. Behind the split-folding bench seat lay the spare tire and a passageway to the luggage compartment. 4. Typical of the '40s, dashboards carried a symmetrical theme. 5. On weekends, the business coupe could become a "camping coupe," able to hold huge amounts of gear.

3

4

5

1

2

3

**1-2.** DeSotos remained a step ahead of Dodge on the Chrysler Corp. ladder, with a slightly bigger engine (though still only a six cylinder) and slightly higher prices. A classy Custom convertible cost $1240; this example wears period accessories including fog lamps, spot lights, and bumper override bars. **3.** The most-popular DeSoto was the Custom sedan, priced at $1085, $50 more than its DeLuxe counterpart. **4.** An unidentified police jurisdiction takes delivery of a fleet of DeSoto DeLuxe sedans. Despite being pricier than comparable Dodges and Plymouths, DeSotos were popular for police and taxi use.

4

# Dodge

Styling is updated with more-horizontal heart-shaped grille, but wheelbases remain the same

Model names change from Special and DeLuxe to DeLuxe and Custom

Taillights, now perched atop the rear fenders, are visible from the side

Turn signals now optional on all models

Engine remains a 218-cid six-cylinder, but horsepower is up by four to 91

Fluid Drive transmission, originally offered by Chrysler and then DeSoto, finally arrives as a Dodge option for all models

Town sedan body style with blind rear quarters added; becomes the most-expensive standard-wheelbase Dodge sedan

Longer seven-passenger models remain in line, though wheelbase shrinks by two inches; still 18 inches longer than standard models

Model-year production up 21 percent to 237,002, yet Dodge falls one position to 7th in industry sales

1

2

3

4                                5

1-2. Company ads of the period stressed the smoothness of Dodge's powertrain, citing the benefits of "Floating Power" engine mounts combined with the "shock-absorbing cushion of oil" found in the newly optional "Fluid Drive" transmission—the latter a bargain at only $25 extra. Fluid Drive incorporated a fluid coupling between the engine and transmission that allowed the car to be brought to a stop and driven off again in any gear without depressing the clutch. 3. The five-millionth Dodge was built in 1941, a production milestone that took the company 27 years to achieve. 4. Sales increased sharply in 1941 for the convertible, which remained the most-expensive standard-wheelbase car in the Dodge lineup. Still, only 3554 were built, with prices starting at $1162. 5. Options that could boost that price included the bumper overriders and rear fender skirts shown on this jaunty example.

1. New to the line for '41 was the town sedan, with its blanked-out rear quarter windows. Unlike other Dodge sedans, the rear doors hinged at the front and included a small vent window. 2. A Custom club coupe shows off its optional two-tone paint, along with the low-mounted center brake light new to all Dodges for '41. 3. Long-wheelbase models, like this seven-passenger Custom, were waning in popularity, as fewer than 700 sedans and limousines were sold. 4. A predecessor of Dodge's famous Power Wagon was this four-wheel-drive ½-ton command car built for military use.

# Plymouth

New fenders and grille freshen Plymouth's look

Roadking and DeLuxe give way to standard, DeLuxe, and Special DeLuxe models

Safety wheel rims introduced; intended to keep tires on their rims in the event of a blowout

"Powermatic" vacuum-assisted shifting made optional; no match for the semiautomatic transmissions or even Fluid Drive used in other Chrysler Corp. cars, it simply makes the shift lever easier to move

Still the only engine offered, Plymouth's 201-cid six gains three horsepower to 87

Model-year production up 29 percent to 545,811; Plymouth sets new company record and hold at its perennial 3rd-place position in industry sales

1

2

3

4

**1-4.** Although Plymouth was the "low-price leader" of the Chrysler Corp. quartet, you wouldn't know it by the look of the Special DeLuxe convertible. As in other Chrysler Corp. cars for '41, dashboards took on a symmetrical look. Easily seen on these examples are the single vertical bumper guards used on higher-line Plymouths that year.

1

2

3

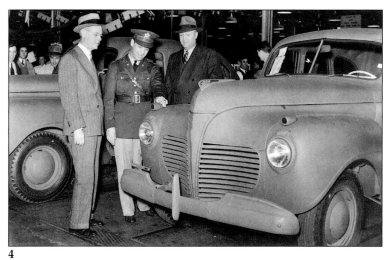

4

5

6

7

8

9

10

1. Due to their low price and reputation for reliability, Plymouths were often used as taxis. Note that, as on most other Chrysler Corp. sedans, the rear doors hinged at the back, "suicide" style. 2. In the standard and DeLuxe series, two-door sedans outsold their four-door counterparts—just the opposite of the Special DeLuxe, and of all other Chrysler Corp. makes. This DeLuxe two-door sedan wears optional rear fender skirts. In the rear window is a banner carrying Plymouth's slogan: "The 'One' for '41." 3. By far the most-popular model was the Special DeLuxe four-door sedan, shown here with optional two-tone paint. 4. Quite on the opposite end of the spectrum were the blackout models built for military use. 5. A Plymouth undergoes a water-leakage test. 6. The panel delivery was popular for door-to-door sales; shown here is one used by the Jewel Tea Company. 7. The most-expensive of the standard-wheelbase cars was the Special DeLuxe "woody" wagon at $1031. 8. Actor Mickey Rooney (*behind windshield*) helps Plymouth celebrate its four-millionth car, a $1007 Special DeLuxe convertible. 9. Front- and rear-fender "speedlines" (new for '41) notwithstanding, Plymouths were hardly impressive performers, yet often found homes with police departments. 10. A snappy Special DeLuxe business coupe went for $795.

# Ford Motor Company

Ford bodies looked about the same in the middle as they had in 1941, but what a difference the revised front and rear ends made! A new flathead six-cylinder engine replaced the underpowered V-8/60; at 90 horsepower, it was actually more powerful than the fabled Ford V-8.

Nothing Ford did seemed to help sales against arch-rival Chevrolet, however. Ford ended the model year a distant second, trailing Chevrolet by more than 300,000 units.

As the big Series K faded out of the picture, Lincoln launched a long-wheelbase Custom sedan, with powered front seats. Continental became a separate model from the lower-priced Zephyr, which was indisputably the focus of Lincoln's attention. Zephyrs kept the division on course financially.

Pushbutton-operated doors on the 1941 Continental gave Lincoln marketers something to talk about. So did a new power convertible top. Not that Continentals needed much of a push to attract attention.

Filling the gap between Ford and Zephyr, Mercury was developing a reputation for performance. A few more horsepower than Fords made quite a difference when pushing on the pedal. Restyled for 1941, Mercury models again were basically Ford-like, but they looked bigger.

# Ford

New front and rear styling introduces "square box" look; wheelbase increases

Ford V-8/60 is replaced by flathead six with 90 more cubic inches and 30 more horsepower

Three trim levels (Special, DeLuxe, and Super DeLuxe) now offered in two series (Six and V8)

29-millionth Ford produced

Model-year production up 28 percent to 691,455; Ford is 2nd in industry

1

1. Posing cars with aircraft has been a popular promotional idea since the 1930s. Here, a Super DeLuxe club coupe poses with the most-advanced airliner of its day, the Douglas DC-3. A military tie-in can also be made here because the DC-3 served as the C47 military transport plane.
2. The new "square box" styling was less-aerodynamic than the previous Fords. Two-piece fenders

2

were used for one year only. This Fordor sedan can be identified as a Super DeLuxe model by its nose script and fully chromed grille. At $859, the V8 sold for $16 more than the Six.

1

2

3

1. Unusual for the time, no military reference was made in this 1941 Ford ad. Instead, Ford noted its new cars' innovations and reminded consumers who had started the auto business as they knew it. 2. Ford's best-seller for 1941 was the Super DeLuxe Tudor sedan. Six and V8 sales totaled more than 185,000 cars. 3. Ford used power tops on its convertibles for the first time. The chrome fender strips on this car identify it as a late 1941 model. Ragtops were offered only with Super DeLuxe trim. 4. Interiors were up to seven inches wider for greater comfort and glass area was increased to aid visibility. Super DeLuxe models had a glovebox-mounted clock, a steering-wheel chrome trim ring, crank-controlled vent windows, plastic "Kelobra"-grain dash trim, and twin visors.

4

1

2

**1-3.** The $807 Super DeLuxe five-passenger coupe was also known as an "opera" coupe because of its folding rear seats. Plastic was becoming more prominent in Ford interiors. **4-10.** 1941 Ford body styles: (4) Fordor sedan. (5) Tudor sedan. (6) Five-passenger coupe. (7) Convertible club coupe. (8) Sedan-coupe. (9) Station wagon. (10) Three-passenger coupe. **11.** A smoking 1942 Ford represented lost dollars in this ad for Havoline motor oil. Havoline advertised that it was insulated and distilled to prevent burning at a time when it was important to conserve both gas and oil. **12.** Station wagons were built at Ford's Iron Mountain, Upper Michigan facility (close to the source of the lumber). The $1013 Super DeLuxe wagon was the first Ford to surpass $1000 since the 1930 Model A Town Car. **13.** Ford truck design lagged behind the cars. The pickups were facelifted in 1941 to reflect 1939-40 car styling. **14-15.** DeLuxe models had chrome center grilles with body-color side grilles, and wheels were black no matter what the body color. Note the crank hole; motorists hadn't been manually turning cranks since the late 1920s. **16.** Ford experimented with plastic, and later built a plastic-bodied car. Here, 75-year-old Henry Ford hits a plastic decklid with an axe to demonstrate its strength. The trunklid didn't break, but no production cars ever came so equipped.

3

4

5

6

7

8

9

10

12

13

14    15

16

# Lincoln

Bodies largely unchanged; slightly revised grilles and other minor updates

Continental becomes its own series

Custom series introduced; Customs are essentially Zephyrs on 13-inch longer, 138-inch wheelbase

Larger of two V-12 engines dropped from lineup

Electric automatic over-drive made optional

Industry's first push-button door releases offered

Babe Ruth owns a 1941 Continental

Model-year production of 21,994, good for 17th in industry

Sales down slightly from 1940; Lincoln is losing market share to Cadillac

1

2

3

1. Zephyrs received only minor exterior changes for 1941. The parking lights, which doubled as turn signals, moved to the top of the fenders. The grille now had fewer bars and a more-pronounced outline. 2. Zephyr rear ends sported a combination license-plate light/orna-ment/stop light and the trunk handle became a separate part. Club coupes were the second most-popular Zephyrs behind four-door sedans. Club coupes could be ordered with a cus-tom interior, which included a fold-down rear-seat armrest. 3. Lincoln interiors received the industry's first pushbutton door releases and a hood release, which had moved from the hood ornament. 4-5. Zephyr ads concentrated on the image of owning a sleek, powerful Lincoln and promised "more fun per gallon" than any car buyers had ever owned.

4

5

1

2

3

4

5

**1.** The most-expensive Zephyr was the convertible coupe at $1858. Only 725 were built. All Lincoln convertibles now had electric-powered tops instead of vacuum assist. Despite Zephyr's good looks, Cadillacs were newly restyled and had more power, adding up to a sales decline for Lincoln. **2.** "Lincoln Continental" script appeared for the first time on the Continental, which now had its own series. Production of the $2812 club coupes totaled 850, and only 400 cabriolets were built. **3-5.** All Continentals shared the Zephyr's 125-inch wheelbase and 120-bhp, 292-cid V-12 engine. Note the gold interior trim. This cabriolet cost $2865 new.

# Mercury

Redesigned bodies (shared with Ford) are longer, wider, taller; new rectangular front grilles with boxy fenders

Wheelbase increases two inches to 118

Running boards now concealed

Mercury remains one-trim-level/one-engine make

New body styles consist of station wagon and two coupes: a three-passenger and a five-passenger with two auxiliary rear seats

Early models use three-price front fenders; late models use two-piece fenders with stainless-steel strip

Convertible sedan no longer offered

Convertibles get electrically powered tops

Model-year production up slightly to 82,391, but Mercury falls one spot to 13th in industry

1

2

3

4

5

6

7

8

1-2. Fords and Mercurys shared bodies in 1941. The new design featured squared-off fenders, twin rectangular grilles, and concealed running boards. This convertible coupe was priced at $1100. **3.** The '41 interior sported a new horizontal cluster with the speedometer and other gauges under one lens. Clutch and brake pedals became round. **4.** Mobiloil urged consumers to prevent the embarrassment of squeaks and rattles with consistent oil and lubrication changes. The car in question is generic, but has a Mercury flavor. **5.** One of the new body styles for '41 was a three-passenger coupe. The A/S (auxiliary seat) coupe looked the same but had two fold-down "opera" seats. **6.** Simoniz was "defense for any car's beauty" at a time when maintaining cars was important. A 1941 Mercury makes an appearance in this ad. **7.** Mercury's best-seller was the four-door or "town" sedan. Priced at $987, it was the last four-door that would sell for less than $1000. **8.** The birch- and maple-bodied station wagon was Mercury's most-expensive car at $1141. **9.** Leather interiors came in tan, red, or blue.

9

# General Motors

Compound Carburetion was the big news at Buick. Optional for the Special and standard on other cars, a pair of carburetors extracted more power from the Fireball straight-eight. Opulent custom bodies by Brunn drew praise, but the regular models sent Buick to fourth place in production. Fastback models emerged at Buick, as well as at Chevrolet, Oldsmobile, and Pontiac.

Hydra-Matic was now available in Cadillacs. Close to one-third of buyers said "yes" to automatic shifting. Gas caps hid under taillights, and the '41 facelift made this one of Cadillac's best design years. Production hit a record, too. Unlike Lincoln and Packard, which emphasized less-costly models, Cadillac stuck to luxury.

More than a million Chevrolets rolled out, helped by an appetizing restyle at Harley Earl's Art & Colour Studio. All models now had Knee-Action independent front suspension. A formal-looking Fleetline sedan debuted midseason.

Inboard-mounted headlights put Oldsmobiles among the most-distinctive cars on the street. Olds adopted new numerical model designations that would soon become familiar.

Positioned just above Chevrolet, Pontiac again ranked fifth in production—behind Buick, but comfortably ahead of Oldsmobile. Facelifting for 1941 followed the GM pattern.

# Buick

Cars get minor facelift

Widest array of Buicks yet—26 body styles on five separate series

Engines tuned for more horsepower; "Compound Carburetion" introduced

Century and Special lines get new fastback bodies

Final year for convertible phaetons

Series 80 folded into Series 90 Limited on 139-inch wheelbase

Model-year production up 34 percent to record 374,196; Buick is 4th in industry

1

2

3

1. Headlights were incorporated into new fenders for '41; running boards were gone for good. 2. Engine-turned metal panels flanked a central radio speaker. The plastic steering wheel cracked over time. 3. The Series 40B SE Special (*shown*) featured a 121-inch wheelbase, Buick's new fastback body style (shared with Century), Compound Carburetion, and a Super level interior.

1

2

3

4

5

6

1-2. Buick sold more convertibles than any automaker except Ford in 1941. This Series 40A ragtop rides a 118-inch wheelbase. 3. Sales of the 126-inch wheelbase Century were reduced by competition from Series 40B Specials. Here, the $1241 Century sedanet. 4. All Centuries had Compound Carburetion, which helped boost horsepower of the "Fireball 8" to 165. Favorable horsepower-to-weight ratios made Century the factory hot rod of the day. 5. Supers (sport coupe shown) shared the Series 40B 121-inch wheelbase 6. A white ash, mahogany, and birch-bodied Estate Wagon joined the 40B lineup.

1

1. Buick's best-selling convertible was the Series 50 Super at 12,391 units. This car is equipped with the optional factory fog lights, which were gaining in popularity. The new two-way hood could be opened from either side. 2. Series 50 Super and Series 70 Roadmaster lines had the final convertible phaetons Buick would ever offer. The two lines combined for only 834 sales. This is the $1555 Super. All Supers were powered by a 248-cid straight eight that produced 115 bhp or 125 bhp with Compound Carburetion. 3. The Super convertible phaeton used the same trunk as the Super sedan. Buick offered 19 different two-tone combinations for $41.50 extra.

2

3

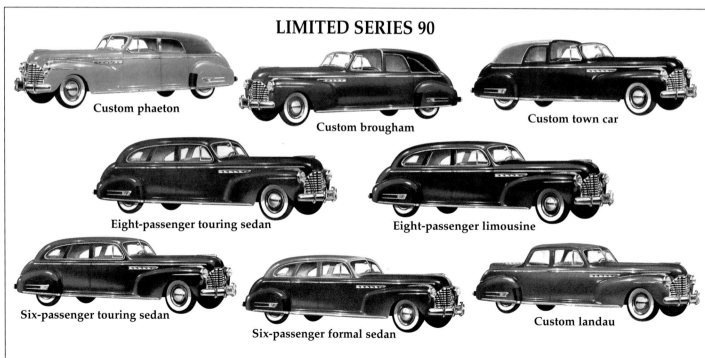

## LIMITED SERIES 90

Custom phaeton

Custom brougham

Custom town car

Eight-passenger touring sedan

Eight-passenger limousine

Six-passenger touring sedan

Six-passenger formal sedan

Custom landau

# Cadillac

New front-end styling introduces Cadillac's trademark rectangular eggcrate grille

Cadillac now one-make, one-engine division; LaSalle is gone

Olds Hydra-Matic automatic transmission offered as option

Air conditioning introduced; ordered in limited numbers

Series 61 revived to replace LaSalle as medium-price offering

Series 61 models use Fisher's new fastback bodies

New Series 67 replaces Series 72

Single body-style Series 63 added

Series 90 Sixteen is no more

Model-year production up 80 percent to 66,130; Cadillac ranks 15th in industry during record sales year

1

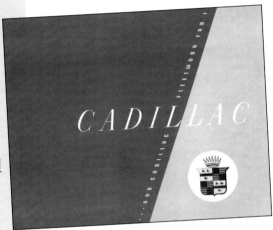

2

3

4

**1.** A new face introduced the rectangular eggcrate grille that would be Cadillac's trademark for years. New fenders fully incorporated the headlights as per the styling trend of the day. The Series 62 convertible coupe outsold the convertible sedan almost eight-to-one. **2.** Cadillac's 1941 brochure claimed its cars were the "Standard of the World" in terms of performance, handling, economy, comfort, and safety. **3.** A higher compression ratio raised horsepower of the 346-cid L-head V-8 to 150. **4.** Only 132 of the $3150 Series 75 division sedans were built. These cars featured a glass divider between the front and rear seats. The chauffeur's compartment was upholstered in black leather, while the rear featured tan wool. **5.** The new Series 63, which was available only as a four-door sedan, filled a price void between the Series 62 below it and the Series Sixty Special above it. All of these cars, as well as the Series 61, rode a 126-inch wheelbase.

5

1

2

3

1. Cadillac's Fleetwood Sixty Special sported front fenders that flowed into the doors. This styling cue began a trend that would be widely copied. 1941 was the final year for the unique Sixty Special in its original William Mitchell-designed 1938 configuration; the '42 was a more-mainstream car.
2. Cadillac interiors set the standard for all General Motors cars to emulate. Symmetry played a big part in dashboard design, with a passenger-side clock offsetting the driver's speedometer. 3. Rear seats were built for comfort as many Cadillac owners had chauffeurs. 4. Sixty Specials lacked running boards and the three chrome strips found on each fender of the other '41 Cadillacs. Sixty Specials listed at $2195 or $2395 with a "formal" glass division.
5. Coachcraft Ltd. built this customized Sixty Special for the Duke of Windsor. The swept-back fenders would appear on the Buick Roadmaster a year later.

4

5

1

2

3

4

**1.** Cadillac Series 62 moved down in wheelbase and price and up dramatically in sales, outdistancing 1940's sales by a factor of four. Convertible sedans were fading fast industrywide, and '41 was the final year for Cadillac's version; sales reached only 400. Like all 1941 Cadillacs, the gas cap was hidden under the left taillight. This car has a single backup light, a $7.50 option. **2-3.** The convertible sedan's elegant interior featured two-tone leather, woodgrain dashboard, and a fold-down rear armrest. Convertible tops now worked with the aid of vacuum assist. **4.** Cadillac station wagons are rare, and fastback wagons are even more so. Los Angeles-based Coachcraft Ltd. built this woody wagon for cowboy movie star Charles Starrett on a Series 61 chassis. Unlike most woodies, this one lacked side slats on the wood body.

# Chevrolet

Redesigned body rides a three-inch longer wheelbase

Master 85 series gone from roster

All Chevrolets have "Knee Action" independent front suspension

Fleetline introduced midyear as Special Deluxe subseries

16-millionth Chevrolet produced

Running boards concealed

Pickup trucks redesigned, offered with optional 235-cid inline six

Engine modifications raise output of "Victory Six" to 90 horsepower

Model-year production of 1,008,976 good for 1st in industry; up 32 percent for new company record

1

2

3

4

**1.** Ads stressed quality for the price, and America agreed. Sales topped 1 million for the first time. Chevrolets were known as well-built, reliable, easy-to-repair cars at a fair price. **2.** Royal Master tires, shown on a '41 Chevy, were known for quality at a time when buyers didn't know when they'd be able to get their next set. **3.** Chevrolet's second redesign in as many years stretched the wheelbase to 116 inches, concealed the running boards, incorporated the headlights into the fenders, and gave the front and rear windows a greater slope—all resulting in great-looking cars. **4.** Recovered from the Depression, America now fought inflation. This Special DeLuxe sport sedan cost $851, six percent more than in '40.

1

1. With a new roof that lacked rear quarter windows, the Fleetline four-door sedan was styled like a Buick Special. Introduced midyear as Chevy's most-expensive sedan, Fleetline garnered a respectable 34,162 orders. 2. Chevrolet interiors followed Cadillac style. Special DeLuxe models had a clock opposite the speedometer and woodgrain paint. Master DeLuxe cars had a metal disc in place of the clock and a single dashboard color. 3. A 6.5:1 compression ratio, a new head, and flat-top pistons helped boost horsepower of the 216-cid inline six to 90. With war on the horizon, the engine took on the name "Victory Six." 4. The rear glass was more-curved for '41, and two-tones were available. This Special DeLuxe business coupe has the optional bumper wing guards, bumper guards, and exhaust deflector that prevented bumper discoloration.

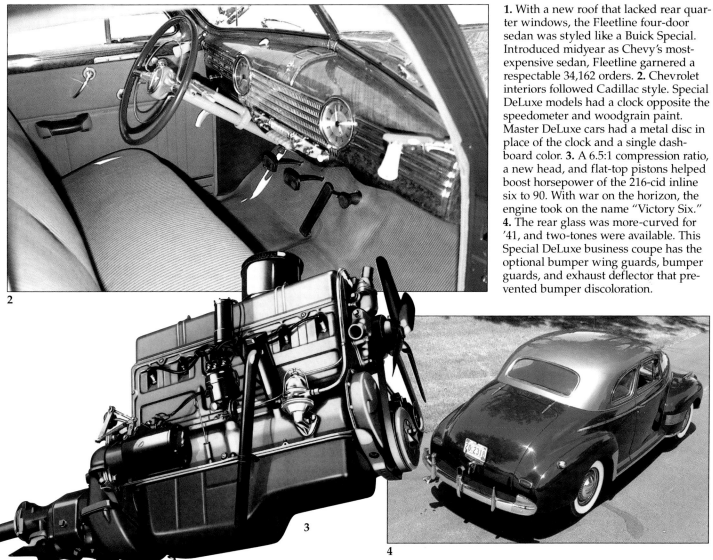

2

3

4

1. Standard and optional chrome-trim items dressed up the low-priced Chevys. This special DeLuxe convertible coupe features optional fog lamps, stainless-steel fender trim, bumper wing guards, chrome wheel-trim rings, and an accessory hood ornament. Note the chrome's red accents. This was a short-lived trend that didn't last past the war. 2. With the door open, you can see the concealed rubber-covered sill plates that replaced running boards on all 1941 Chevrolets. 3. The sedan delivery shared styling with the car line and was offered in both series. This Special DeLuxe model has the standard single taillight and side-opening rear door; options include full-wheel discs and trim rings. 4. The white ash and mahogany woody station wagon bodies were provided by Cantrell or Ionia Manufacturing. Only available in Special DeLuxe trim, the wagon was the costliest of all 1941 Chevrolets, selling for $995. 5. Based on the Master DeLuxe business coupe, the coupe pickup sold 1145 examples. The pickup box rolled out like a dresser drawer, and an independent taillight was provided. 6. Chevy trucks were redesigned for 1941, also producing an attractive, if toothy, look. An optional 235-cid inline six that made 93 horsepower was available for pickup truck buyers.

1

2

3

4

5

6

# Oldsmobile

Cars redesigned with new hood, grille, and longer wheelbases

60 series also known as Specials; 70 series models take on Dynamic Cruiser name

All cars offered with six- or eight-cylinder power for the first time

Fastback styling introduced on Dynamic Cruiser 70 series

Hydra-Matic automatic transmission installed on 50 percent of cars

L-head six-cylinder engine bored to 238 cid and boosted to 100 horsepower

Two-millionth Olds rolls off assembly line

Olds offers sleeper option, *a la* Nash; one year only

Final year for four-door convertibles in all GM divisions

Model-year production of 270,040 good for 6th in industry; up 46 percent for new company record

**1.** Olds ads, with the tagline "The Car Ahead," concentrated on modern features, including Hydra-Matic automatic transmission and fastback styling. **2.** The new grilles weren't much different than those of '40. The head- and marker lights were repositioned, fenders were redesigned, and the grille became more rectangular. **3.** The symmetrical Olds dash simulated American walnut for the Special series and Bayou wood for other models.

1

2

3

4

5

6

1. Like all Oldsmobiles for 1941, series 60 Special sedans came with a 238-cid, 100-bhp inline six-cylinder engine or a 257-cid, 110-bhp straight eight. Externally, there was no difference between 66s and 68s. 2. All Specials rode a 119-inch wheelbase. Sixes outsold eights by a wide margin. 3. Two 60 Special coupes were offered: the club coupe and the business coupe, which lacked a back seat. Club coupes were much more popular. 4. Only 776 series 68 convertible coupes were built. 5. At $1048, the 66 convertible coupe cost $41 less than the eight-cylinder version. 6. A deluxe package was offered for $20 on any 60 series car. It included a plastic hood ornament, deluxe instrument cluster, deluxe clock and glovebox door, glovebox light, and deluxe steering wheel. 7. Forward-thinking fastback styling was featured on series 70 Dynamic Cruisers, all of which rode a 125-inch wheelbase.

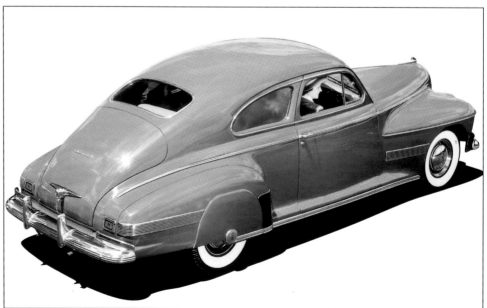

7

**1**

**2**

**3**

**4**

1. Two series 60 four-doors were offered, the traditional sedan and the new "town" sedan. The latter had rear vent windows. 2. The most popular '41 Olds was the 76 Dynamic Cruiser club sedan. Priced at $954, 46,885 units left dealership floors. 3. This 76 club sedan's interior features deluxe trim, including the passenger-side clock and chrome steering-wheel ring. 4. Interiors of 70 series cars were upholstered in leather or one of two types of cloth. 5. This press photo shows a 70 series fastback coupe undergoing testing at Oldsmobile's Milford Proving Grounds. The script behind the front fender identifies this as a Hydra-Matic-equipped car. 6. Olds offered wagons only in the 60 series. All had second- and third-row seats that could be easily removed. 7. Priced at $1575, the 98 convertible phaeton was the most-expensive Olds in '41. 8. The Dynamic Cruiser four-door sedan had "modern" fastback styling. Note the red striping in the trim.

**5**

**6**

**7**

**8**

# Pontiac

Cars redesigned with new grilles, fenders, trim, and one-piece hoods

Six series now offered—all called Torpedo: DeLuxe, Streamliner, and Custom, each with six- or eight-cylinder power

DeLuxe models use Chevy A-body; Streamliners have Olds/Buick B-body; Customs mount Cadillac C-body

Fastback styling introduced on Streamliner Torpedo series

L-head six-cylinder engine bored to 239 cid and boosted to 90 horsepower

Running boards concealed

Pontiac becomes best-selling car in medium-price field

Model-year production of 330,061 good for 5th in industry; up 52 percent for new company record

1

2

3

4

5

6

**1.** Pontiac had a car for all low- and medium-price buyers in 1941. Three series were offered, each with six- or eight-cylinder power. **2-3.** New Pontiac styling consisted of higher fenders with more silver streaks, horizontal grilles, and concealed running boards. The DeLuxe Torpedo Eight convertible coupe cost $1048, $25 more than the Six. **4.** Six-cylinder cars could be distinguished from Eights by their trim. Sixes had "Pontiac" lettering in the hood trim; Eights said "Pontiac Eight." DeLuxe models, like this coupe, used Chevy's A-body on a 119-inch wheelbase. **5-6.** Pontiac made two DeLuxe coupe body styles: business coupe and sedan coupe, also known as sport coupe. This is the $864 sport coupe. The front seats were 2½-inches wider than in '40. Business coupe trunks were 53½ inches deep, 14½ inches longer than sport coupe trunks. **7.** Metropolitan four-door sedans came out midyear as DeLuxe series cars. Designed with Cadillac Series 61 styling, they rode a less-costly platform. **8.** Pontiac Streamliners, like this four-door sedan, utilized Olds/Buick B-bodies with fastback styling on a 122-inch wheelbase. **9.** Custom series cars had Cadillac C-bodies. This Custom Torpedo Eight station wagon was the most-expensive Pontiac at $1250.

7

8

9

# Hudson

Judged by profits alone, 1941 turned out to be an exceptional year for Hudson, invariably one of the prominent independent manufacturers. In reality, most of that profit—totaling almost $4 million—was earned through defense contracts rather than regular car production. Whatever the source, total sales escalated by some 10 percent this year. Hudson again ended the model year in 11th place, ahead of Nash.

Not only were Hudsons facelifted again, but the lineup included some new models—led by a fresh Commodore series that would continue after the war. A station wagon appeared for the first time. So did a "Big Boy" car/pickup, following the lead of the combination car-truck models that Studebaker had been issuing for the past few years. Convertible sedans remained available, too, if not for long.

Almost all sheetmetal but the front fenders is new

Rooflines are lowered

New manual 3-speed synchromesh transmission is introduced

Convertibles pick up power-operated tops

"Symphonic Styling" greatly increases color choices, particularly interior/exterior combinations

*Safety Engineering* magazine cites Hudson as America's safest body design

Model-year production of 91,769 up 4 percent and good for 11th place in industry

4

5

6

1. Lowered, less-rounded rooflines and more-pronounced trunks were notice-able Hudson styling changes this year, as on this Super Six. 2. The Commodore Eight convertible differed from its Six counterpart only in engine size. 3. A Six DeLuxe touring sedan, with extra-cost two-tone paint. 4. This burly, but not inelegant, four-door Commodore Eight touring sedan sold new for $1035. Other Commodore Eight models included a convertible, station wagon, three-passen-ger coupe, and club and touring coupes. 5. The Commodore Eight dash was clean, with an eye-catching concavity at the center. Although this interior is a subdued gray, Hudson pushed complementary body-interior color combina-tions called "Symphonic Styling." 6-8. Another Commodore Eight, this one in Majestic Maroon, showing the sharp nose that recalled contemporaneous Fords and Studebakers. 9-10. Hudson promoted its wagons as passenger and com-mercial cars. The Super Six wagon seated eight, though the center and rear seats could be removed to accommodate cargo. Bodies were by Cantrell.

7

8

9

10

# Nash

Nash-Kelvinator brought in a $4.6-million profit for fiscal 1941, and a healthy chunk of those dollars were due to economy-car sales. Immediately after discontinuing the Lafayette, Nash introduced a new 600 series to attract budget-minded buyers. Built with unitized construction on a relatively short wheelbase, the 600 served as a crucial breakthrough for the company, helping to pave the way for additional efficient, economical models in the future—though Nash also continued to produce the bigger Ambassadors. Oddly, the Ambassadors now featured a unitized body *and* a frame.

The "600" designation wasn't a random number. It stood for the possibility of driving 600 miles on the car's 20-gallon fuel tank. Even though it evolved from prior models, with a moderate styling change, *Time* magazine called the 600 "the only completely new car in 1941." In fact, the coupes and sedans were quite handsome. The 600s were remarkably priced—lower than a Ford at the time.

Raymond Loewy styling dumps running boards, and adds "electric-shaver" grilles that flank the prow

New "600" series has unit-body on 112-inch wheelbase; boasts 25-plus mpg

Small 173-cid, 75-bhp Flying Scot L-head six engine introduced

Ambassador has unitized body *and* a frame

Ambassador is first low-price car with coil springs all around

Ambassador Eight rides on Ambassador Six's 121-inch wheelbase

Model-year production of 84,007 up 35 percent as Nash climbs to 12th place in industry

1

2

3

4

5

6

7

**1.** Nash went to unibody construction for 1941, and gained a "New Kind" of selling point. Curiously, only the entry-level 600 series had this innovation. Uplevel Ambassadors shared 600 bodies, but were assembled on-frame. **2.** This two-tone 600 sedan and others in the series were promoted as gas-sippers, claiming 25 to 30 mpg; the "600" name suggested 600 miles on a 20-gallon tank of gas. **3.** Novelty continued to be stressed in this ad, which helpfully noted beneath the image of the top car, "Actual color photograph of the Nash DeLuxe Trunk Back four door sedan, only $860." **4-6.** A rakish Ambassador Eight ragtop, with optional factory fog lamps and a 261-cid ohv inline eight developing 115 horsepower. Note the platelike steering-wheel hub. Although this car's dual exhausts are nonstock, the right-side mirror is a (seldom seen) factory option. **7-8.** The Ambassador Six rode a 121-inch wheelbase shared with the 600. Like the eight-cylinder engine, the 235-cid Nash six had overhead valves, long-stroke design, and laudable smoothness.

8

# Packard

At Packard, the future came early, in the form of a brand-new Clipper series. Launched at mid-year, the four-door Clipper predicted postwar styling and marked a sharp break with the past. Low and wide, the fastback sedan featured a narrow grille, faired-in fenders, a tapered tail and skirted rear wheels. Designed primarily by Howard "Dutch" Darrin, the Clipper was modified by Werner Gubitz. All 1941 Packards were classified internally as the Nineteenth series.

Not that the regular Packard models weren't beautiful. They were, but in the old-fashioned squared-up mode rather than the flowing modern shape. Unlike Cadillac, Packard continued to emphasize midprice models, effectively canceling its long tradition as a maker of fine motorcars.

Packard was the first auto company to offer air conditioning, though at an eye-popping price: $1080, which was enough to buy the most-costly Ford and still have change left over. An automatic clutch, called Electromatic, cost $37.50, but the driver still had to shift gears.

New front-end styling incorporates headlamps into fendertops; all models are lowered, eliminating running boards

A new model, midpriced Clipper, bows at midyear on 127-inch wheelbase

New semiautomatic clutch dubbed "Electromatic"

New overdrive system called "Aero-Drive"

First factory air conditioning introduced, but it's very expensive at $1080

Midlevel One Twenty line is reduced from 13 models to eight

Model-year production of 72,855 down 26 percent; Packard falls to 14th in industry

1

2

3

4

5

**1.** Packard carried on with its vertical-grille treatment for 1941, flying in the face of a new industry emphasis on horizontal design, and giving the line a look that was not just prestigiously "traditional" but faintly old-fashioned, as well. Packard did integrate its headlamps with the fenders, abandoning the outdated freestanding units. One of many innovations touted in this mildly tech-oriented period ad is the Electro-matic clutch, an extra-cost option with on-demand automatic or manual operation. **2.** Despite their pedigree, Packards were not uncommon as cabs. Roominess was a plus. **3-4.** Although considered Packard's "junior" series, the One Twenty sold at a price comparable to Buicks and Chryslers. This One Twenty convertible epitomized Packard performance, smooth operation, and high build quality. **5-6.** Here, a Packard woody wagon, with an inline 282-cid eight mated to a three-speed overdrive transmission. Rated brake horsepower was 125.

6

1

1. The imposing One Eighty line was a special-order variant of the One Sixty. This One Eighty touring sedan produced 160 horsepower from its 356-cubic-inch inline eight. Optional accessories on this example include bumper guards, right-side mirror, and hood ornament. 2-4. This built-to-order One Eighty convertible adds extreme scarcity to impeccable styling and smoothness. The bumper guards, radio, and hood cormorant are factory options; the fog lights are custom add-ons. The original purchaser was actress/ballerina Vera Zorina. 5-6. This 1941 convertible sedan parade car, with bronze body and brown and tan interior, came off the Packard line, "Dutch" Darrin custom windshield included, as a formal sedan, and was converted to a ragtop around 1983. 7. Packard ad art emphasized the smoothness of Air-Glide ride and Safe-T-fleX suspension. 8. Readers of this ad pondered the "beaut-ility" of the dash and "Multi-toned harmonies" of the interior. 9. A One Eighty formal sedan, with factory armrest cigarette lighters, note pads, perfume bottles, folding seat, Selectronic radio, rear-seat heater, and padded top. Luxury awaits!

2

3

4

5

7

8

6

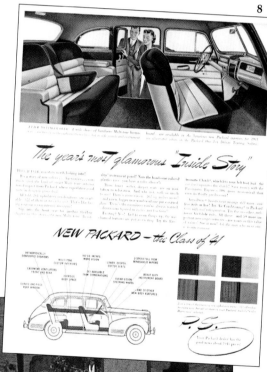

9

# Studebaker

Stylist Raymond Loewy reworked the entire Studebaker line for 1941, giving each model—low-priced Champion, Commander, and posh President—a more formal, elegant look with a sharper nose. A new Land Cruiser version featured closed-in rear roof quarters. Other automakers were introducing comparable formal sedans.

Loewy also introduced two-tone paint on the body sides of Studebakers, consisting of a slim color sweep just below the beltline. His name was becoming almost synonymous with Studebaker, and the two would become more-closely tied in the postwar years when stunning new models emerged.

In March 1941, new Skyway editions of the Commander and President debuted, abundantly trimmed and wearing neat fender skirts. Studebaker ended the model year dropping from 8th to 9th place, with 133,900 cars built—nearly 85,000 of them frugality-focused Champions, the top-selling line in Studebaker history.

Linewide styling update by Raymond Loewy dumps running boards

Champion, Commander, and President engines increase from 78, 90, and 100 hp to 80, 94, and 117, respectively

Wheelbase of top model, President, is 124.5 inches, up from 122 in 1940

Paint and upholstery combinations are significantly increased

Model-year production of 133,900 up 25 percent, but Studebaker falls to 9th in industry

1

2

3

4

8

9

10

6

11

7

12

**1.** The contrasting trim on this 1941 Champion Delux-tone sedan was an innovation of Studebaker design consultant Raymond Loewy, who made his name with corporate logos, streamlined industrial design, and memorable packaging (like the Lucky Strike pack). Champs started at $710, plus another $5 if you wanted Loewy's "contrasting color belt." **2-4.** Champions, like this four-door sedan, had a 170-cid, 80 horsepower flathead six. Art Deco treatment of inner door panels gave a touch a class. **5-7.** Studebaker advertising for '41 stressed the line's overall economy and roominess, but couldn't resist less-than-subtle status pitches to women. **8-9.** The Delux-tone cruising sedan was positioned at the middle of the Commander line. 1941 Studebakers had one- or two-piece windshields, without regard to model level. **10-11.** Here, a President Land Cruiser sedan, with President's striking double-curve rear fenders, by the Loewy Studio. **12.** At $1260, the President Skyway sedan topped the '41 Studebaker price list. Skirts, whitewalls, and hubcaps were standard.

# Minor Makes

Crosleys now had U-joints, after bad experiences with the initial driveshaft design. Rather than being sold (and serviced) at appliance stores, they were now available at regular car dealerships. Engines were smaller this year, but the cars themselves were considerably improved technically, promising greater durability and dependability.

A handful of final Graham Hollywoods and Hupp Skylarks went to customers, but they were leftovers. The joint-venture company had gone under in October 1940. American Bantam was also gone, with a few leftovers reaching customers as the company turned full attention to Jeep production.

Appeals to patriotism were a fact of 1941 life, prompting Willys to rename its passenger line the Americar. Up-front styling appeared more Ford-like, with a sharply pointed nose above a small grille. Sales were moderate but respectable as Willys-Overland geared up for military-vehicle production.

# Graham

Horsepower of super-charged L-head six rises from 120 to 124; normally aspirated six gains two bhp, to 95

Graham-Paige shuts the auto factory in November, but finds new economic life with war contracts

Unusually complex dies acquired from Cord delay production

Proposed convertible models exist only as prototypes

Model-year production approximately 860

1

2

3

4

5

**1-2.** Here, a Graham Hollywood, with a 124-horse supercharged six. The fashionable red wheels were stock, and were widely imitated by customizers. This year's Grahams were based on the coffin-nose Cord, but were rear- rather than front-wheel drive. Graham managed minuscule production, because of low demand and the troublesome complexity of the Cord dies. The 1940-41 total for all Hollywood models was just 1859. **3-5.** Another supercharged Hollywood six. These were handsome cars, but suicide doors and free-standing headlamps (replacing the Cord's hidden units of 1936-37) looked dated by 1941. Graham stopped car production after the '41 models, then prospered with defense contracts before selling its moribund auto division to Kaiser-Frazer in 1947.

# Hupmobile

Hupp production is carried out by Graham-Paige, in exchange for access to old Cord dies that have been acquired by Hupp

Only one convertible leaves the factory in 1940-41

Hupmobile ends operations in October 1940, three weeks into 1941 model year

Model-year production only 319

Hupmobile, like its partner, Graham, based its final cars on the Cord but did not offer a supercharger. Worse, the Cord dies made Hupmobile struggle to get its assembly line up and running for the '41s, and many once-interested buyers canceled advance orders. The Skylark Custom, seen here, was the only model offered for '41; only 319 were built, and of that number only one was a convertible. You're looking at it.

1

3

4

2

**1-4.** Another 1941 Hupmobile Skylark Custom, this one in eye-catching maroon, and with the vertical crest in the divided grille proudly proclaiming "HUPP." The textured-look dash fascia went a short way toward distinguishing the dash from that of the '41 Grahams. The final Skylarks were built in July 1940, and Hupmobile auto production was officially ended three months later. Only 103 Hupps were registered in 1941. Following reorganization under bankruptcy, Hupp eventually became a heating and air-conditioning subsidiary of White Consolidated Industries.

# Willys

Willys assumes patriotic "Americar" moniker and Ford-like styling

L-head four gains two bhp to 63; wheelbase grows two inches, to 104

Model line adds uplevel coupe, sedan

Model-year production of

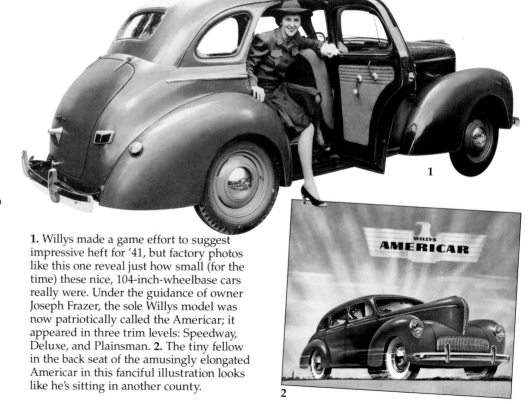

1

1. Willys made a game effort to suggest impressive heft for '41, but factory photos like this one reveal just how small (for the time) these nice, 104-inch-wheelbase cars really were. Under the guidance of owner Joseph Frazer, the sole Willys model was now patriotically called the Americar; it appeared in three trim levels: Speedway, Deluxe, and Plainsman. **2.** The tiny fellow in the back seat of the amusingly elongated Americar in this fanciful illustration looks like he's sitting in another county.

2

1

2

3

**1-3.** This 1941 Willys Americar DeLuxe coupe, with its shark-nose hood and faired-in headlamps, reveals the styling debt to Ford. The one-piece, vertical-strake grille had been a two-piece unit a year earlier. The coupe ran with a 63-horse, L-head four that displaced 134 cid. **4.** Willys' ½-ton pickup carried on the carlike styling. **5.** The Model MA jeep, variations of which kept Willys afloat during WW II. **6.** Not bad trunk space, but where's he going to put that satchel? **7.** Roughing it with the DeLuxe wagon, which retailed for $916. **8.** An Americar sedan, snapped on May 7, 1941, at New York's Roosevelt Field. This and similar promo images suggested Willys' no-nonsense, do-anything nature. Buyers, though, shunned small cars.

4

5

6

7

8

In the months following the Japanese attack on Pearl Harbor on December 7, 1941, the U.S. exercised astounding swiftness in transforming a civilian society into a nation on a solid military footing. Automobiles played a notable role in the changes to daily life. Government officials realized early on that private transport would have to be curtailed if the U.S. was going to function as the "arsenal of democracy" that President Franklin Delano Roosevelt had called for in 1940. Conservation of scarce resources—including petroleum, rubber, and steel—would play a major part in the war effort.

To get the new policy underway, as of January 1, 1942, the federal government ordered automakers to issue only "blackout" cars, using painted parts rather than the usual chrome on trim pieces (bumpers could still be chrome). Cars that had been built late in 1941 sported their regular trim, but those that left the assembly lines in the early days of 1942 adopted an austere appearance.

Whether chromed or plainly trimmed, most of the 1942 models looked lower, longer, and more massive than in '41, even if actual dimensions didn't change appreciably. Grilles became more gaudy and "busy," not nearly as clean-looking. Few, if any, models seemed as attractive or fashionable as their 1941 predecessors.

DeSoto scored points for distinctive styling, strictly on the basis of its covered headlights—an innovation borrowed from the 1936-37 Cord and used only for 1942 models. All Chrysler products adopted "alligator-style" hoods that opened from the front, and running boards were fully hidden.

Chevrolet launched a new line of Fleetline fastback sedans. Hudson introduced a DriveMaster semiautomatic transmission. Studebaker called its new semiautomatic unit Turbo-matic. Nash offered its last straight-eight engines.

Civilian auto production officially came to a halt on February 10, 1942, though trucks kept rolling off the assembly lines until March 3. GM and Ford released their final cars right around deadline time.

Not only were new automobiles strictly rationed for the duration of the war, but the government imposed a national 40-mph speed limit as a measure to conserve gasoline and rubber. Later, the limit would be cut to 35 miles per hour.

Gasoline rationing was ordered in January 1942, starting in northeastern states. Americans were unaccustomed to wartime sacrifice. During World War I, civilian life had been largely undisturbed as the battles—harsh though they were—took place far from American shores, with no mass communication to keep people informed. In this more-modern war, radio broadcasts would be issued regularly, bringing news from each battle front.

Despite continuous government calls for sacrifice in the name of patriotism, not everyone was eager to face a restricted lifestyle. Gas rationing went nationwide on December 1, 1942. Most drivers got an "A" sticker for the windshield, permitting the purchase of three or four gallons per week. War workers in car pools got "B" stickers, good for a bit extra. "C" stickers went to doctors and corporate executives, while the seldom-seen "X" sticker was restricted to government officials.

Urban dwellers took streetcars, or walked to work. Families shunned automobile vacations and pleasure trips.

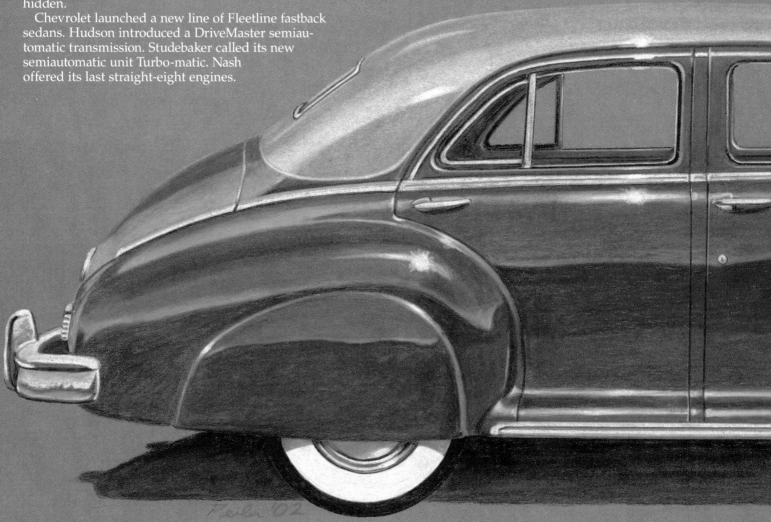

With no replacements available, bald tires and frequently patched inner tubes became unavoidable. Many people put their cars up on blocks for the duration, choosing not to drive at all.

Gasoline and tires weren't the only restricted commodities. The Office of Price Administration (OPA) established a rationing point system for foods, including meat, butter, coffee, and sugar—many of the edibles that Americans enjoyed most. Without a ration book and the appropriate coupons, no purchases could be made.

As the year ended, though, gas-rationing cheaters were rampant. Nefarious folks who refused to accept the legal limit uncovered sneaky ways to obtain more gasoline than their neighbors. Government agents spent considerable effort tracking down the culprits. A thriving "black market" had developed in rationed items. Nevertheless, as a result of gasoline rationing, automobile usage was eventually cut by 40 percent.

As more young men went off to war as G.I.s, fewer were left on the home front. Those who were classified 4-F (medically unfit for service) by their draft boards typically had their pick of jobs—and often of girls as well at the nation's dance halls and other recreational spots.

War-themed movies filled the nation's theaters in 1942. Frank Capra, best known for directing populist comedies in the 1930s, turned out a series of seven inspirational—if not propagandistic—films called *Why We Fight*.

Humphrey Bogart, Ingrid Bergman, and Claude Rains exchanged witty banter in the movie *Casablanca*, which took place in early wartime North Africa, with a strong Nazi presence. Popular songs, too, took on a wartime theme, with

titles such as *This Is the Army Mr. Jones, Der Fuehrer's Face*, and *Praise the Lord and Pass the Ammunition*.

On a lighter note, Bing Crosby crooned *White Christmas* in the movie *Holiday Inn*. Big-Band musician Glenn Miller stood high on the pop-music charts with his brand of swing; but while entertaining the troops as a military officer, Miller would be killed in 1944.

On February 19, 1942, President Roosevelt ordered the forced evacuation of as many as 120,000 people of Japanese descent from their homes on the West Coast. About 77,000 of the evacuees, who were sent to internment camps in the desert, were American citizens. Most of them would remain interned until the war was over in 1945, but in '43 the U.S. government permitted male internees of appropriate age to join the military. Many did, fighting with distinction in all-Japanese units.

In May, Secretary of War Henry Lewis Stimson authorized the Women's Army Auxiliary Corps (WACS). Each of the military services began to recruit women for service. By the time the war ended, more than 300,000 would serve.

In late-1941 and early 1942, Allied forces lost one territory after another in the Pacific: Guam, Wake, Hong Kong, Singapore—and perhaps most ominously, the Philippines. Then, the U.S. began a turnaround on the Pacific front, undertaking major offensives at Midway, the Coral Sea, and Guadalcanal. In the other area of war, as part of their battle against Adolf Hitler and Italian dictator Benito Mussolini, the Allies invaded North Africa in November.

World War II had effectively ended the Great Depression as U.S. industry ramped up for wartime production. Yet, although the tide of war was slowly beginning to turn in the Allies' favor, America faced a long, hard battle ahead—on land, sea, and air, as well as on the home front.

# Chrysler Corporation

Front-end facelifting gave Chrysler a modestly new look for the abbreviated 1942 model year. A new "alligator" hood opened from the front, not the side. After introducing several new upholstery patterns for 1941, Chrysler added another one this year called Thunderbird, with a Native American motif. Running boards were hidden beneath flared door bottoms on all models.

Concealed "Airfoil" headlights made DeSoto one of the most-distinctive makes of 1942. Operating like the hidden lights on the 1936-37 Cord, DeSoto's lasted only this one season. "Out of sight, except at night" was the promotional slogan, and they imparted a clean look to the facelifted front end. A plush new Fifth Avenue edition of the Custom town sedan joined the DeSoto lineup.

Dodge cars got a bigger six-cylinder engine and a massive grille as part of the substantial facelift. Styling was less-radical than DeSoto's, but optional fender skirts could give the body a rakish stance. As on other Chrysler products, Plymouth doors now covered the running boards, and the grille had a more-massive look.

Chrysler Corporation earned its first Army-Navy "E" Award in 1942 for wartime production.

# Chrysler

Facelift has taller, squarer front fenders and wrap-around grille bars that also appear on rear fenders; running boards concealed

Six-cylinder grows to 251 cid and 120 horsepower

Highlander interior joined by Thunderbird design

Chrysler suspends civilian operations Jan. 29, 1942

Cars sold after Jan. 1, 1942, are "blackout specials" with painted trim

Production limited to 36,586 in short model year

1

2

3

1. A Chrysler promotional shot includes sketches depicting "the cars of tomorrow." 2. Derham modified a few Crown Imperial sedans into stately looking town cars. 3. An unknown builder produced this custom phaeton from a Town & Country wagon; it was used in at least one movie. 4. Another Derham town car, this one with squared-off roofline and tapered rear deck.

4

1

2

3

4

5

6

7

8

9

1-5. The Town & Country woody returned for '42, and despite a higher price (up more than $100 to $1595) and short production run, sales stayed about the same at just under 1000 units. Again, it came only with a six-cylinder engine. 6. Crown Imperials continued in six- and eight-passenger versions on a 145.5-inch wheelbase. 7. A "blackout" New Yorker sedan still sports chrome bumpers, but most exterior trim is painted. Note the white plastic trim rings on the wheels; these were intended to simulate whitewalls. 8. Another blackout model, this one a 121.5-inch wheelbase Windsor club coupe. 9. Dennis "Frenchy" Demomy drives the last prewar Chrysler off the assembly line on Jan. 29, 1942. Chrysler executives (*left to right*) Stewart W. Munroe, David A. Wallace, Charles L. Jacobson, A. M. Fleming, and H. V. Hilborg give it a proper send-off.

# DeSoto

Bold new look comes courtesy of hidden headlights, the first to be used on a production car since the 1936-37 Cord

Massive front and rear bumpers replace thinner ones; cars gain wraparound trim strips

Running boards concealed

Six-cylinder engine grows from 228 cid to 237, gaining ten horsepower in the process, now 115

DeLuxe model gains convertible and town sedan body styles

Ashtray, map, and glovebox lights added

DeSoto suspends civilian operations Feb. 9, 1942

Cars sold after Jan. 1, 1942, are "blackout specials" with chrome bumpers and painted trim

Model-year production limited to 24,015 as DeSoto switches to wartime production

1

2

3

**1-2.** At $1317, a Custom convertible was the most-expensive regular-wheelbase DeSoto for 1942, but it made for a stunning ride. Only 489 were built in the shortened model year. Note that this example wears the optional plastic wheel-trim rings that were used to simulate whitewall tires. **3.** By contrast, a Custom two-door sedan listed for $1142 and found 913 buyers. **4.** DeSoto's expansive sales brochure included these colorful drawings depicting the various body styles available. **5-6.** "Out of sight except at night," DeSoto's hidden headlights were controlled by an under-dash lever. When the lever was activated, the doors retracted upward and the lights turned on. **7.** The Custom four-door sedan was DeSoto's biggest seller for 1942. A total of 7974 were built starting at $1152.

# DeSoto
## Custom & DeLuxe
## Body Styles for 1942

Custom convertible club coupe

Custom four-door sedan

Custom 7-passenger sedan & limousine

DeLuxe business coupe

Custom Brougham

Custom club coupe

DeLuxe 6-passenger coupe

DeLuxe four-door sedan

DeLuxe 7-passenger sedan

Custom coupe

Custom town sedan

DeLuxe two-door sedan

DeLuxe town sedan

4

5

6

7

# Dodge

New styling includes massive rectangular grille, front fenders more smoothly integrated into body

Running boards concealed

Cars are all new mechanically, but retain 119.5-inch standard wheelbase and 137.5-inch senior-line wheelbase

Six-cylinder engine gets increased displacement, growing from 218 to 230 cid; horsepower climbs from 91 to 105; now called "Power-Flow"

DeLuxe series adds a club coupe

Dodge suspends civilian operations in early February 1942

Cars sold after Jan. 1, 1942, are "blackout specials" with chrome bumpers and painted trim

Model-year production limited to 68,522 as Dodge switches to wartime production

1

2

3

4

5

6

7

8

9

10

11

**1-2.** A smart-looking Custom club coupe cost $1045. Though its dashboard layout was little changed from '41, gauges had light—instead of dark—colored faces, and the surrounding metal was painted with a new woodgrain effect. Drivers faced a rather elaborate new three-spoke steering wheel with full horn ring. **3-4.** New for '42 was a DeLuxe club coupe, which cost $50 less than its ritzier Custom counterpart. **5.** Dodge's most-popular car was the Custom four-door sedan. At $1048, it sold 22,055 copies. **6-7.** For just $895, customers could drive a DeLuxe business coupe—and live in the trunk. **8-11.** Again the most-expensive standard-wheelbase Dodge, the Custom convertible listed for $1245. This car has Fluid Drive, which incorporated a fluid coupling between the engine and transmission. It allowed the car to be brought to a stop and driven off again in any gear without having to declutch, though the clutch was still used when shifting from one gear to another. The greater use of brightwork on '42s brought a richer look.

# Plymouth

Redesign brings lower, wider bodies with broader grilles; weights increase by about 90 pounds

Six-cylinder engine grows from 201 to 218 cubic inches, with higher compression ratio; horsepower jumps from 87 to 95

X-brace chassis replaced by boxed side rail unit

Long-wheelbase, seven-passenger models dropped

Town sedan body style added to Special DeLuxe series

Civilian production ends on Jan. 31, 1942

Cars sold after Jan. 1, 1942, are "blackout specials" with chrome bumpers and painted trim

With model-year production of 152,427, Plymouth retains its 3rd-place ranking in the industry, ending up only about 8000 units shy of 2nd-place Ford

1

2

3

4

1. All Plymouths were garnished with more exterior brightwork for '42, as evidenced by this top-line Special DeLuxe club coupe, which listed for $928. 2-4. New for Plymouth was a town sedan with blanked-out rear roof quarters; it arrived in the Special DeLuxe series at $980. Like other town sedans in the Chrysler Corp. family, it used front-hinged rear doors rather than the traditional sedan's "suicide" rear-hinged doors. 5. New Plymouths are shown undergoing final inspection 6. A Special DeLuxe convertible cost $1078. Most noticeable on light-colored cars was the new sheetmetal "apron" that appeared below the front bumper. 7. With the demise of the long-wheelbase models, the wood-sided Special DeLuxe wagon became the most-expensive Plymouth at $1145. 8. Plymouth two-door sedans were used by the Michigan State Police, even though the new 95-horsepower six was outgunned by most rivals. 9. Dashboards carried the symmetrical styling and wood-grain paintwork common to Chrysler Corp. cars for '42. 10-11. Per government mandate, "blackout" versions were built in the final days of prewar assembly, with virtually all exterior trim, save the bumpers, being painted rather than chromed.

5

6

7

8

9

10

11

# Ford Motor Company

Ads promised "America's Most Modern 6 [and] America's lowest-priced 8." Ford ranked number two again, behind Chevrolet, in the short 1942 season. Changes were few, beyond the revised lower and wider grille—a favorite way of making the 1942 models look different than their predecessors. In Ford's case, helped by fresh front fenders, the new grille imparted a more-cohesive look.

Design and engineering modifications were more notable in the Lincoln division. Not only did Lincoln's V-12 engine grow in displacement, but it was made more reliable. Flashy facelifting

of all Lincoln models (Zephyr and Continental) predicted postwar styling. Little twin parking lights flanked each of the cars' headlights this year, and fenders were longer and taller. Continentals gained seven inches in length, though the difference wasn't so easy to see, and all models were heavier than before.

Mercury cars had a "busier" and more massive appearance, resulting from a more-substantial facelift than many had received for 1942. Following the trend toward gearshifting ease, Mercury introduced a "Liquamatic" semiautomatic transmission, but it wouldn't last long.

# Ford

New front end has one-piece fenders and fully horizontal grille

First turn signals and windshield washers

Low-priced Specials come only with 6-cylinder power

Ford suspends civilian operations Feb. 2, 1942

Cars sold after Jan. 1, 1942, are "blackout specials" with chrome bumpers and painted trim

Model-year production of 160,432, good for second in industry

1

2

3

4    1941

1942

5

6

7

**1-2.** Ford's 1942 ads claimed new materials used due to defense considerations were equal to or better than previous materials. Time showed otherwise. **3.** Fenders were now one-piece units, which saved money. To conserve zinc and aluminum, the grille was stamped rather than diecast. The body and doors swept out at the bottom, concealing the running boards. Special DeLuxe Fordor sedans (*shown*) were outsold by only the Tudor sedans. **4.** Fords were still police favorites. This is the Lincolnwood, Illinois, police department of 1942. **5.** The Super DeLuxe station wagon remained the most-expensive Ford at $1115 with the flathead six or $1125 with the eight. **6.** Sedan deliveries received passenger-car styling and joined the DeLuxe series. **7.** Ford dashboards were redesigned, using round gauges in a symmetrical layout like GM cars.

1

2

3

4

5

**1.** Only 2920 convertibles were produced, all with Lincoln-built bodies in the Super DeLuxe series. Ragtop buyers had the choice of black or beige tops, and red, blue, or tan leather interiors. Engine choices continued as the 226-cid, 90-bhp flathead inline six or the 221-cid, 90-bhp flathead V-8. Cars outfitted with Special level trim could only be ordered with six-cylinder power. **2.** DeLuxe series cars had painted grille surrounds and "DeLuxe" spelled out vertically in the center grille bar. Parking lights on all '42s moved to the catwalk area above the grille. The "8" in the hood emblem on this Fordor sedan identifies it as the $885 eight-cylinder car. **3.** Taillight pods were now painted (instead of chrome-plated) and had a horizontal design, though they stayed in about the same place as '41. **4.** Ford was making every effort to conserve metal, so more plastic, which was viewed as an advanced material, was used in dashboards, radio grilles, and door handles. **5.** The Super DeLuxe five-passenger sedan coupe was characterized by a slight humpback look in its rear quarter panels. Ford also offered three-passenger coupes in Special DeLuxe trim. **6.** Ford's ½-ton pickup was restyled for the second straight year, taking on heavy-duty truck design. It also rode a new truck-style chassis, making the pickup more rugged and moving it further from its passenger-car roots.

6

# Lincoln

Heavy facelift features new grille, wider fenders, longer overall length

Vacuum-operated power windows standard

V-12 engine bored to 305 cid and horsepower boosted to 130

"Liquamatic" semiautomatic transmission debuts, but is recalled due to mechanical problems

Price increases reflect elevated status of Lincoln cars within Ford corporate lineup

Wheels change from 16-inch diameter to 15

Lincoln suspends civilian operations Jan. 31, 1942

Cars sold after Jan. 1, 1942, are "blackout specials" with chrome bumpers and painted trim

Model-year production limited to 6547 as Lincoln switches to wartime production

1

2

3

1. The new face featured Cadillac-like "tombstone" styling, with a split grille and heavier nose. Zephyr price increases placed them in Cadillac Series 62 and 63 territory. Convertibles now had roll-down rear quarter windows. 2. Known as the "Sunshine Special," president Franklin Delano Roosevelt's 1939 K Series was shipped to Detroit to be updated and armor plated. Lincoln replaced the front end with '42-style fenders and grille, and added 17-inch wheels. 3. At $3075, the Custom limousine was the most-expensive Lincoln for '42. Pushbutton door latches replaced '41's pull handles. 4. The final '42 Lincoln rolled off the assembly line Jan. 31, 1942. 5-7. Unlike most automotive advertising, these 1942 ads make no mention of Lincoln's war effort. Instead they say the '42 Lincoln is the best ever, and boast about its smooth ride and available "automatic" transmission. 8. Continentals lacked the hood and beltline moldings of the Zephyrs and Customs. Only 136 cabriolets were built, compared to 200 club coupes. 9-10. Vacuum-operated power windows now came standard on all Lincolns, and Continentals continued to use gold-plated trim.

4

5

6

7

8

9

10

# 1942

# Mercury

Facelifted models get new horizontal grille and more-massive front fenders

New styling takes on a Lincoln appearance

"Liquamatic" semiautomatic transmission debuts, but is recalled due to mechanical problems; very few Mercurys were so equipped

Flathead V-8 upgraded to 6.4:1 compression and 100 horsepower

Turn signals offered as option

A/S five-passenger coupe dropped from lineup

Mercury suspends civilian operations Feb. 10, 1942

Cars sold after Jan. 1, 1942, are "blackout specials" with chrome bumpers and painted trim

Model-year production limited to 22,722 as Mercury switches to wartime production

1

1. Mercury's 1942 interiors took on a General Motors-inspired symmetrical look with a round clock balancing off the speedometer on either side of a central speaker grille. 2. Texaco gas stations advertised the cleanliness of their restrooms to help build brand loyalty. 3. A split-horizontal grille, a new bumper, and inboard parking lights marked the 1942 Mercury face. The multiple-piece fenders of 1941 were gone, and new dual chrome strips adorned each fender. Prices for the station wagon were up $119 to $1260, making it the most-expensive model that year. It was also the heaviest and longest Mercury. Station wagons had roll-up windows instead of the sliding type. 4. Four-door or "town" sedans outsold two-door sedans two-to-one. The rear vent windows in this two-door sedan were functional. 5. Roll-up rear quarter windows were added to the club convertible, which listed at $1215. Tan or black tops were offered, but production was only 969 due to the war. After the government banned whitewalls (*shown*), white wheel-trim bands could be ordered. 6. The only remaining pure coupe was the three-passenger, or business, coupe. Rear quarter windows were now functional.

2

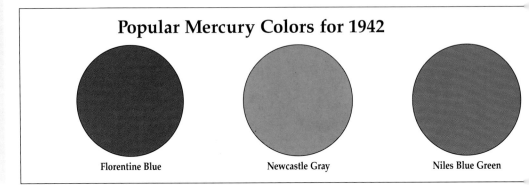

## Popular Mercury Colors for 1942

Florentine Blue    Newcastle Gray    Niles Blue Green

Fathom Blue          Moselle Maroon          Village Green          Phoebe Gray Metallic

# General Motors

Unlike most makes for 1942, Buick came out with a brand-new body, not a mere touch-up job. Restyling followed the lead of Harley Earl's 1938 Y-Job show car. With its low, wide, vertical-bar grille complemented by "Airfoil" fenders that swept along the body to the rear fenders, the Buick body would still look fresh in 1946-48.

Cadillacs got all-new styling with long pontoon fenders that ran back into the front doors. On four-door models, similar rear fenders blended into the back doors. As on other GM makes, the fastback body style was expanding, now offered on Series 62.

New Fleetline "torpedo" style Chevrolet models included a two-door Aerosedan and four-door Sportmaster. Fenders blended into the front doors, as on more-costly GMs. Compared to its 1941 predecessor, the '42 grille looked cleaner, if in many eyes, less dramatic.

Oldsmobile officially became a GM division this year, abandoning the Olds Motor Works name used since the 1890s. Headlights reverted to the normal position, after a one-year stint with inboard lights.

Pontiac was the first automaker to earn the U.S. Navy's "E" Award for military production. Restyling for 1942 mimicked other GM divisions, but considerable shuffling of models took place.

# Buick

Complete redesign inspired by 1938 Buick Y-Job show car; Super and Roadmaster get longer wheelbases

Government orders small-block pistons changed from aluminum to cast iron; horsepower suffers

Buick suspends civilian operations Feb. 2, 1942

Cars sold after Jan. 1, 1942, are "blackout specials" with chrome bumpers and painted trim

Model-year production of 94,442 good for 4th in industry

1

2

3

4

5

6

**1.** New styling brought the Super four-door sedan's front fenders into the doors. Other Supers, and all Roadmasters, featured sweptback, or "Airfoil," fenders that flowed all the way into the rear fenders. **2.** All Buicks used the same dash, but refinement varied. This Super dash features woodgrain and "B-U-I-C-K" radio pushbuttons. **3.** Roadmasters rode a 129-inch wheelbase. The convertible sold for $1675 and came with a power top. **4.** Buick ads stressed quality in a time of unsurity, but all automotive quality was suffering as automakers geared up for war. **5.** Buick's waterfall grilles and huge bumpers were very modern. Supers (*sedanet shown*), Roadmasters, and Limiteds were powered by the Fireball 8, which remained unchanged at 320 cid and 165 bhp. The government mandated that cast-iron pistons replace the aluminum units in Buick's 248-cid straight eight, taking horsepower down to 110 or 118 with Compound Carburetion. **6.** A Special "blackout special" was the final Buick built before factories were completely converted to defense work on Feb. 3, 1942.

# Buick Body Styles for 1942

Special Series 40A 6-pass. family sedanet

Special Series 40A 3-pass. business sedanet

Special Series 40A 6-pass. four-door sedan

Special Series 40A 6-passenger convertible

Special Series 40A 3-passenger utility coupe

Special Series 40B business sedanet

Special Series 40B 6-pass. four-door sedan

Special Series 40B Estate Wagon

Super 6-passenger four-door sedan

Super 6-passenger sedanet

Super 6-passenger convertible

Century 6-passenger four-door sedan

Century 6-passenger sedanet

Roadmaster 6-passenger four-door sedan

Roadmaster 6-passenger sedanet

Roadmaster 6-passenger convertible

Limited 6-passenger four-door sedan

Limited 8-passenger touring sedan

Limited 6-passenger formal sedan

Limited 8-passenger limousine

# Cadillac

Massive restyling based on 1941 bodies for everything except Series 75; grille revised and pontoon fenders added

Cadillac's 40th anniversary

Optional Hydra-Matic installed on 60 percent of cars

Longer wheelbases for Series 62 and Sixty Special

Final year for Series 63 and 67 models

Rear fender skirts made standard on all models

Cars sold after Jan. 1, 1942, are "Blackout Specials" with chrome bumpers and painted trim

Car production ends Feb. 4, 1942, as Cadillac switches to wartime production

Model-year production of 16,511, including 2150 "Blackout Specials"

1. The new grille advanced what had begun in '41. The rectangular shape was gone, the bars were wider, rectangular marker lights were incorporated, and bumper guards with chrome bullets appeared. 2. Series Sixty Specials and Series 62s had reworked dashboards. Round gauges changed to rectangular, but symmetry was still evident. 3. Series 62 models moved up to a 129-inch wheelbase. 1941's triple fender strips gave way to single strips.

1. Custom coachbuilt cars were fading by the 1940s because factory-built cars could approach their quality and performance at more-reasonable prices. This Fleetwood Sixty Special town car was most likely built by Derham, the coachbuilder that also built six Series 75 town cars in '42. 2-3. Pontoon fenders were the major change for Cadillac in 1942. Fastback Series 61 body styles had been introduced in '41, but now Cadillac offered fastback Series 62 models. This Series 61 coupe was the lowest-priced Cadillac at $1450. Its four-door sedan counterpart sold for $1530 and was the most-popular Caddy that year, selling 3218 units. Fog lamps were a popular option; when they weren't ordered, chrome circles filled their prominent position on the grille. 4. Series 75 was the only Cadillac to maintain squared-off fenders with triple chrome trim. This body would remain in production until 1949. All '42 Cadillacs continued with the 346-cid L-head V-8 that had been upgraded to 150 bhp in 1941.

# Chevrolet

Facelifted cars get new grilles, hoods, fenders

Chevrolet claims one out of every four cars on American roads is a Chevy

Fleetline becomes its own separate subseries, gains a second body style called Aerosedan

Cars sold after Jan. 1, 1942, are "Blackout Specials" with chrome bumpers and painted trim

Civilian car production ends Feb. 9, 1942; Chevrolet continues to make "Blackout" military-staff vehicles

Model-year production of 258,795 good for 1st in industry

1-2. War was imminent; it was just a matter of time. Chevrolet responded by advertising its war effort and the quality and reliability of its cars. 3. Fastbacks in GM's senior divisions proved so popular in '41 that Chevy got a fastback, called Aerosedan, in '42. Despite an $880 price tag, it was the most-popular Chevy for the short model year. 4. New styling cues included fenders that stretched into the doors, longer hoods that reached the doors, and a revised grille. Cadillac-inspired chrome fender "speedlines" came on Fleetlines.

1

2

1. A mere 1742 Special DeLuxe cabriolets were built before car production ended February 9, 1942. Convertibles now had rear quarter windows that aided visibility. 2. A new Chevrolet emblem adorned the hood; it looked remarkably like a military decoration. 3. The Fleetline Aerosedan's rear quarter windows rolled down, and all Fleetlines came with Chevrolet's "Fleet-weave" broadcloth upholstery. 4. The 1942 Chevrolet brochure said of the valve-in-head inline six: "It's the same good engine with the same good pistons." Actually, the pistons were cast iron; cast-iron (instead of aluminum) pistons caused 1942 Buicks to lose horsepower. 5-6. Note the painted headlight bezels, side trim, hubcaps, and trunk handle on this rare surviving "Black-out Special" Fleetline Aerosedan. Despite materials shortages, bumpers, bumper guards, and windshield wipers were still chrome. 7. The Fleetline Sportmaster sedan carried over from 1941 with its rear vent windows. This car is restored to look like a military-staff car; all that chrome would be inappropriate—and most likely unavailable—for a military vehicle.

3

CHEVROLET FOR 1942

Fleetline
Special De Luxe
Master De Luxe

4

5

6

7

## 1942 Chevrolet Colors

Martial Maroon Metallic

Santone Beige Metallic

Fortress Gray

Torpedo Gray

Fleet Blue Metallic

Seafoam Green

Ensign Blue Metallic

Wing Blue

Scout Brown

Sport Beige

Volunteer Green Metallic

Maple Brown Metallic

# Oldsmobile

Bodies get facelift with new fenders and two-tier bumpers

Name changes from Olds Motor Works to Oldsmobile division of General Motors

Nearing war, cars bear "B-44" designation, marking Oldsmobile's 44 years in business

General manager Sherrod E. Skinner takes six-month hiatus to serve as Director of the Product Division of the War Department's Office of Materiel

Fastback body styles offered in all series

Custom Cruiser 96 dropped

Custom Cruiser 98 wheelbase up to 127 inches

Cars sold after Jan. 1, 1942, are "Blackout Specials" with chrome bumpers and painted trim

Civilian car production ends Feb. 5, 1942

Model-year production limited to 67,999 as Olds shifts to wartime production

1

2

3

4

5

6

7

8

1. Militaristic Olds ads claimed its cars had "fuse-lage" fenders, "dreadnaught" frames, and an engine of greater "fire power." 2-4. New styling included fenders that extended into the doors, a "double duty" two-tier bumper/grille, and out-board headlights. This is the $960 66 two-door sedan. Series 60 models had rippled bedford cloth or mohair upholstery. 5-6. Rationing was controlled with stickers applied to windshields; they warned car owners to conserve resources and determined how much gas motorists could buy in a given month. 7-8. The 98 line was down to three models, including this four-door sedan. The hood was lengthened to eliminate the cowl, and the wheelbase was stretched two inches. 9. A "Blackout Special" 98 club sedan was the last Olds built before conversion to war produc-tion. 10. Hydra-Matic was still a selling point, but military efforts crept into almost all 1942 ads.

9

10

123

# Pontiac

Bodies get new grilles, pontoon fenders, longer hoods

C-bodied Custom line eliminated

Station wagon changes to Streamliner series

Chieftain designation denotes deluxe trim level on Streamliners

Fastback body styles offered in all series, with addition of Torpedo sedan coupe or sedanet

Six- and eight-cylinder cars split sales 50/50

Cars sold after Jan. 1, 1942, are "Blackout Specials" with chrome bumpers and painted trim

Civilian car production ends Feb. 10, 1942

15,404 cars built in calendar-year 1942

Model-year production of 83,555 good for 5th in industry

1

2

3

4

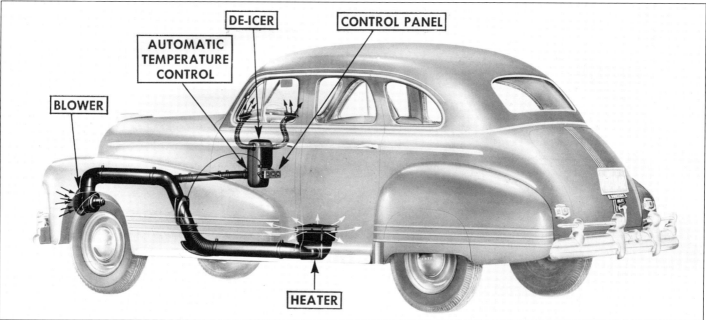

BLOWER

AUTOMATIC TEMPERATURE CONTROL

DE-ICER

CONTROL PANEL

HEATER

5

**1.** Like all General Motors ads of the day, Pontiac advertisements noted quality in unsure times and the company's war effort. **2.** Pontiacs were wider, heavier, and longer in 1942. The grilles, although running the width of the car, had a vertical center section that mimicked the hood line. **3.** Pontoon-style fenders extended into the doors. This is the $1010 Torpedo eight four-door sedan with notchback styling. Streamliner models with Chieftain level trim had fender badges in the speedlines behind the front wheel wells. **4.** GM's styling studio was looking forward in 1942. With the silver streaks on the trunk, the blue fastback on the left is most likely a Pontiac concept. The three models along the far wall are probably Cadillacs; that rear-fender design was introduced in '48. **5.** Pontiac had developed a new heating and ventilating system over a two-year period. Fresh outside air was used to heat the car and defrost the windows. **6.** 1942 ads claimed Pontiac had made 15 improvements, though no mention was made of what they were.

Most important announcement PONTIAC has ever made!

In addition to 15 important improvements, the 1942 Pontiacs _still_ offer _all_ the quality features for which Pontiac has long been famous!

6

# Hudson

While some cars regressed in styling in the final prewar model year, Hudson launched one of its most-attractive lineups ever—smoother of line, if a little more chubby than before. Richly appointed inside, Hudsons had a lowered grille and hidden running boards, as part of another, though highly appealing, facelift. Hudson's white-triangle logo appeared on both sides of the prow, and would light up at night.

Both an automatic clutch and a semiautomatic transmission were available this year, controlled by buttons on the dashboard. Only General Motors offered a true automatic transmission, but most car companies sought to find stopgap ways to make gear-changing easier.

Station wagons were discontinued, but a handful of final convertible sedans left the Hudson factory during the abbreviated 1942 season. Since early 1941, Hudson had been heavily involved in production for the war effort.

Grilles are wider and now wrap around front fenders; lower rear springs bring down overall height about 1.5 inches

Semiautomatic Drive-Master transmission is introduced

Running boards concealed

Prices increase 20 percent

Luster of chrome pieces is progressively dulled, then eliminated altogether in favor of paint

Cars sold after Jan. 1, 1942, are "Blackout Specials" with chrome bumpers and painted trim

Civilian car production ends Feb. 5, 1942

Production limited to 40,661 in short model year

1

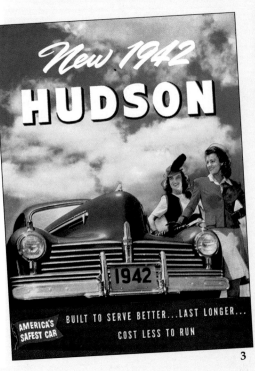

2

3

1-2. The Hudson Commodore Custom Eight four-door seated six, and was the most-expensive closed car in the '41 line. Power came from a 128-bhp, 254-cid straight eight. Traditional running boards were hidden behind flared lower doors that turned out to be rust-prone. 3. Hudson sported new horizontal grilles this year. Drive-Master automatic transmission was an extra-cost option. 4-6. The Commodore Six convertible rode a 121-inch wheelbase. Note the band of color beneath the uppermost chrome strip. 7. The last Hudson before conversion to wartime production.

4

5

6

7

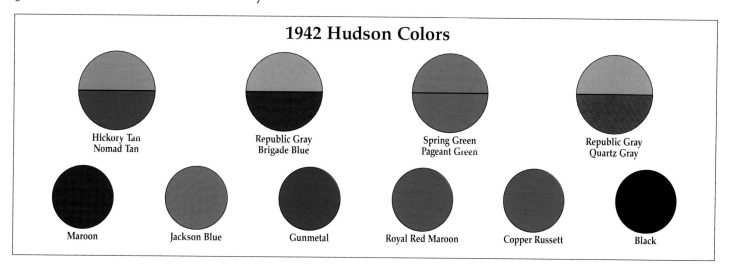

## 1942 Hudson Colors

Hickory Tan
Nomad Tan

Republic Gray
Brigade Blue

Spring Green
Pageant Green

Republic Gray
Quartz Gray

Maroon

Jackson Blue

Gunmetal

Royal Red Maroon

Copper Russett

Black

# Nash

Charles W. Nash, with a long history in the auto business, continued to preside over the Nash-Kelvinator organization as World War II loomed. George W. Mason remained as the corporation's president. As a result of their leadership through the late 1930s, Nash was in satisfying financial shape.

Nash issued straight-eight engines for the last time in 1942 in its Ambassador line, but the smaller, economy-oriented six-cylinder 600 series continued to draw the greatest attention and garner the most sales. A major facelift of all cars resulted in especially distinctive styling, centered on a low, wraparound grille with a little auxiliary grille planted above. Nash front ends would keep this basic layout after the war from 1946 to '48. Trim on some models played off the wraparound theme.

Fewer body styles were available than before, but that didn't matter so much when the model year ended abruptly in late winter of 1942. Nash was already focusing on production of military materiel, including aircraft engines, munitions, and cargo trailers.

Facelift includes wrap-around grille with three horizontal bars; some models have matching side trim; parking lights move to fenders above headlights

Final year for the Nash straight eight

No convertible as Nash offers fewer body styles

Cars sold after Jan. 1, 1942, are "Blackout Specials" with chrome bumpers and painted trim

Civilian car production ends early February 1942

Model-year production limited to 31,780 as Nash switches to wartime production

1

2

3

4

5

6

1. Nash ads emphasized fuel economy (500 miles on a single fill-up), two-way Roller Steering, and welded body and frame. 2. The new horizontal grille followed the industry trend; its lower wraparound owed a debt to Chrysler. This is a 600 four-door sedan. 3-5. Quality engineering was a hall-mark of Nash's Ambassador series, but the cars were prone to tinworm, too. Power for this fastback Ambassador Six came from a smooth, 105-bhp, 235-cid ohv L-head six. By now the Six shared a 121-inch wheel-base with its big brother, the Ambassador Eight. 6. With its resolutely monochrome exterior, this 600 four-door sedan has the simple appeal of a plain Jane you'd like to take.home—and at $918, that wouldn't have been too difficult. 600s rode a tidy 112-inch wheelbase. 7. Nash archives are vague, but this 600 two-door brougham may have been the last Nash built before wartime conversion. 8. Conditioned Air was touted as a real plus for hot summertime trips.

7

8

# Packard

All but a few Packard models adopted the Clipper styling that had been introduced in mid-1941. Only the One Twenty convertible and the plush One Eighty series stuck with the old-fashioned look. Clippers came with either a six- or eight-cylinder inline engine, the latter offered in two sizes. General Motors cars adopted "pontoon" fenderlines, but Packard Clippers maintained a distinctive appearance, unlikely to be mistaken for a Buick or Cadillac. Packard referred to all '42s as Twentieth Series cars.

Even though Packard management leaned heavily on its moderately priced automobiles, custom creations from the likes of Rollston and LeBaron still drew oohs and aahs in their rare appearances at dealerships or on the street. Despite growing prosperity, few Americans could even consider a Packard One Twenty sedan, much less an ultra-posh custom job.

When automotive production ended in early February 1942, Packard turned to war materiel, including Rolls-Royce Merlin aero engines.

Clipper styling dominates across entire line

Base One Ten line now called Packard Six

Midlevel One Twenty line now called Packard Eight

Station wagon and convertible sedan are dropped

Packard quickly establishes itself as a specialist in large, hardy military engines

Cars sold after Jan. 1, 1942, are "Blackout Specials" with chrome bumpers and painted trim

Civilian car production ends early February 1942

Model-year production limited to 33,776 as Packard switches to wartime production

1

2

For 1942, *new Clipper styling* - in even the lowest-priced Packards!

*How Clipper beauty pays off...* in more miles per gallon!

1942 PACKARD CLIPPER

1. Packard introduced the Clipper midway through the 1941 model year, positioning it between the One Twenty and One Sixty. By '42, every Packard carried the Clipper name, though designations such as One Twenty and One Eighty continued. This One Twenty sedan rides a 120-inch wheelbase, the shortest of five from the model year. 2. A One Eighty sedan sold new for $2196, in marked contrast to the less-plush but otherwise identical $1688 One Sixty. 3. Clipper's "Super-slipstreamed" design and "Fade-away" fenders hinted at the slab-sided styling that would characterize postwar automobiles. 4. The public could guess that gas rationing was coming, but for Packard, a luxury make, to emphasize economy may have been a marketing faux pas. 5-7. The convertible coupe was a stand-alone One Ten model, and was the only car of the series to ride a 122- rather than 120-inch wheelbase. Though pretty, it eschewed "Fade-away" styling for an upright, older look. 8. General MacArthur's military-blackout One Twenty staff car still survives. Note the five-star license plate.

131

# Studebaker

Before abandoning regular passenger-car production for the duration of the war, Studebaker turned out a modestly restyled lineup, in the same three series as 1941. As before, the economy-minded Champion took the lead in sales. Higher-priced Commander and President models had their own modest legions of fans.

Semiautomatic transmissions constituted an undeniable trend in 1942, and Studebaker was no exception. Following the pattern of Chrysler's semiautomatic unit, Turbo-matic Drive was a short-lived option for the Commander and President. Like all manufacturers, Studebaker cut the 1942 model year short, to gear up for wartime production.

After some lean years early in the Depression period, including receivership in 1933, Studebaker was in good financial shape under the leadership of company president Paul G. Hoffman and chairman Harold S. Vance. Studebaker was also poised to become the first American automobile manufacturer to introduce a brand-new model after the war.

President and Commander models get new grille and front sheetmetal

New Turbo-matic automatic transmission available on Commander and President

New radio has tuning buttons on steering column

Cars sold after Jan. 1, 1942, are "Blackout Specials" with painted trim

Civilian car production ends Jan. 31, 1942

Production limited to 50,678 in short model year

1

2

3

7

8

9

10

**NEW 1942 SKYWAY SERIES**
*Studebaker Commander*

1. The $744, three-passenger Champion Custom coupe was Studebaker's entry-level model for the shortened production year. 2. This Custom club sedan and other Champions had a 170-cid inline six. 3. The three model levels for '42, left to right, President Skyway Land Cruiser (with white "beauty rims" in lieu of scarce whitewalls), Commodore Skyway cruising sedan (note suicide doors), and the low-priced Champion DeLuxstyle Cruising Sedan. 4-6. Ads stressed aircraftlike styling, Turbo-matic Drive, and, especially, Studebaker's role in defense manufacturing. 7. Here, the Commander Skyway coupe, which produced 94 bhp from a 226-cid L-head six. 8. A six-passenger Commander Custom Cruising Sedan could be had for $1095. 9. The President Deluxstyle Land Cruiser sold for $1241, and weighed 3540 pounds. The back glass had ventilating wings. 10. Hey, sailor! The Skyway Commander Land Cruiser meets the Navy.

133

# Willys

As the 1942 model year began, Willys-Overland continued to turn out passenger cars in small numbers—again named Americar to correspond with the patriotic mood of the country. In the wake of the Pearl Harbor attack on December 7, 1941, production ground to a halt even earlier than for most automobile manufacturers because the Willys-Overland company was already turning out utility Jeeps for the U.S. Army.

Naturally, total Americar sales dipped significantly with such a short production season. Furthermore, small passenger cars would not be part of the picture when Willys-Overland resumed operations after World War II ended. In fact, the company wouldn't offer a passenger car again until 1952.

Although the Jeep had been designed primarily by American Bantam, Willys-Overland became the dominant producer of those critical military vehicles through the war years. When the war was over, Willys-Overland would use that experience to create a series of civilian offshoots of the jeep.

Americar grille picks up prominent vertical bar

Americar is promoted as "The People's Car"

Running boards no longer standard on all models

Cars sold after Jan. 1, 1942, are "Blackout Specials" with chrome bumpers and painted trim

Civilian passenger-car production ends Jan. 24, 1942

Passenger-car model-year production limited to 11,910 as Willys switches to wartime jeep production

1

2

3

THE VICTORY CAR
A DESIGN FOR
AN ALL-WHEEL
DRIVE CIVILIAN
'JEEP'
SCALE: $\frac{1}{8}$="1"      APRIL,1942

Styled by Brooks Stevens

**1.** With war looming, and Willys poised to build jeeps under government contract, no changes were made to the 1942 lineup. The ½-ton pickup carried on as functionally as before. **2.** Ads for '42 dubbed the Americar (*sedan shown*), "The People's Car," imparting an unintended Russian feel. But the Americar line, with its stolid, lumpy styling and faintly odd proportions, did have a Soviet air of drab practicality. **3.** The '42 coupe was economical and, to its credit, a nimble little handler. The 1942 models had improved sound-deadening materials and switched to molybdenum pistons. **4.** Although Willys resumed civilian production for the 1948 model year, it didn't offer a traditional auto until 1952. The reason was the enormous postwar demand for variants of the wartime Willys jeep. Here, Willys chief Joseph Frazer pilots an early jeep MA, with prominent Willys nameplate. **5-7.** In April 1942, designer Brooks Stevens looked ahead to the postwar period, when Willys might offer an all-wheel-drive "Victory Car" based on jeep mechanicals. Stevens' assumption was that buyers would love a tiny streamliner as much as they loved the jeep—a significant leap of faith. The '52 Aero-Willys was far nicer.

As Allied forces fought in Europe and the Pacific, the auto industry continued to focus its complete attention on the war effort. Instead of stylish coupes and practical sedans, the automakers used their factories to produce armaments and war materiel.

In 1943, a total of 139 passenger cars were built in America, intended for military and government use. The figure grew to 610 in 1944.

About three-quarters of aircraft engines were made by automobile and truck manufacturers during the war, as were 87 percent of bombs. In the five-year period starting in July 1940, American industry built 296,429 airplanes, 76,487 naval and cargo ships, 5.8 million tons of bombs, more than 2.4 million tanks, and 41.6 billion rounds of ammunition for the war effort.

It was a blending of private industry and government on a scale never before seen—or imagined. By 1944, American factories were turning out a B-24 plane every hour, and a Jeep every two minutes. Ford Motor Company produced 8675 B-24 Liberator bombers at its Willow Run plant in Michigan. Ford also produced 277,896 Jeeps.

Lincoln turned out 255,332 twin-cam 500-horsepower engines for Sherman tanks and antitank vehicles, while Buick manufactured more than three million cylinder heads for Pratt & Whitney aircraft engines. Hudson was heavily into aircraft production, while Studebaker concentrated on trucks and amphibious troop carriers.

Women played a vital role in war production. Between 1940 and 1944, the num-ber of women in the work force grew from 12 million to 18.2 million. A real woman was the model for Norman Rockwell's drawing of "Rosie the Riveter," a prototype of the wartime assembly-plant worker. Sadly, their contributions were considered temporary. After the war ended, most of those women lost their jobs to returning veterans.

Plastic, considered an experimental substance before the war, saw increasing use in production as availability of traditional raw materials—steel, tin, lead, rubber—diminished. General Motors' Hydra-Matic transmission improved greatly during the war, as a result of its use in tanks and other military transport.

Patriotism was not the sole motivator. Fat defense contracts helped keep manufacturers on their toes and yielded big profits, while good wages helped keep war plant workers satisfied.

On January 28, 1943, Secretary of War Henry Stimson said the Army would accept Japanese-American volunteers to serve in segregated

units. Some 8000 did so, with distinction. African-American servicemen were kept separate from other military personnel.

In May 1943, Edsel Ford died of complications due to stomach cancer. His father, Henry, reassumed the presidency of Ford Motor Company. Before long, though, Henry Ford II was discharged from the U.S. Navy to head the firm.

On what became known as D-Day, June 6, 1944, Allied forces crossed the English Channel to reach Normandy, in France. Dwight D. Eisenhower, the Allied supreme commander, issued the order for this secret operation that turned the tide of the conflict.

Back on the home front, war news took center stage. *Time* magazine called World War II "the most reported war in history," with some 5000 correspondents sending back stories.

A million and a half spotters participated in the Civilian Defense Corps, though no enemy planes were ever seen. Air Raid wardens roamed the neighborhoods, ready for possible enemy attack.

Victory Gardens sprang up everywhere, many of them on unlikely patches of ground in the nation's cities. In 1943, they yielded one-third of the country's fresh vegetables, grown on more than 20 million separate plots. Paper and scrap-metal drives contributed material for recycling into war production.

Despite the ongoing war, Americans did the best they could to enjoy life. Frank Sinatra, singing with the Tommy Dorsey Orchestra, drew legions of young female "bobby soxers" to his concerts in the early 1940s. In 1944, more than 3600 girls crowded the Paramount Theater in New York to see "Frankie." Outside, at Times Square, thousands more created a stir—sufficient to bring in riot police.

People were reading *A Tree Grows in Brooklyn* in 1943, and seeing the new Rodgers & Hammerstein musical *Oklahoma* on Broadway. Two years later, showgoers got to see another of their legendary musicals, *Carousel*.

War movies were popular in 1944, including Ernie Pyle's *Story of G.I. Joe*, based on the correspondents' close-up observations of ordinary soldiers at the front. Cartoonist Bill Mauldin became a favorite of those regular soldiers as a result of his "Willie and Joe" series in the military newspaper, *Stars and Stripes*. One of his best-known cartoons depicts a forlorn soldier aiming his pistol at his broken-down Jeep, as if it were an injured horse that had to be put out of its misery.

Even comic strips were part of the war effort, with many characters in uniform—except for Superman, oddly enough, who was classified 4-F.

Twelve-year-old Elizabeth Taylor starred in *National Velvet*, released in 1944. Margaret O'Brien, another child star of the war years, appeared in *Meet Me In St. Louis*, along with Judy Garland.

Servicemen on leave visited USO Centers, while entertainers such as Bob Hope kept the troops laughing overseas. Actress/singer Marlene Dietrich entertained the troops right at the front lines in Europe.

Soldiers overseas hung pinup photos of Betty Grable in a swimsuit and Rita Hayworth in a nightgown in their lockers and on walls of Quonset huts. Ostensibly, they did so as reminders of what they were fighting for back home. Sexy pinups by artists at *Esquire* magazine saw similar service.

President Roosevelt, suffering from the aftereffects of polio since his youth and in ill health during the war years, died on April 12, 1945. The war in Europe officially ended on May 7, 1945, dubbed V-E Day, as Germany surrendered. V-J (Victory in Japan) Day finally came on August 14, 1945, five days after the U.S. dropped its second atomic bomb on Nagasaki, and eight days after the initial strike on Hiroshima.

By war's end, the auto industry had turned out $29 billion worth of military goods—about one-fifth of the total. Americans had bought $49 billion worth of War Bonds, and 16 million people had served in the military.

Now, both civilians and veterans needed to readjust to peacetime life. Automakers were scurrying to get the first new cars onto the market, with Ford taking the lead.

1

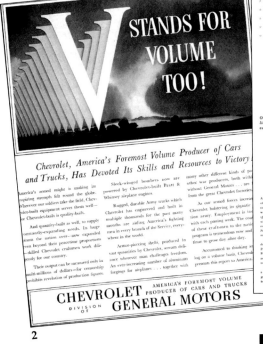

**V STANDS FOR VOLUME TOO!**

Chevrolet, America's Foremost Volume Producer of Cars and Trucks, Has Devoted Its Skills and Resources to Victory!

**CHEVROLET** AMERICA'S FOREMOST VOLUME PRODUCER OF CARS AND TRUCKS
DIVISION OF **GENERAL MOTORS**

2

*Pontiac Reports to the Nation on Arms Production!*

On April 30th, at 11:30 P.M., Pontiac delivered its ____th automatic anti-aircraft cannon to the United States Navy.

The contract covering this important war assignment called for the production of only ____ guns up to that date.

Thus, Pontiac deliveries of these vitally-needed weapons have exceeded the rate of production specified in the contract by 13 times and the time specification by 7 months.

**Pontiac** DIVISION
**General Mot**

3

*From the highways of peace to the skyways of war...*

The highest honor that could be paid any motor car manufacturer...

*Studebaker* BUILDS CYCLONE ENGINES FOR THE *Flying Fortress*

★ STUDEBAKER'S 90TH ANNIVERSARY 1852-1942 ★

4

**1.** Ford fulfilled many military contracts, turning out the B-24 Liberator bomber, jeeps, trucks, light tanks, and gliders (*shown*).
**2-4.** Patriotic ads gave automakers valuable exposure during a period when new autos weren't available. **5.** Final assembly of artillery-shell casings is handled by one of thousands of American women who entered the workforce. **6.** More than 16,000 NR Macks were built from 1940 to '45, making it the most-common wartime Mack vehicle.
**7.** Converted auto plants needed vast quantities of rubber for war production. That meant a dearth of new tires for the public, and a grassroots collection-and-recycling effort. Kids scrounged for rubber tubing and discarded tires. **8.** Ford jeeps were built to Willys-Overland specs. High ground clearance aided off-loading into water, as Gen. George C. Marshall (*right*) discovered in North Africa. **9.** Workers at Chrysler's Evansville, Indiana, facility machine and box .30- and .45-caliber ammunition.
**10.** "Rosies" assemble aircraft wings at Chrysler's Jefferson Ave. plant in Detroit.

5

6

7

8

9

10

1

2

3

1. Workers at the enormous new Ford factory at Willow Run, near Detroit, had turned out 5000 B-24 Liberator bombers by the summer of 1944. On a single day, August 31, 1944, the plant produced 432 of the 32,065-pound planes. 2. Hudson, which would create wonderfully innovative cars postwar, did its bit with precision manufacture of aircraft pistons. Note the bright fluorescent lighting, a must for quality control. 3. With a "ceiling" spec of nearly 32,000 feet, a B-29 Superfortress needed four 2200-horsepower Wright Duplex Cyclone engines, many of which Chrysler manufactured. The Cyclone was an 18-cylinder radial fitted with a pair of exhaust-driven turbochargers. 4. Workers put the finishing touches on light trucks at a GM plant. During the war, the company made 854,000 trucks of all types.

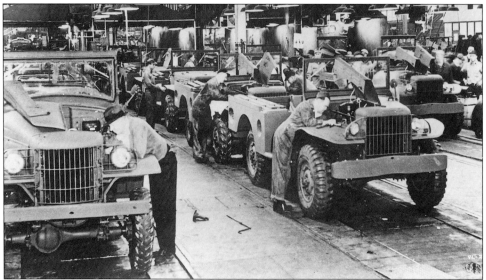

4

5

6

7

5. A quarter of all aircraft engines produced by America during the war were made by GM. Among the 206,000 that left GM plants were numerous V-12 Allison V-1710s that powered Lockheed's tough P-38 Lightning. Each 1710 was fitted with a General Electric turbo-supercharger, and produced 1475 horsepower, which gave the Lightning the speed (414 mph, max) and climbing capability (2850 feet per minute) the U.S. Army Air Corps demanded. A fighter, bomber escort, attack, and recon aircraft, the P-38 was the only single-seat, twin-engine airplane to be mass produced during WW II. 6. Heavy-built air-raid sirens were another piece of materiel from Chrysler's Jefferson Ave. plant. 7. More unglamorous but very useful equipment built by Chrysler: a smokescreen trailer, which, when towed, provided mobile ground cover. 8. GM's Truck & Coach division developed the hardy "Duck," an amphibious craft that saw combat duty across the globe. 9. The bottom photo shows, from left to right, the 2-ton, 4-ton, and 8-ton models. A much smaller Marmon-Herrington variant was dubbed the "Seep."

8

9

1

2

3

4

5

**1.** On June 12, 1944—less than a week after D-Day—naval transport craft disgorged jeeps at Omaha Beach, Normandy, France. The jeeps' custom exhaust stacks prevented fouling by water. **2-4.** A 1944 Ford GPW military jeep, buttoned and unbuttoned. "GPW" designates Government ("G"), 80-inch wheelbase ("P"), and Willys model ("W"). **5.** "Utilitarian" best describes the cockpit of Ford's '44 GPW. Staff officers and others smart enough to know better rode in front, for the cramped back seat was famous for causing hemorrhoids. **6.** The behemoth seen here is one of 2053 wartime Mack NO models, a 7½-ton 6×6. **7.** New GM trucks await rail shipment and eventual transport overseas. **8.** Hudson electricians carefully wire B-29 bombers. **9.** Studebaker brags on its Weasel personnel and cargo carrier, and the company's role in the production of Wright R-1820 engines used by the B-17. **10.** Nash-Kelvinator made props, aircraft engines, Sikorsky helicopters, binoculars, and more.

6

7

8

*It's a jungle "Weasel" too!*

9

## IN WHICH WE SERVE FREEDOM...

10

1

2

3

4

5

6

7

8

9

10

1. Gen. Douglas MacArthur takes a jeep tour of blasted Corregidor in March 1945.
2. Mack's NM3 served double duty as a personnel or cargo carrier. Folding benches in the back could be stowed to allow more cargo capacity. 3 & 5. Willys MB jeeps were manufactured in Toledo, Ohio, and had a 60-horse, iron-block four. 4. World War II had not yet ended when this Buick ad appeared in 1945, but all of Detroit anticipated a great postwar demand for new cars. 6. This effectively sentimental Studebaker ad from 1945 celebrated the first peaceful Christmas since 1938. 7. "I don't want to kill any more," the copy says. Nash hoped what he really wanted to do was drive a new car. 8. A Jeep for the masses: Willys' '45 CJ-2A. 9. In 1945, 29-year-old Henry Ford II (with grandparents) inherited a company in deep trouble. 10. Henrys I and II sign the 5000th Ford "Liberty" aircraft.

Euphoria had reigned as the war came to an end in the summer of 1945. The U.S. came out of the conflict as the dominant global force, both militarily and economically. As the coming year dawned, however, the excitement began to wane and ordinary Americans were less certain about the future.

Wartime wage and price controls soon were eased, sending prices up sharply. Winston Churchill warned of Soviet expansion in the postwar period, noting that "an iron curtain has descended across the Continent." Before long, concern about the spread of Communism—despite the fact that the Soviet Union had been a U.S. ally during World War II—would result in a "Cold War," destined to last for half a century.

Americans wanted—and expected—a much better life than they'd seen during the depressed 1930s. Even though they'd been readily available, many people had been unable to buy cars and other commodities during those harsh economic times.

After receiving their welcome-home kisses from family members, fiancées, and eager young women, returning veterans faced some practical problems. Jobs weren't as easy to find as they had been during the war. After enduring years of military hardship, some veterans weren't that eager to rejoin the workforce right away. Housing shortages loomed across the country, at a time when record numbers of couples were ready to start families.

The federal government promised that 2.7 million new housing units would be constructed by 1948. For the time being, though, married couples wound up living in trailers, with friends and relatives—even in hastily erected Quonset huts, not unlike those used for shelter in the European war.

What became known as the GI Bill of Rights, passed in 1944, provided a year of unemployment benefits to returning veterans. They could also get money for college or job training, including $500 for annual tuition and monthly living allowance, as well as low-interest loans for home purchases. A married vet could receive $90 a month.

During 1946, some 2.2 million couples were married—twice the figure for any previous year—and 3.8 million babies were born, setting off the postwar "baby boom." For the decade of the 1940s, 32 million babies were born—eight million more than in the Depression of the 1930s.

Soon after Germany collapsed in 1945, the U.S. government authorized the production of 200,000 cars. Those limits ended as the Pacific war came to a close.

All of the 1946 automobiles were little more than warmed-over '42s. They wore spruced-up grilles and some modified trim, but little changed underneath. Nothing was truly new, apart from a few specification changes.

Ford was first to the market with a 1946 model, which went into production on July 3, 1945, two days after the government-sanctioned resumption of production. Ford's flathead V-8 engines had internal improvements, resulting from the war effort. As a result of their wartime production, the automakers had learned a lot in terms of technology.

General Motors cars went on sale in October, but GM endured a 119-day strike shortly thereafter, keeping production down. Hudson reentered the market in August; Nash in September; Packard in October. Chrysler produced only a small number of cars during 1945. At first, the Office of Price Administration ordered that cars built in 1945 had to be sold at 1942 prices, but price restrictions were soon eliminated.

Strikes and materials shortages plagued the industry in

the early postwar years. There were sporadic shortages of glass, doors, locks, and many other components. Supplier strikes were especially bothersome.

Change was coming, however. Henry J. Kaiser and Joseph Frazer were developing a brand-new car for 1947. In fact, they exhibited a front-wheel-drive prototype (*shown*) of the forthcoming Kaiser sedan in January 1946, at the Waldorf-Astoria Hotel in New York. They even considered using a fiberglass body, and managed a $44 million loan to acquire Ford's Willow Run plant. By the time production got underway, however, the car was more conventional in layout, with the usual front engine and rear-wheel drive.

An all-out "seller's market" was already in full swing, and would continue through the end of the decade. Anyone who had a new car to sell could easily find a buyer—one willing to pay far above the usual retail price for the privilege of being among the first with a postwar automobile in the garage.

Over half of the cars on the road, after all, were more than 10 years old. Vehicle registrations declined by four million during the war years. After such a lengthy automotive drought, shoppers were eager to accept anything they could get—even if it came out of the "black" or "gray" markets. Less-than-scrupulous dealers would get a new automobile from the factory, put a few miles on it, and sell it as a used

car—perhaps at a higher price than the government permitted for a new one.

Though most automakers came out of the wartime period in healthy financial condition, Ford Motor Company was suffering economically as a result of management problems and internal squabbles. Henry Ford II had been named president of the company as the war raged, and in February 1945, he hired a group of former military officer "Whiz Kids" to turn the company around.

K. T. Keller remained the president of Chrysler Corporation, as he had through the war era. Detroit celebrated its Automotive Golden Jubilee in 1946. Total output for the 1946 model year topped 2.2 million cars—and that was just the beginning of the postwar production boom.

One of the millions of returning veterans was John F. Kennedy, who ran for Congress—and won—in his home state of Massachusetts. Joe DiMaggio and Stan Musial were back on their baseball diamonds.

Penicillin had been used during the war to treat infections, and was gradually becoming available to civilians. Electric clothes driers made their first appearance on the market.

Top-selling books of 1945-46 included *Forever Amber* and *The Robe*. Ethel Merman thrilled audiences on Broadway with her portrayal of Annie Oakley, in *Annie Get Your Gun*. Sales of 78-rpm records shot upward.

Postwar prosperity was underway, if off to a slow start. Before long, some brand-new, never-before-seen automobiles would be rolling into dealerships to tempt those with extra dollars in their pockets. For the first time, America had more miles of surfaced roads than nonsurfaced paths. Those new highways seemed to be aching to transport some stunning new vehicles.

# Chrysler Corporation

In addition to introducing carryover models with less fender brightwork, Chrysler expanded the idea of the Town & Country wagon to a new sedan and convertible. Produced with plenty of hand work, postwar T&C models had structural white ash framing with shaped plywood panels.

Designers even came up with a Town & Country hardtop convertible, but only seven were built. All Chrysler models displayed one of the most intricate chromed grilles on the market.

DeSoto abandoned the hidden headlights of 1942, launching '46 models with heavier, wider "toothy" grilles and fenders that flowed into the doors. New for 1946 was a long Suburban sedan, developed for stylish hauling of patrons at hotels and airports and fitted with a metal/wood roof rack. Lack of a trunk partition produced a huge cargo hold when the back seat was folded down.

Although wartime stylists had come up with plenty of ideas for postwar bodies with rounder shapes and thin door pillars, Dodge and Plymouth models got only mild facelifts of the 1942 designs. Still, Dodge finished fourth in the production race, while Plymouth took third place. DeLuxe and Special DeLuxe models continued, but with fewer body choices.

# Chrysler

Unchanged bodies gain crosshatch grille and stand-up taillights

Town & Country now its own series, offering a range of wood-sided models in both six- and eight-cylinder versions; the original wagon model, however, is dropped

First true hardtop debuts in very limited supply

Also in limited supply are steel and other materials, which limit model-year production to 83,310; Chrysler ranks 11th in industry

1

2

3

4

5

6

7

8

**1.** Comedian Bob Hope stands with a wood-sided Town & Country convertible, which came only in eight-cylinder form. As Chrysler's most-expensive regular-length model for '46, it listed for $2743. **2.** Famous racing driver Barney Oldfield (*in car, far right*) takes an uncharacteristic back seat while being chauffeured in a Chrysler convertible. A '46 New Yorker ragtop cost $2193, substantially less than its T & C counterpart. **3-4.** Although Buick is often credited with building the first hardtop, Chrysler beat it to the punch by more than three model years. The Chryslers slipped into obscurity, however, because only seven were built, all in wood-sided T & C form. **5-6.** Even more rare was the Continental, built by Derham to mimic Lincoln's car of the same name. Just two were produced, both on the Saratoga chassis. **7.** Chrysler's Town & Country brochure listed five body styles, but only two were widely available: the convertible and the four-door sedan, the latter in six- and eight-cylinder form. T & Cs of any stripe were expensive, generally listing for $200-$400 more than comparable Cadillac Series 62s. **8.** Rarest of all was the T & C two-door brougham; you're looking at the only one built.

149

# DeSoto

Unlike most 1946 cars, DeSotos carry significant sheetmetal changes; taller, wider waterfall grille tops a wraparound front bumper; elongated front fenders reach midway into the front doors

Hidden headlights replaced by conventionally mounted units

DeLuxe and Custom series return, but with fewer body styles

Both series still powered by 237-cid six-cylinder engine, but horsepower drops from 115 to 109

Suburban "semi-station wagon" added to Custom line

Production drops and prices rise substantially due to labor troubles and material shortages

First cars hit the market in March 1946

Exact figures aren't kept, but estimated model-year production is 66,900; DeSoto ranks 12th in industry

1. The Custom four-door sedan—traditionally DeSoto's most-popular model—saw a postwar price increase of more than 30 percent. But cars were in short supply, so the $1511 sticker didn't hurt sales. 2. Ethyl Corporation, maker of antiknock additives for gasoline, promoted safe driving practices with an ad depicting examples of various infractions. 3. After years of rubber rationing, tire manufacturers experienced a booming market for both original equipment and replacement tires. 4. New to the Custom series was the eight-passenger Suburban. It had no partition between the trunk and passenger compartment, so folding away the second- and third-row seats resulted in a huge cargo hold. It was DeSoto's most-expensive model at $2093, and it weighed in at more than two tons. 5-6. With the difficulty in purchasing any new car in the booming postwar period, it was a lucky buyer, indeed, who managed to drive off in a flashy Custom convertible. Though the list price was $1761, chances are that cars such as this brought whatever the market would bear.

5

6

151

# Dodge

Cars get significant styling changes; front fenders extend into doors; huge eggcrate grille replaces horizontal bars

Lowered wheel cutout in rear fender gives semi-skirted look

DeLuxe and Custom have fewer body styles; DeLuxe drops its club coupe, Custom its two-door sedan

Same 230-cid six-cylinder engine loses three horse-power, now 102

Actual model-year production figures not kept, but estimated sales of 163,490 put Dodge 4th in industry

1

1. From $1245 in 1942, a Custom convertible jumped to $1649 in '46. But with demand far exceeding supply, the price increase didn't deter buyers. Note that white plastic wheel-trim rings still substituted for proper whitewalls. 2. A 1946 ad claimed that "Goodyear holds its place for the 31st consecutive year as America's first-choice tire." The two tread patterns shown are the "De Luxe Rib" (*left*) and "De Luxe All-Weather." 3-4. Another Custom convertible, this one with traditional whitewalls, which were hard to come by. Dashboard design carried over from '42, though the formerly square speedometer and clock were replaced by round units. 5. The Custom four-door sedan had traditionally been Dodge's top-seller; for 1946 it cost $1389. 6-7. With separate headlights perched atop its front fenders, the WC pickup looked dated even upon its introduction in 1939. Yet postwar sales were strong, with 1947 being its peak year. The WC was powered by the same 218-cid six used in Dodge cars prior to 1942, here rated at 95 horsepower. Like the rest of the truck, the interior was very utilitarian.

3

4

5

6

7

# Plymouth

Unlike some other Chrysler Corporation cars, postwar Plymouths differ little from their prewar predecessors in appearance

Grille is most noticeable change, receiving alternating thick and thin bars; sheetmetal pan deleted from beneath front bumper

New rear fenders have lower wheel cutouts for a semiskirted look

DeLuxe and Special DeLuxe return

DeLuxe loses its utility sedan, Special DeLuxe its town sedan

Engine remains a 218-cid six with 95 horsepower

First cars hit the market in February 1946

Actual model-year production figures not kept, but estimated sales of 264,660 put Plymouth 3rd in industry

1

2

3

4

5

6

7

1-2. Convertibles were once again offered only in the top-line Special DeLuxe series, and their prices had risen considerably: from $1078 in 1942 to $1439 in '46. Note the thick "pillars" and tiny rear window in the convertible top, which severely limited the view aft. 3. "It fits and matches the car you're driving," claimed this ad for an aftermarket Motorola radio. While the control panel was small enough, the large box, which contained the radio itself, must have been difficult to conceal behind the dashboard. 4. White plastic wheel-trim rings can be seen on this Special DeLuxe four-door sedan, which listed for $1239. 5. The most-expensive Plymouth—both before and after the war—was the station wagon. Still wood sided, it listed at $1539. 6-7. Many a postwar buyer would have been thrilled to get their hands on this Special DeLuxe two-door sedan. Due to a shortage of cars, it often took luck in addition to the $1199 list price to acquire such a car. Postwar Chrysler dashboards wore heavy chrome trim.

# Ford Motor Company

Henry Ford II became president of Ford Motor Company in 1945 and hired a group of "Whiz Kids" to get the organization firmly on course. Ford had pondered the idea of a small car during the war, but decided against that move. Ford led the industry in returning to civilian production, issuing 1946 models right after V-J Day in 1945.

A Sportsman convertible debuted, with structural white ash and mahogany wood panels mounted over the doors, trunk, and rear end. Mercury issued an equivalent wood-paneled ragtop, but only for one season; Ford's continued through 1948. The design emerged from wartime sketches by E.T. "Bob" Gregorie. Like Chrysler's

Town & Country, the Sportsman cost plenty to produce, but drew a lot of traffic into showrooms.

Ford borrowed a bigger flathead V-8 engine from Mercury, coupled by significant mechanical changes. Mercury lost its business coupe.

Lincoln designers had developed a "bathtub" look during the war, producing dozens of scale models and hundreds of renderings—some lacking eye-appeal. Like other automakers, however, Lincoln stuck with the '42 body dies for its '46 models, adding a fresh grille and dropping the Zephyr designation. Continentals got a lower hood and tapered rear deck, with a protective spare-tire mount.

# Ford

Cars are essentially 1942 models with new grilles

Special series dropped

Woody-bodied Sportsman convertible coupe debuts

President Edsel Ford died of stomach cancer in 1943; replaced by 80-year-old Henry Ford; Henry Ford II takes over in 1945

Ford production resumes July 3, 1945; long model year lasts until February '47

Ford claims 1st in industry with model-year production of 467,413, but posts an $8.1 million loss

1. Ford's best-selling body style in 1946 was the Tudor sedan; 238,324 rolled off the line in DeLuxe and Super DeLuxe trim. This car can be identified as a Special DeLuxe by the chromed windshield moldings and script on the left front fender. 2. The 29-year-old Henry Ford II needed more than a crystal ball to see Ford through shaky times. To stir things up, Henry II hired 10 Army air-corps officers, known as the "Whiz Kids." Two of them, Arjay Miller and Robert McNamara, later became Ford presidents; McNamara was also Secretary of Defense. 3-5. With few improvements to the cars, Ford ads concentrated on styling, and attempted to get people talking about the '46 models. 6. The six-

There's a *Ford* in your future

passenger sedan coupe, or "close-coupled" coupe, came only in Super DeLuxe trim. 7. Twin stainless-steel trim pieces graced the rear deck for one year only. 8. All closed Super DeLuxe models were upholstered in gray broadcloth or gray mohair, both striped.

3

IN THE STYLE PARADE
FORD'S OUT FRONT!

There's a Ford in your future

Ford's out Front
IN EVERYTHING!

4

Talk about style
— it's got it!

There's a Ford in your future!

5

6

7

8

157

1

1. Introduced midyear as the most-expensive Ford, the Sportsman convertible coupe sold for $1982. Ford's new horizontal-bar grille featured red striping for one year only. 2. Super DeLuxe models had a horn ring instead of a button and an electric dashboard clock. Sportsman models came with power windows standard. All convertibles had V-8 power and offered the choice of red, tan, or gray leather upholstery. 3. Instead of the prewar 221-cid, 90-bhp engine, 1946 Fords used the Mercury 239-cid flathead V-8 that produced 100 horsepower. A "6" or "8" embossed into the hood ornament identified the engine that lurked beneath. 4. The 226-cid flathead inline six remained at 90 horsepower. The six used a Holley single-barrel carburetor, while the eight ran a Holley two barrel. 5. 1941 sedan delivery rear fenders and taillights were used on the Sportsman convertibles to achieve a proper fit. Though attractive, the high price and maintenance required by the wood panels meant low sales numbers. Only 1209 left showroom floors in its inaugural year. 6. Consumers snapped up cars as soon as automakers could build them in the first few postwar years. The Super DeLuxe Tudor sedan outsold its DeLuxe counterpart more than two-to-one because more of the high line cars were built. 7. In the immediate postwar period, whitewalls were difficult to find. Most Fords, like this Super DeLuxe Fordor sedan, came with blackwalls. 8. Decent performers in stock form, Fords were popular with police departments. They also attracted a legion of hot rodders, who took advantage of the growing aftermarket of hop-up accessories for the V-8.

2

3

4

5

6

7

8

# Lincoln

Cars are essentially 1942 models with new grilles and bumpers

Zephyr name dropped; same cars now called, simply, "Lincoln"

Custom series dropped

Jack Benny, Bob Hope, Greer Garson, and Jimmy Durante own 1946 Lincoln Continentals

Edsel Ford, president and father of Continental, died of stomach cancer in 1943; replaced by 80-year-old Henry Ford; Henry Ford II takes over in 1945

Henry Ford II paces 1946 Indianapolis 500 in yellow Continental cabriolet

Oct. 22, 1945: Lincoln-Mercury becomes a separate Ford Motor Co. division

Engine bore reduced due to problems; horsepower down to 120

Power windows standard on all models

Long model year lasts until February 1947

Model-year production of 16,645 good for 16th in industry

1

2

3

**1.** New company president Henry Ford II paced the 1946 Indianapolis 500 in a special yellow Continental cabriolet. Yellow later became available on production models. A total of 201 cabriolets were built compared to 265 club coupes. **2.** All Lincolns received new bumpers with integral wing guards, diecast eggcrate grilles, and recessed fog-lamp mounts. Although optional, many cars came equipped with fog lamps from the factory. **3.** Continental rear bumper styling was slightly updated with fender guards and partial rails. **4-6.** "Nothing could be finer" than a 1946 Lincoln. Ads claimed these were the best Lincolns yet; materials-wise, they were better than prewar cars. **7.** Base-model Lincolns shared the Continental's 125-inch wheelbase, but sported hood side trim and a different hood ornament. **8.** Lincoln rear ends now had bumpers with full upper rails. Fender skirts were standard. **9.** The price for the Lincoln club coupe was $2318, up $618 from the comparable '42 Zephyr. **10.** Window division bars were now fixed; they had been attached to the vent windows. Inside, silver-gray paint was used instead of mahogany woodgrain, and burgundy was the accent color.

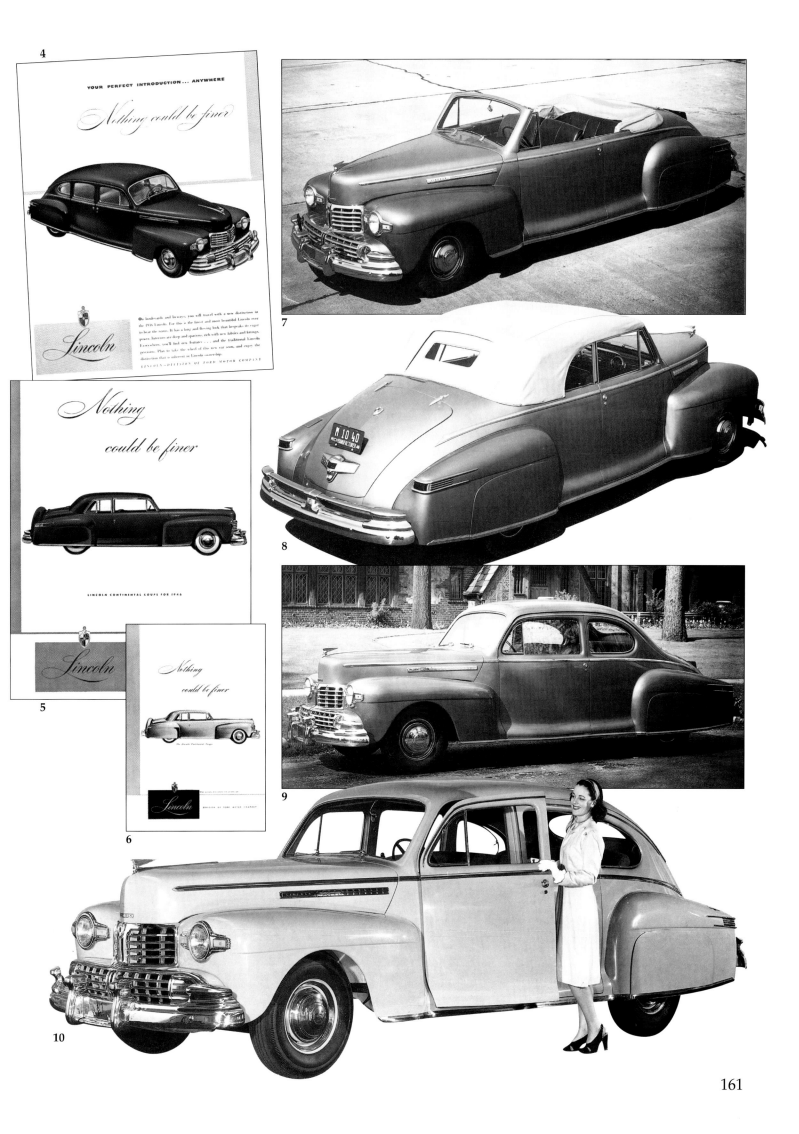

4

YOUR PERFECT INTRODUCTION ... ANYWHERE

*Nothing could be finer*

Lincoln

5

*Nothing*

*could be finer*

LINCOLN CONTINENTAL COUPE FOR 1946

Lincoln

6

*Nothing*

*could be finer*

Lincoln

7

8

9

10

# Mercury

Cars are essentially 1942 models with new grilles, hoods, and trim

Three-passenger business coupe dropped

Woody-bodied Sportsman convertible coupe debuts

"Liquamatic" semiautomatic transmission not offered

Engine improvements don't affect horsepower, but improve reliability

President Edsel Ford, who conceived Mercury in 1937, died of stomach cancer in 1943; replaced by 80-year-old Henry Ford; Henry Ford II takes over in 1945

Lincoln-Mercury becomes a separate Ford Motor Co. division on Oct. 22, 1945

Mercury production resumes Nov. 1, 1945

Long model year lasts until February 1947

Model-year production of 86,608 good for 10th in industry

1

2

3

**5**

**6**

**7**

**1-2.** Introduced midyear, the Sportsman convertible coupe was a one-hit wonder as it didn't return for 1947. It shared its body with a similar Ford. The costliest '46 Merc at $2209, only 205 were sold. **3.** Sportsman models came standard with Mercury's first power windows. Like the club convertible, upholstery choices were tan, red, or gray leather. **4.** Willard "Safety-Fill" batteries were popular replacement parts of the day. **5.** Warmed-over '42s, 1946 Mercurys had new grilles with "Eight" spelled out vertically in the center and fewer, lower grille bars. The vestigial crank hole was still there, but now it was covered. Wheelbase for all Mercs remained 118 inches and horsepower stayed put at 100. **6.** The most popular two-door was the sedan coupe: 24,163 were sold. **7.** "Mercury" and "Eight" badges now adorned the trunk. The tail-lamp housings were clad with stainless steel instead of paint at midyear. **8.** Like all Mercurys, two-door sedan prices rose 40 percent from 1942 models. **9.** This spare tire was probably retrofitted during restoration. No early postwar Mercs had spares due to a rubber shortage.

**8**

**9**

# General Motors

Seriously redesigned for 1942, the '46 Buicks looked fresher than most competitors. The first "gunsight" hood ornaments appeared, above a simpler grille. Century and Limited models were gone, body styles were fewer, and no more exotic customs were issued. Compound Carburetion didn't return, either.

Cadillac slimmed down its selection, but appearance changed little. The divider-window Sixty Special was extinct, but a luxurious Series 75 remained, gaining full-length running boards with stainless-steel trim.

Chevrolet designers under Maurice Olley had experimented with a small rear-engined car, code-named the Cadet. Management decided

against such a car, but it's notable for the first use of MacPherson struts. Because of strikes and materials shortages, Chevrolet fell behind Ford in production. In June, Nicholas Dreystadt, former Cadillac general manager, took the helm. He predicted sports cars, a hardtop convertible, and an all-steel wagon for Chevrolet's future.

Oldsmobiles again came in six series with prewar styling. George Snyder created a simple four-bar grille to replace the gaudy 1942 unit. This design would identify Oldsmobiles into the 1950s. Oddly, parking lights were omitted.

Pontiacs added a massive full-width grille but retained the prewar look, with the same engines, suspension, and body styles.

# Buick

Bodies largely unchanged; slightly revised grilles and minor trim changes; "Airfoil" fenders extended to four-door models

Century, Limited dropped

Specials return late in year with pontoon fenders: 118-inch-wheelbase models dropped; 121-inch offerings pared down

Compound Carburetion discontinued; 320-cid V-8 horsepower drops to 144

Model-year production of 158,728, good for 5th in industry

1. The '46s had less trim than '42s, and the new grille had fewer teeth spaced farther apart. The new "bombsight" hood ornament became a popular aftermarket item. Supers, like this convertible, rode 16-inch tires, as did Specials; Roadmasters used 15s. 2. The 248-cid straight eight returned in Supers and Specials, still rated at 110 bhp. 3. Ragtop dashboards were painted body color. 4. Compound Carburetion was gone, and horsepower for the 320-cid inline eight slid from 165 to 144, but it still had 9 horsepower more than its closest competitor. 5-6. "Airfoil" fenders now stretched the length of four-door models. Here, the $2110 Roadmaster sedan. 7. Early '46 Buicks (*top to bottom*): Super four-door sedan, Estate Wagon, sedanet, and convertible sedan; Roadmaster four-door sedan, convertible sedan, and sedanet. 8. Rayon cords made Firestone tires stronger and longer lasting than prewar tires.

## Yes, its Engine is still out Front

PROBABLY it is no real surprise to you that the new cars for '46 have their engines out front where good engineering sense puts them.

Certainly it is no surprise to old-time Buick followers that the long, reaching bonnet of this car houses a power plant that is still out front in its field as it is in the car.

It's a '46 Fireball straight-eight that employs the matchless valve-in-head principle used in the engines of every American warplane.

It's a power plant, indeed, which in a fistful of vital dimensions is actually made to closer tolerances than modern aircraft engines are.

Put foot to treadle, and in the leaping response of weight-thrifty Fliteweight pistons you find still more lift and life than in the last Buicks to come your way.

It's an engine frugal on oil to the point of amazement — silkily smooth and ready

from the very minute your car rolls from the line.

Yes, in spite of the times, we've found ways to do things to this Buick power plant — things you'll feel and thrill over the first time you can try it out.

The eyes are right in putting this Buick lovely at the head of the style parade; but nowhere more than in the engine is it plain that this 1946 honey is the *best Buick yet*.

BUY VICTORY BONDS

4

5

7

6

# Cadillac

Slight facelift includes new bumpers, minor grille changes

Series 63 and 67 do not return

Series 61 and 62 models no longer available with DeLuxe trim

Series Sixty Special loses division window

GM hit by UAW strike that shuts down production for more than four months

"Pooling" begins: two or more people buy one Cadillac and share it

John F. Gordon succeeds Nicholas Dreystadt as general manager

First Cadillac rolls off assembly line October 17, 1945

Only Series 62 four-door sedan built for first few months; accounts for more than half of model-year production

Model-year production of 29,214 good for 14th in industry

1. The Sixty Special was down to one model, the five-passenger, four-door sedan without a division window. New "Cadillac" block letters adorned the front fenders, and the chrome fender louvers of '42 were gone. 2-4. The "Interceptor" concept of 1946 was a styling proposal for '48 Cadillacs. The concept incorporated one flowing line from front to back. Sketches were done, clay models made, and even two running versions built, but the idea was scrapped because it was too radical for the day. 5. The Series 62 club coupe, with its fastback styling, returned, but not until a few months into production. Chrome fender guards replaced rubber units as a running change throughout the year. 6. Grille changes were minimal. The parking lights became rectangular instead of round, and the bars were slightly heavier and spread farther apart. The front and rear bumpers now wrapped farther around the body. 7. War advanced some technologies, butyl rubber being one of them. This new synthetic rubber improved inner tubes. 8. Series 62 dashboards reverted to the 1941 style with round gauges instead of rectangular as in 1942. 9. The familiar Cadillac "V" emblem appeared with the crest on the hood and trunk for the first time.

5

6

7

8

9

# Chevrolet

Cars are basically warmed-over '42s with new grilles

Series renamed: Master DeLuxe now Stylemaster; Special DeLuxe becomes Fleetmaster; Fleetline moves to top of line

First Chevrolet rolls off assembly line October 3, 1945

GM hit by UAW strike that shuts down production for more than four months

Government steps in to settle strike and UAW chief Walter Reuther emerges as powerful labor leader

M. E. Coyle moves from president of Chevrolet to executive vice president of General Motors; replaced by Nicholas Dreystadt from Cadillac

Model-year production of 398,028; Chevy falls to 2nd in industry behind Ford due to strike

1

2

3

4

5

6

7

1-2. Big-car quality at low prices was Chevrolet's main selling point for 1946. Not that Chevy needed to promote its cars; pent up demand created a sellers' market. 3. GM production lines shut down on November 21, 1945. Workers wanted a 30-percent pay increase to match inflation. GM wouldn't budge and eventually the government ordered a 17.5-percent increase. Production resumed on March 29, 1946. 4. Fleetmasters featured notchback styling and "Fleetmaster" block lettering in the hood's chrome trim. Priced at $1250, the Fleetmaster four-door sport sedan was Chevrolet's second-best-seller. 5. Suburban Carryalls received truck styling, which also remained essentially unchanged from 1942. 6. Municipalities had the first choice of cars after the war. Most police cars were Fords, but individual departments chose Chevrolets, like this Stylemaster four-door sport sedan driven by Erv Peiler, father of Publications International publisher Frank Peiler. 7. Chevrolet resumed civilian truck production on August 20, 1945, prior to Japan's surrender. The same cab could be found on everything from ½-ton pickups to heavy-duty trucks.

# Oldsmobile

Cars are warmed-over 1942 models with new grilles

Fastback styling extended to low-line 60 Special series cars

60 Specials available with six-cylinder only

Oldsmobile offers "Valiant" controls designed to aid disabled war veterans

Engine enhanced for durability, but no performance increase

A few hand-built cars appear in July, but Oldsmobile resumes full production October 15, 1945

GM hit by UAW strike that shuts down production for more than four months

Model-year production of 117,623 good for 7th in industry

4

1

2

3

1. Although the 1946 models amounted to warmed-over '42s, the new "frowning" grille imparted a much different look. Simple and stylish, this grille became a favorite of customizers. 2-3. Notchback styling was available in all series (here, the 98 four-door sedan), while fastback styling (shown on a 98) was now used for the low-end 60 Specials on the two-door sedan. 4-5. Style and Hydra-Matic drive were Oldsmobile's selling points in 1946. Aside from the revised grille, neither trait was new. 6. Custom Cruiser 98 mechanicals remained the same as prewar models: 127-inch wheelbase with a 257-cid, 110-bhp straight-eight engine. 7. "DeLuxe" meant quality in the 1940s. Like many automakers, Firestone used the term for its DeLuxe Champion tires. 8. The rarest and most-expensive Olds was the 98 convertible coupe. Priced at $2040, only 875 left showroom floors. 9. D. E. Raltson and S. E. Skinner greeted the first postwar factory-produced Oldsmobile as it came off the line. Hand-built cars appeared as early as July, making them the first postwar GM automobiles. 10-11. Without a Valiant-equipped 1946 Olds to show, Oldsmobile previewed the hand-control interior on a '42 Olds at this 1946 display. With Hydra-Matic drive already available, Olds was a natural to offer "Valiant" controls that

allowed veterans and others with disabilities to drive. 12. Jack Thompson became a well-known Chicago-area Oldsmobile dealer, but he had a successful used-car dealership in 1946.

6

7

8

9

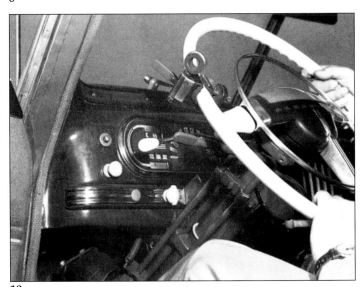

10

11

12

# Pontiac

Cars are basically warmed-over '42s with new grilles, bumpers, and trim

Pontiac produces only Streamliner two-door sedan coupe for first few months

First Pontiac rolls off assembly line September 13, 1945

Torpedoes use GM A-body on 119-inch wheelbase; Streamliners run GM B-body on 122-inch wheelbase

Engine options remain 239-cid, 90-bhp inline six or 249-cid, 103-bhp inline eight

Sales manager L.W. Ward reorganizes dealer network; pays off in postwar sellers' market

GM hit by UAW strike that shuts down production for more than four months

Full production resumes in June 1946

Model-year production of 137,640; Pontiac is 6th in industry

1

2

1. Pontiac's new grille eliminated the vertical bars below the headlights. The parking lights moved and the Pontiac nameplate was redone. 2. 1946's "new" Pontiac wasn't really new. A few trim changes and technical improvements were made, but the cars were basically reissued '42s. 3. A spear-shaped hood-side nameplate replaced '42's full-length side trim and revealed which engine lurked under the hood. This Streamliner Eight four-door sedan sold for $1538, $478 more than the '42. 4. Streamliners got chrome-plated speedline side trim. Torpedoes lacked chrome on the speed-lines; instead the streaks were stamped into the fenders. 5. With the war over, the nation turned to play. Pontiac, like many automakers, issued factory photos showing active lifestyles. Here, the $1335 Torpedo Eight convertible coupe. 6. Firestone ads stressed technical information and the company's racing efforts. 7. This Torpedo Eight two-door sedan is stock, except for the Chrysler Corporation hubcaps.

3

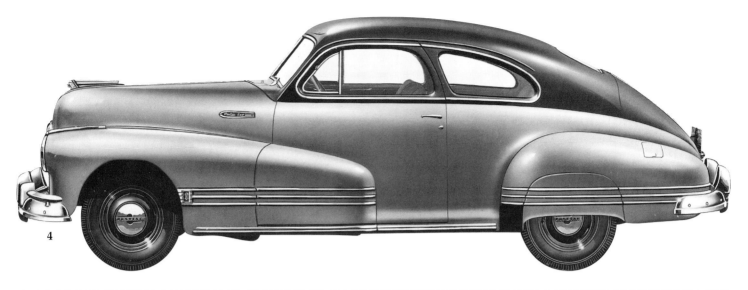

4

5

6

7

# Hudson

Facelifted only slightly for 1946, Hudsons again came with six- or eight-cylinder engines. As usual, Hudson models had a distinctive appearance, both in profile and up front—different enough from the other makes on the market to give them a special edge.

In addition to a batch of passenger cars, the Super Six line included a Carrier car/pickup truck. Nothing equivalent to GM's Hydra-Matic had been developed, but three transmission options were available: overdrive for $101, Drive-Master semiautomatic at $112, and Vacumotive Drive (an automatic clutch) for just $47.

Hudson finished the 1946 model year in ninth place in the production race, with just over 91,000 cars. Total sales in 1946 topped $12 million, earning Hudson a profit of more than $2.3 million—a welcome sum to a company that had been financially insecure in the latter days of the Great Depression.

1946 models are warmed-over '42s; grilles and trim are slightly reworked

Hudson abandons lowest-price market by dropping Traveler and Deluxe

Eight-cylinder models delayed until late in year

Materials shortages and suppliers' labor problems slow Hudson production

Speed engineer Reid Railton joins Hudson as a consultant, and will remain until the formation of AMC in 1954

Hudson resumes production in September 1945

Model-year production total of 91,039 good for 9th in industry

1

2

3

4

5

6

7

**1.** The 1946 Hudson line offered styling that was only modestly facelifted from prewar cars, with a recessed center-grille portion the most noticeable change. Few shoppers were bothered by the *deja vu*, because Americans wanted new cars—now. About two-thirds of the 91,000 Hudsons built for 1946 were Super Sixes, like this convertible. **2.** Here, the ¾-ton Big Boy pickup, with a 212-cid flathead six. **3 & 5.** The two-tone paint on this plump and curvaceous, 3085-pound Super Six sedan was an extra-cost option. **4.** With the end of wartime rubber restrictions, tiremakers were able to keep prewar cars on the road a while longer. **6.** At $1879, the Super Six convertible brougham sat near the top of the Hudson price list for '46; only the $2050 Commodore Eight convertible brougham was more expensive. **7.** The unorthodox Super Six dash, with speedometer offset far left. **8.** A September day in 1945 was big one for Hudson: The first shipment of new '46 models left the company's Detroit plant.

8

175

# Nash

Still in charge of the company that bore his name, Charles W. Nash was one of a dozen still-living industry pioneers who were honored at the Golden Jubilee of the auto industry in Detroit. George Mason served as president, closer to the everyday running of the company.

Eight-cylinder models were deleted from the lineup, so Nash cars now came in only two series, including the budget-priced 600. No convertibles were produced this year. Nash managed an eighth-place ranking for the 1946 model year, with about 94,000 cars produced.

Nash joined a couple of competitors in turning out something special for the first postwar season. The Ambassador Six line included a Sedan Suburban, lavishly wood-trimmed in the mode of the Chrysler Town & Country and Ford and Mercury Sportsman. Because considerable handwork was needed to assemble such a model, production costs were high.

1946 models are warmed-over '42s with slightly revised grilles and inboard parking lamps

Ambassador Eight models dropped

Four-door "woody" sedan debuts

173-cid inline six boosted to 82 bhp; 235-cid six up to 112 horsepower

Nash dealers are unable to meet demand

Model-year production of 94,000 good for 8th in industry

1. Nash ads for '46 used images of subtly upscale people to complement news of underbody innovations, notably unibody construction, which, as this ad put it, was "twist-proof, rattle-proof, squeak-proof." All this "in a car that sells in the low-price field": $1342 for the pictured trunkback sedan. 2. As before the war, ads emphasized Nash's gas-sipping ways and value: "A 500 to 600-mile week-end trip on a single tankful of fuel!" Unibody construction, the copy claimed, eliminated a ¼-ton of "lazy weight." 3. Nash's entry-level line, the 600 didn't look like a stripper, but it was priced like one; that, plus consumer demand, kept sales chugging. 4. The Ambassador trunkback sedan had a 112-horse, 235-cid L-head six. 5. Race-proven Champion plugs were popular replacements for Nash and other makes. 6. Only 272 of the $1929 '46 Suburban were built. 7. A carefully retouched factory photo of the Ambassador trunkback four-door sedan shows off Nash's appealing two-tier, horizontal grille and quizzical-looking headlight surrounds.

3

4

5

6

7

177

# Packard

Internally, Packard called all of its 1946 models (as well as the little-changed '47s) Twenty-First Series cars. All postwar Packards were Clippers—the modernistic design that had debuted in 1941. Body dies for the Senior Eight series were sold to the Soviet Union, which used them to manufacture the Zis. Packard was the only independent automobile manufacturer to emerge from World War II debt-free.

Despite a satisfying financial position, management made what turned out to be a questionable decision. They chose to back away even further from the luxury end of the spectrum, and concentrate instead on midprice cars—postwar equivalents of the One Twenty series that had helped keep the company alive through the late 1930s. As a result, Packard's image suffered and Cadillac wound up as the largely undisputed leader in the prestige-car field.

Not that prestigious automobiles were ignored completely. A Packard Custom, for instance, was richly trimmed with plush broadcloth and leather seat upholstery. For the calendar year, Packard produced more than 42,000 automobiles.

Only minor trim details distinguish 1946 models from '42s

Only one model, the Clipper Eight sedan, is available from October 1945 to April 1946

All models now feature Clipper styling because standard dies had been sent to USSR as part of war effort

Seven-passenger bodies are built in Freeport, Illinois; all others in Detroit

Model-year production totals 30,793; good for 1th in industry

1

1. The Packard line hums with low-price, six-cylinder, Series 2100 Clippers. Unfortunately, Packard shot itself in the foot when it diluted its luxury cachet with these models during a prosperous period when "economy" cars were no longer necessary for the company's survival. Clipper Sixes accounted for more than half of 1946 model-year sales. Cadillac stayed the luxury course, and eventually overtook Packard as America's premier luxury make. 2. While Packard scrambled to build new '46s, ads urged buyers to patiently wait. 3. The Super Clipper Eight touring sedan ($2290) ran with a 356-cid straight eight that cranked out 165 horsepower. 4. The eight had a two-barrel Carter carburetor, and was mated to an improved Electromatic clutch. 5. Packard was justifiably proud of its "fade-away fenders," which added to interior width. This is a Clipper Six club sedan. 6. 1946 Packard interiors had wool broadcloth and a general air of understatement.

# "HOW SOON CAN I BUY A NEW 1946 PACKARD?"

Knowing that more than 12 million* American motorists urgently *need* new cars, you probably wonder just what *your* chances are.

Not everybody can buy one of the first cars built. Some will have to wait—and some will have to wait longer than they think.

Packard production will be increased just as rapidly as available materials permit.

To help meet the overwhelming demand, we have expanded our facilities and set our production sights on 200,000 cars a year. This output is double our best pre-war production. Most manufacturers are planning to increase output only fifty per cent.

Meanwhile, take good care of your present car!

See your Packard dealer, regularly, for a car-health check up. He knows a hundred-and-one ways to keep your car safe and dependable—to protect its trade-in value—until your new Packard is ready for delivery!

*Many competent authorities estimate the demand at 15,000,000 cars!

2

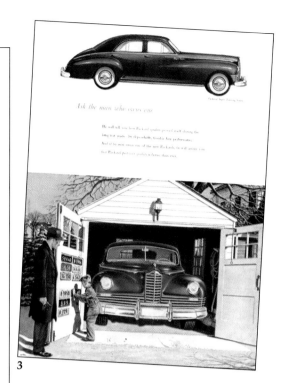

3

4

Styled and powered
for real economy

THE NEW PACKARD *Clipper Six*

5

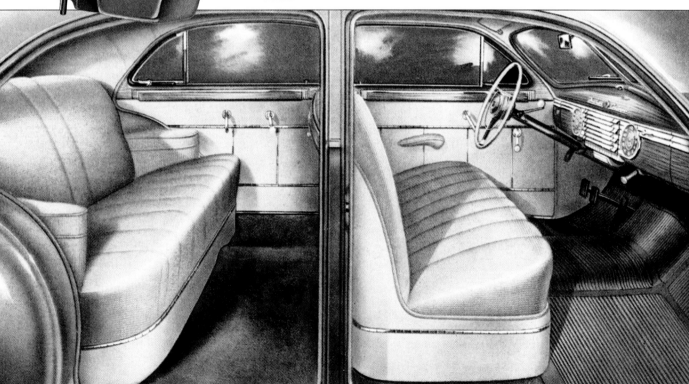

6

# Studebaker

In the race for brand-new models after the war ended, Studebaker had what turned out to be an advantage. Before World War II, styling had been the province of Loewy Associates, an outside consulting firm, rather than undertaken in-house. During the war, the Loewy organization was less involved with military projects than were Studebaker and the other automakers. Therefore, its stylists could devote more attention to a design for the postwar period.

For that reason, Studebaker would be ready with a completely new model in the spring of 1946. In the early months of that year, however, Studebaker returned to the marketplace with a single series, based on the prewar design. Little more than 19,000 Skyway Champions were produced in that period, all of which were essentially mildly facelifted versions of 1942's economy-minded Champion. Overdrive was an option on the short-lived 1946 models.

Grilles and bumpers are revised, made larger

Because of materials shortages, Champion is the only model; Commander and President aren't offered

Stainless steel shortage eliminates beltline trim

Model-year production of 19,275 good for 15th in industry

1

2

3

1. Studebaker's 1946 line consisted only of the Skyway Champion series due to a nationwide steel shortage and the fact that Studebaker was readying itself for the midyear introduction of a strikingly restyled '47 line. The priciest '46 model, the $1097 cruising sedan seen here, was also the most popular, with slightly more than 10,500 units coming off the line. All '46 Studes ran with a 170-cid L-head six that developed 80 horsepower. 2. A sparkling Studebaker service area, complete with late-deco lettering and a Champion cruising sedan. Except for stainless steel rocker trim and elevated parking lights, this is essentially a '42. 3-5. The price leader for the year was the three-passenger coupe, available for $1002. The nearly identical five-passenger coupe had a back seat instead of a copious storage area. The three-passenger outsold the five, 2465 to 1285.

4

5

# Minor Makes
## AND IMPORTS

Several developers were making plans for brand-new makes after the war, but most would take a while to get started. Kaiser-Frazer was the exception, preparing to introduce a pair of new makes as 1947 models. At a more basic level, the new King Midget was a buckboard-style vehicle, first offered only in kit form.

Willys-Overland sent a Jeep station wagon into the civilian market, along with a Universal offshoot of the familiar military vehicle. Defiantly trucklike, the Jeep station wagon was the first true all-steel wagon ever produced.

Crosley reentered the postwar market a little late, with a new carbon-brazed engine. Built around a copper/steel block, the four-cylinder COBRA engine had an innovative overhead-cam design but proved to be troublesome. During the war, it had been developed for use by the U.S. Navy. Crosley bodies were made by the Murray company. Almost 5000 Crosleys went to customers during the 1946 model year.

In war-torn Italy, Maserati was just starting production of the A6/1500 sports car. Britain was turning out MG TC sports cars and prewar-styled Jaguar saloons, some of which reached the United States.

Willys introduces metal-bodied Jeep station wagon and civilian Jeep CJ-2A

Crosley develops COBRA 4-cylinder engine; proves problematic

Tiny King Midget debuts with 6-bhp, 1-cylinder engine

Many GIs driving British MG TCs they shipped home during the war

Other foreign makes—Maserati and Jaguar among them—make their way to United States

1

2

3

4

5

6  7

8  9

CROSLEY NOW HAS THAT "New Look"

**1-2.** Willys rolled into the postwar era with jeep variants, initially for civilian "working" use. The Universal Jeep, or CJ-2A, was produced from 1945 to '49. **3.** Early SUV: Willys' wonderful 1946 Jeep station wagon. The vehicle had an all-new frame, and did without 4WD. **4.** A mostly finished August 1943 clay of the Willys 6/66, a Brooks Stevens proposal for a postwar car to be based on jeep underpinnings. Wheelbase was just 98⅜ inches. While this separate-fender car might have had a slim chance for short-term survival in the postwar sellers' market, the proposal was dumped in favor of a line of Willys Jeeps. **5.** Styling of Jaguar's '46 SS Saloon Mark IV carried on the look of the '39 SS; 0-60 mph took about 17 seconds. **6.** The King Midget, built in Athens, Ohio, used a 6-bhp rear-mounted engine, and sold for $350. **7.** Maserati's A6 1500 was bodied by Pinin Farina. Just 61 were built. **8.** Powel Crosley's eponymous mini sold for $905. **9.** America fell hard for the MG TC, after GIs returning from England began to ship them home.

183

Two names—one old and one new—lit the automotive skyline of 1947: Studebaker and Kaiser-Frazer. Studebaker was the first familiar automaker to release a brand-new model after the war. In addition, a wholly new company, Kaiser-Frazer, was ready to enter the marketplace with a series of modern-looking sedans. Independent automakers seemed ready to forge a strong spot in the industry standings, taking advantage of their ability to get new vehicles to market faster than the "Big Three" manufacturers.

"Is it coming or going?" That's what any number of onlookers asked when they first saw the new Studes, which were nothing like Studebakers—or any automobiles—of the past. Actually introduced in May 1946, after a short run of carry-over '46 models, the new Studebaker was designed by Raymond Loewy and Virgil Exner, with a short hood, long trunk, and wraparound rear window. The most striking example of the new design was the Starlight coupe, which featured a huge, four-section wraparound back window.

Although plenty of independent companies would turn up in the late 1940s, none achieved anything close to the success demonstrated by Kaiser-Frazer. Though conventional in rear-drive configuration underneath the new skin, the Kaiser—and its more-costly Frazer companion—displayed slab-sided styling created by Howard "Dutch" Darrin. In February, Kaiser-Frazer bought the assets of the old Graham-Paige Motor Corporation. Production soon moved to a plant the company had acquired from Ford in Willow Run, Michigan.

Another notable independent was getting underway, too, though the end result would be less pleasing. In January, the U.S. government agreed to let the Tucker Corporation lease a former Dodge war plant in Chicago. Later that year, the first Tucker car was exhibited in that city—unlike anything that anyone had seen before. Preston Tucker gathered stockholders with the intention of entering full-scale production, though his efforts would soon be thwarted.

The Davis Motor Car Company was formed to produce a three-wheeled automobile, with the first example turned out in October. Playboy Motor Car Corporation also issued a three-wheeler, but neither firm would produce more than a handful of vehicles. Another new independent, the Bobbi Company, changed its name to Keller Motors Corporation and moved to Alabama to make its stab at manufacturing.

Automobiles had trickled into the U.S. from foreign lands before World War II, but their numbers rose in the later 1940s as more Americans grew to love their idiosyncrasies, as well as their economy. Most of the imported models came from Britain, including little Austin A40s, Hillman Minxes, and Ford Anglias, as well as sports cars like the MG TC and an occasional Triumph 1800 or Jaguar. Naturally, Bentleys and Rolls-Royces also turned up occasionally at Atlantic-coast ports.

For most car makes, 1947 was a continuation of 1946. In fact, the differences were so slight that it was difficult to tell many models from the previous year's offerings. Domestic automakers' development teams scurried toward production, but most totally new models were still a year or two away from being introduced.

Packard introduced hydraulically operated power windows and seats. Synthetic rubber was developed by the Phillips Petroleum Company. Chrysler cars rode Goodyear low-pressure "Super Cushion" tires.

Henry Ford I passed on in April 1947, at age 83. Although he had certainly not "invented" the automobile, as many Americans seemed to believe, few industry leaders had been

anywhere near as influential. Led by grandson Henry Ford II, Ford Motor Company still faced financial troubles. The Lincoln brand celebrated its 25th anniversary with the Ford Motor Company.

In June, Ford and the United Auto Workers Union reached a tentative agreement on a foremen's strike. Chrysler and General Motors signed new UAW contracts. Also in June, the U.S. Senate overrode President Truman's veto and passed the Taft-Hartley act, which would outlaw the closed shop, encourage "right-to-work" state laws, and effectively abolish strikes.

Car demand still exceeded output, keeping the "sellers' market" in full swing. Inflation was a serious problem through the economy, but especially noticeable at car dealerships as list prices reached all-time high levels.

The American auto industry turned out 3,555,792 cars in calendar-year 1947. The total included more than 164,000 convertibles and 82,000 station wagons.

Chevrolet wound up number one again, with 671,546 cars built. Ford ranked second with 429,674, followed by Plymouth, Buick, and Dodge. Kaiser-Frazer finished the year with 139,249 cars built—the highest output of any independent automaker.

World War II might have been over, but a new "Cold War," destined to last into the 1990s, was well underway in 1947. In June, Secretary of State George Marshall described a new Marshall Plan—designed to give massive economic aid to Europe—at Harvard University.

Not all was joyful in the entertainment world. The House Un-American Activities Committee began hearings on the movie industry. Ten Hollywood people were jailed for contempt of Congress for refusing to answer the committee's questions.

On a brighter theatrical note, Marlon Brando starred on Broadway in Tennessee Williams' dark play *A Streetcar Named Desire*. Howdy Doody, a jovial red-haired puppet, appeared on TV for the first time with Buffalo Bob Smith. The first World Series telecast was in 1947, the same year that Jackie Robinson became the first African American player in Major League Baseball. Jimmy Stewart and Donna Reed starred in what would become a perennial Christmas favorite: *It's a Wonderful Life*. Another Christmas classic, *Miracle on 34th Street*, came out in summer.

Fashions were making a comeback, building on the "New Look" that had been created by French designer Christian Dior as the war ended. At the same time, nearly two million working women lost their jobs this year.

A report by the Bureau of Labor Statistics revealed that half of adult females didn't work. Nearly 20 million women over 40, with no children under 18 at home, were declared "idle." Despite women's toil during the war, the typical postwar family was expected to include a husband who went off to work each day and a wife who served as homemaker.

Housing was still in short supply. Plenty of young married couples were moving in with family or friends, or occupying hastily-erected Quonset huts as a temporary stopgap. Developers began to eye vacant farmland in the areas surrounding cities, envisioning handsome profits from low-cost homes.

One-car families were still the norm—but that limitation was destined to disappear as Suburbia grew across the nation in the late 1940s and beyond. California authorized the construction of an expressway between San Francisco and Los Angeles—another harbinger of the auto-oriented nation that was beginning to grow.

# Chrysler Corporation

Chryslers saw no more than detail changes, in fender trim, hubcaps, colors, wheels, and carburetion. Goodyear low-pressure Super Cushion tires were installed. Instruments were different, too. Critics referred to the "jukebox" dashboard, laden with chrome and one of the flashiest displays of the postwar era.

A new Chrysler Traveler luxury utility car featured a wood luggage rack. An eight-passenger Crown Imperial sedan also joined the lineup.

Production of the elongated Suburban wagon continued at DeSoto, with fold-down seats and wood floorboards at the rear. Actually, nothing significant was new for 1947. In the 1946-48 period, DeSoto turned out some 11,000 taxicabs.

Unlike Chrysler and DeSoto, which provided a semiautomatic transmission, Dodge stuck with a conventional three-speed column-shifted gearbox. However, Dodge did adopt Fluid Drive as standard equipment. Fluid Drive referred to the fluid coupling that was installed in place of a conventional flywheel, which permitted extra-smooth takeoffs.

Plymouth prices, like those of many 1947 models, rose sharply—as much as $250. Styling was essentially unchanged for the 1946-48 period. Despite an abundance of designs created during the war, the new models introduced in March 1949 would continue to be more square and upright than the competition.

# Chrysler

Styling and mechanicals are unchanged from '46

Six-cylinder Royal and Windsor continue on their 121.5-inch wheelbase, eight-cylinder Saratoga and New Yorker remain on a 127.5-inch chassis, and Crown Imperial keeps its 145.5-inch span

Town & Country lineup trimmed to a six-cylinder sedan and an eight-cylinder convertible

Estimated production of 119,260 moves Chrysler up to 9th in industry sales

**1-2.** Though the Lincoln and Cadillac nameplates generally carried more prestige, Town & Countrys were often the car of choice for Hollywood luminaries. Actor Leo Carillo—who played the Cisco Kid's sidekick Pancho—decorated his Town & Country convertible with a hood-mounted steer head and custom longhorn-upholstered interior. Note the special nose guard fitted to the front bumper. **3.** Not quite as lavishly decorated was the Town & Country convertible of Marie MacDonald.

1

2

3

4

5

6

7

**1-2.** Town & Country convertibles all carried an eight-cylinder engine and rode a 127.5-inch wheelbase. Interiors were lavishly appointed with two-tone materials and chrome accents. The wooden door jamb had chrome hardware. The price of entry rose to $2998. **3.** T&C sedans had a six-cylinder engine and were built on a 121.5-inch wheelbase. They were longer than other six-cylinder sedans, however, thanks to an extended rear deck made of wood. Prices started at $2713. **4.** Extensive hand labor went into each Town & Country, which is one reason they cost far more than their steel-bodied counterparts. **5.** A New Yorker convertible was the basis for a rolling advertisement built for the Zippo Company. **6.** Joining the plaid Highlander interior option was a Navajo design, also at extra cost. **7.** A New Yorker fitted with a white padded top in town sedan style was offered by the J.T. Fisher Motor Co., a Chrysler dealer in Memphis.

# DeSoto

No styling or mechanical changes for the model year, which begins on January 1, 1947

DeLuxe and Custom series return with same body styles

Sole engine remains a 109-horsepower, 237-cid flathead six; wheelbases continue at 121.5 inches standard and 139.5 inches for extended-length cars

Model-year production approximately 87,000; DeSoto maintains 12th place position in industry sales race

1

2

3

1. The heaviest and most-expensive DeSoto was the 2-ton, $2283 Suburban. Riding a long 139.5-inch wheelbase (vs. 121.5 for standard models), the Suburban could hold up to nine passengers. The roof rack was standard. 2. Mobilgas claimed to be "America's favorite," promising "standout pep and power." 3. Dashboards maintained a symmetrical theme with "woodgrain" paint. Note the plastic knobs on the engine-turned control panel beneath the dash. 4-5. A Custom club coupe cost $1591, but that was before adding the optional two-tone paint, right-side mirror, and whitewall tires. Like all Chrysler Corporation cars of this period, it carried a third brake light above the license plate. 6. Even in the late 1940s, many cars didn't come with standard heaters. South Wind offered an add-on unit that burned its own gasoline in a "Safety-Sealed" chamber, promising "hot heat from a cold start in 90 seconds flat."

4

5

6

# Dodge

Cars carry over with virtually no styling or mechanical alterations

New model year starts on January 1, 1947

DeLuxe and Custom series continue with same body styles

A 102-horsepower, 230-cid flathead six remains the sole engine

Estimated model-year production of 243,160 drops Dodge to 5th in industry sales

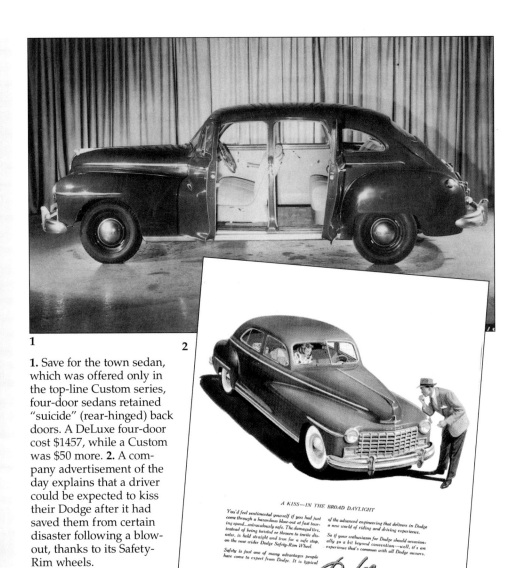

1

2

**1.** Save for the town sedan, which was offered only in the top-line Custom series, four-door sedans retained "suicide" (rear-hinged) back doors. A DeLuxe four-door cost $1457, while a Custom was $50 more. **2.** A company advertisement of the day explains that a driver could be expected to kiss their Dodge after it had saved them from certain disaster following a blow-out, thanks to its Safety-Rim wheels.

## 1947 Dodge Colors

Marine Blue

La Plata Blue

Fortress Gray

Aircruiser Red

Forest Green

Military Maroon

Windward Green

Opal Gray No. 4

Stone Beige No. 1

Gypsy Green

Patrol Blue

Orinoco Green

Squad Red

Panama Sand

Lullaby Blue Dark

1. Save for the long-wheelbase sedan still offered in the Custom series, a Custom convertible was the most-expensive 1947 Dodge at $1871. With the sellers' market still going strong, dealers most likely got much more than the manufacturer's suggested retail price. 2. A lack of chrome trim around the side windows marks this as a DeLuxe two-door sedan, priced at $1417. 3. A Custom interior shows off its woodgrain dash paint and none-too-fancy (by today's standards) door trim. A vertically oriented radio tuner was located to the left of the radio speaker that dominated the center of the dash. 4. In its final year with 1939 styling, this pickup-based ½-ton Canopy could be dressed up with two-tone paint and plenty of bright trim. This was the biggest sales year to date for Dodge trucks. 5. The least-expensive Dodge was the three-passenger DeLuxe business coupe at $1347.

# Plymouth

No visual or mechanical changes; cars are virtual reruns from '46, save for slightly higher prices

DeLuxe and Special DeLuxe return, offering same body styles

Engine remains a 218-cid flathead six with 95 horsepower

Estimated model-year production of 382,290; Plymouth maintains 3rd place ranking in industry sales

1

2

1. A Special DeLuxe business coupe went for $1209, $70 more than its DeLuxe counterpart. As had been the practice since before the war, Plymouth business coupes had rear quarter windows rather than the blind rear quarters of other Chrysler Corporation business coupes. 2. An ad for Prestone antifreeze touts that "One shot lasts all winter." However, that "shot" cost $2.65 per gallon in 1947—pretty pricey. 3-5. A Special DeLuxe sedan, Plymouth's traditional best-seller, went for $1289. Note the optional outside sun visor, a popular period accessory. Topping the tire stems are red crown caps, which were given away by Standard gas stations. 6. Chrysler Corporation considered building this compact on a short (for the time) 105.5-inch wheelbase, but the small-car idea didn't take hold—at least, not until 1960 when the Valiant compact appeared. 7. A Special DeLuxe convertible sold for $1565. Note the trio of front bumper guards.

3

4

5

6

7

# Ford Motor Company

An ad proclaimed "For '47, Ford's out front." Judging by the annual sales totals, that statement wasn't quite accurate. After a brief flirtation with first place in 1946, Ford fell behind Chevrolet once again in model-year output.

Initial 1947 Fords were basically unchanged. In April, marketers announced mildly facelifted "spring models" in the Ford, Lincoln, and Mercury brands. These were the true '47s, with Fords now flaunting round parking lights below the headlights. Fords cost about $100 more than in 1946.

Conventional pull-out door handles replaced the pushbuttons on Lincoln models, except for the Continental. On the corporate side, the Lincoln-Mercury division now operated with a separate dealer network, no longer matched with Ford. This followed the pattern set by General Motors, with distinct divisions.

Mercury now used more raw materials that had been scarce during the war, including aluminum for the pistons and hood. Chrome was readily available, so the grille frame and interior hardware adopted a bright look. After making a handful of two-door sedans, that body style was dropped. Production didn't begin until February 1947.

# Ford

Ford announces in March 1946 that no 1947 model year will be offered

Change of heart by management sets new model year at Feb. 19, 1947

Cars get minor facelift in April with slightly different grilles and trim

Auto industry mourns death of Henry Ford I on April 7, 1947, at age 83

Model-year production of 429,674; Ford falls to 2nd in industry but posts a $64.8 million profit

1

2

3

4

1. Early model-year cars were the same as '46s; slightly updated models didn't appear in showrooms until midyear. 2. Sportsman returned for 1947, but sales of just 2342 cars disappointed dealers. Late model-year changes are evident on this car. The grille no longer has '46's red stripes, the hood emblem is new, the parking lights are located below the headlights (they had been inboard on the top of each fender), and the "Super DeLuxe" script is gone. 3. Station wagons used their own rear fenders, which were similar to those of the sedan delivery and Sportsman. This car has the optional right-side taillight. 4. Instrument panels remained unchanged; Special DeLuxe cars had horn rings, dash-mounted electric clocks, and an armrest on each door. 5. The '46's twin stainless-steel trim decklid strips were replaced by a solid chrome strip above the trunk handle. Accessories on this sedan coupe include a radio, chrome wheel trim rings, whitewall tires, and an exhaust deflector. Six-passenger Special DeLuxe coupe sedans outsold three-passenger business coupes by more than a seven-to-one margin. 6. Super DeLuxe Fordor sedans ranked behind only their Tudor counter-parts in sales popularity. 7. Much of the world mourned the passing of Henry Ford I. Despite his eccentricities and unwillingness to adopt new technology, HF I was a suc-cessful industrialist, a folk hero, and an icon who was credited with "inventing" the automobile in the minds of many Americans.

5

6

7

# Lincoln

Ford announces in March 1946 that no 1947 model year will be offered

Change of heart by management sets new model year at Feb. 19, 1947

Cars get minor facelift in April with with slightly different trim

Lincoln-Mercury dealer network takes root

Midyear engine update boosts horsepower to 125

Model-year production of 21,460, including a record 1569 Continentals, good for 18th in industry

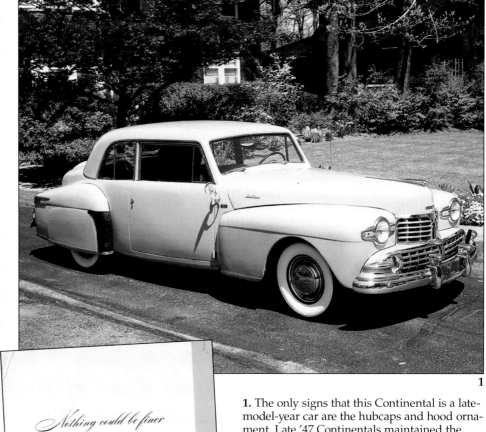

*Nothing could be finer*

THE LINCOLN CONTINENTAL CABRIOLET

*Lincoln*  DIVISION OF FORD MOTOR COMPANY

1

2

1. The only signs that this Continental is a late-model-year car are the hubcaps and hood ornament. Late '47 Continentals maintained the pushbutton door latches, while base Lincolns reverted to pull handles. 2. Image ads stating "Nothing could be finer" were still Lincoln's marketing strategy. Actually, the aging cars could have been improved with a redesign, but Lincoln was still taking advantage of postwar demand. 3. The hubcaps and pushbutton door latches mark this car as an early 1947 Lincoln convertible coupe. The price was $3142, up $259 due to inflation. 4-5. All of the base 1946-48 Lincolns were basically '42 Zephyrs with different grilles. The 292-cid V-12 was bumped to 125 horsepower, after backtracking to 120 in '46. The four-door sedan listed at $2554 or $2772 with the custom interior. 6-7. This interior carries the '46-style silver-gray garnish moldings and burgundy accent color. Late-model cars had walnut-grain garnish moldings and a silver accent color.

3

4

5

6

7

# Mercury

Ford announces in March 1946 that no 1947 model year will be offered

Change of heart by management sets new model year at Feb. 19, 1947

Cars get minor facelift in April with slightly different grilles and trim

Short-lived woody-bodied Sportsman doesn't return

Slow-selling two-door sedan eliminated after only 34 produced

Mercurys and Fords are virtually identical; Mercs sport higher trim level

Lincoln-Mercury dealer network takes root

Mercurys have shorter waiting lists than Fords as Lincoln-Mercury dealers aren't afraid to pad prices

Model-year production of 85,383, down only slightly from 1946, but Mercury drops from 10th to 13th in industry output

1

2

3

4

5

6

7

**1-2.** Early model-year 1947 Mercurys, called the "peach crop" by Mercury executives, were unchanged from the '46s. Changes came later in the model year on spring model cars, like this '47½ coupe sedan. Revisions included a chrome upper grille frame, shorter side trim, a new "Mercury" hood badge, revised hubcaps, standard bumper-tip guards, and a solid decklid molding. **3.** Firestone dealers dealt in much more than tires. Consumers could go to their local Firestone department store for one-stop shopping. As this ad shows, a customer could pick up a set of tires, a refrigerator, a train set, golf clubs, ice skates, an outboard engine, and numerous other products. **4.** The base price for the convertible club coupe was up almost $300 to $2002 for 1947. The background color for the "Mercury" nose emblem was black instead of red for late '47 models. **5-6.** Upholstery choices for ragtops were red or tan leather. The instruments were new and more chrome adorned the interior. The theme was standard Ford (which mimicked GM), though upscale: symmetrical styling with a central radio speaker grille flanked by a round speedometer and a round clock. **7.** Options on this convertible club coupe include the exhaust deflector and the right-side rearview mirror.

# General Motors

Alfred P. Sloan, Jr., named GM's president in 1923, resigned his post as CEO this year but hung on as board chairman. Expansion was in the air. GM opened a new plant in Wilmington, Delaware. Chevrolet added facilities in Flint, Michigan, and Van Nuys, California.

Except for a new "wing-top" grille that imparted a lower look, Buicks were unchanged for the 1947 model year. A more-elaborate Buick crest stood above the grille. All Buicks still had manual transmissions.

Cadillac prices escalated by $150 or more, but little was changed apart from the a script on the fenders and the first "sombrero" wheel covers.

Despite a substantial production boost, Cadillac wound up with 96,000 unfilled car orders. According to *Fortune* magazine, Cadillac was "the division that could return the most dollars per pound of steel."

Chevrolet prices rose, as did nearly all competitors' figures, but the cars themselves showed only detail styling changes. Chevrolet recaptured the number-one spot in model-year volume, with 671,546 cars to Ford's 429,674.

Oldsmobiles and Pontiacs looked essentially the same as in 1946, except for a simpler Pontiac grille. For the first time, eight-cylinder Pontiacs outsold their six-cylinder mates.

# Buick

Cars are basically '46s with new grilles

Station wagon added to Roadmaster series; breaks $3000 price barrier; first Buick to do so since 1921

Buick leads industry in convertible sales

Demand continues to outpace production capacity

Model-year production of 277,134; Buick reclaims 4th place in industry from Dodge

1

2

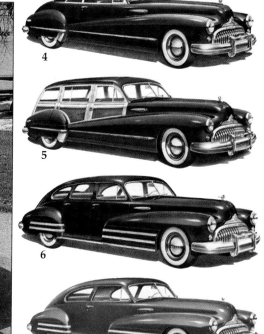

4

5

6

7

8

9

**1.** Two-tone paint was an attractive extra-cost option on all Buicks. The Roadmaster sedanet listed at $2131. **2.** Chrome circles in the front and rear bumper guard crossbars signified the series designation. This is the Super sedanet, which stickered for $288 less than its Roadmaster counterpart. Of course, dealers sold most cars for far above invoice during a time of unprecedented demand for any automobile. **3.** Buick sold more than 40,000 convertibles to lead the industry, including 28,297 Supers (*shown*). **4.** Roadmaster convertible sedan: $2651. **5.** Super Estate wagon: $2940. **6.** Special four-door sedan: $1623. **7.** Special sedanet: $1522. **8.** Interior options were limited to a radio and a heater; otherwise, the design was the same as in 1946. **9.** Like the 1946 models, '47 convertibles had hydraulic-assist tops. The hydraulic cylinders tended to leak over time. **10.** Priced at $1929, the Super four-door sedan was the most-popular Buick for 1947, selling 83,576 units. Engines remained the same: Supers and Specials had the 248-cid, 110-bhp inline eight, and Roadmasters ran the familiar 320-cid, 144-bhp inline eight. Wheelbases also remained the same: 121 inches for Specials, 124 inches for Supers, and 129 inches for the flagship Roadmasters.

10

# Cadillac

Slight facelift includes new grille and minor trim changes

"Sombrero" hubcaps introduced; become popular with other makes and hot rodders

Series 62 and 75 models get Hydro-electric power windows

92 percent of Cadillacs come equipped with Hydra-Matic automatic transmission

Prices increase $100 to $200 due to inflation and continuing demand

Cadillac has 96,000 unfilled orders

Model-year production more than doubles to 61,926; Cadillac ranks 16th in industry

Cadillac sales outpace rival Packard for second time; Cadillac would gain permanent sales superiority over Packard in 1950

1

1. Minimal changes were made for 1947. The block "Cadillac" lettering on the front quarter panels changed to script, and bright chrome "sombrero" wheel covers became available on all models. 2. Stately and dignified, the Fleetwood 75 now featured stainless-steel running board extensions. This seven-passenger sedan appeared in the movie *The Godfather*. 3. Interiors remained top-of-the-line, but no major changes were made as Cadillac rode the wave of high demand. 4. The new grille design included five stamped bars instead of six diecast bars. This Series 62 convertible has rectangular fog lamps; when these weren't ordered, round parking lights took their place. 5-6. Largely unchanged from 1942 models, the only convertible was the Series 62, priced at $2902. 7. Series 62 was home to Cadillac's best-seller in 1947, the four-door touring sedan, which boasted a total output of 23,997 units. The two-door coupe (*shown*) accounted for sales of only 4764 cars. 8. Cadillac advertising in 1947 didn't need to sell potential customers on its cars as demand outpaced production. This ad tells buyers their patience will be rewarded if they wait for a Cadillac.

2

3

4

5

6

7

8

# Chevrolet

Slight facelift includes minor grille and trim changes

Prices jump another 15 to 20 percent

20-millionth Chevrolet vehicle produced

New plants open in Flint, Michigan; Cleveland, Ohio; Los Angeles, California

Engineering Enterprises, Inc., introduces "Country Club" wood-trim kits for several Chevrolet models

Model-year production up 69 percent to 671,546 as Chevrolet posts full year of production and reclaims 1st place in industry

1

2

1. More than 750 Chevrolet dealers paraded through the streets of Flint, Michigan, to celebrate the opening of the town's new Chevrolet assembly plant. 2. Most municipalities bought low-end Stylemasters for use as police cars. Apparently, the state of Idaho had money to spare, as it used a Fleetline Aerosedan for highway-patrol duty. 3. Chevrolet grilles got fewer, thicker bars for 1947. Fleetline Sportmaster sales increased from 7501 to 54,531 units. As before, only Fleetlines featured the triple-chrome fender-trim bars. 4. Fleetmaster models (*like the sport coupe shown*) had chrome window reveals and stainless-steel front and rear window moldings; Stylemasters omitted the window reveals and had body-color front- and rear-window surrounds. All '47s had wraparound trim that started at the front pillars, just below the windows, instead of 1946's body-length beltline trim. 5. Chevrolet dashboards remained basically unchanged. The panel on top of the dash is the ashtray. 6. Chevy's stovebolt six carried over at 217 cid and 90 horsepower. 7. Fleetmaster convertible coupes came with your choice of three leather interior colors. 8. The spare was mounted flat in Chevy trunks. Notice the trim under the taillights: It was new for '47. 9. Convertible sales hit an all-time high of 28,443 units. Offered only in the Fleetmaster series, the ragtop sold for $1628. 10. The least-popular and most-expensive Chevrolet was the wood-bodied Fleetmaster station wagon. Priced at $1893, only 4912 were sold. 11. For $149.50, consumers could buy a Country Club trim kit and have it installed by the dealer. Made by Engineering Enterprises, Inc., these kits were the Chevy buyer's answer to the wood-sided Ford Sportsman.

3

4

5

6

7

8

9

10

11

# Oldsmobile

Cars get minor trim changes; virtually identical to '46s

Eight-cylinder engine available again in 60 Specials

GM research director Charles Kettering installs experimental high-compression V-8 into '47 Olds sedan; the car is a preview of 1949's revolutionary Rocket 88

Model-year production up 65 percent to 193,895; Oldsmobile is 7th in industry

You'll be "in the swim" with the smartest people . . . in a Style-Leader Oldsmobile. This "Custom Cruiser" Convertible, for example, is a stand-out in any gathering . . . in the city . . . at the country club . . . at fashionable summer resorts. And driving this smart looking Oldsmobile— the car with all the automatic features—is as restful as a day at the beach. The top goes up or down automatically. Windows raise or lower hydraulically. The front seat goes forward or back at the touch of a button. And as for the driver . . . all he does is sit and steer, thanks to GM Hydra-Matic Drive*. Gear shifting is fully automatic. There's not even a clutch pedal in the car!

It's *Smart* to own an Olds

Swim suit designed by Tina Leser.
Convertible Coupe by Oldsmobile.

1

2

3

1-2. Without innovation or a new design to sell, Olds touted convenience features, including Hydra-Matic Drive, and style in these 1947 ads. 3. Chairman of General Motors' Board of Directors Alfred P. Sloan, Jr. (*right*), congratulates Ransom E. Olds, builder of the first Oldsmobile in 1897, on his 80th birthday. 4. Priced at $1533, the two-door club sedan was the most-popular 60 Special; a total of 21,366 were sold. An eight-cylinder engine was again available in the 60 Specials (after a one model-year hiatus) as Olds tested the waters for the Rocket 88s that would debut in 1949. 5. With a redesign on the way for '48 and a continuing sellers' market, the 1947 Oldsmobiles didn't change much. From the exterior, the only way to tell a '47 Olds from a '46 was the chrome spear on each front door and fender. The inset with the "Oldsmobile" lettering on the '47 version was larger. 6. Tan cloth was the standard interior for 60 series cars. Five- or six-tube radios, an electric clock, turn signals, a deluxe steering wheel, and a heater/defroster were optional.

4

5

6

# Pontiac

Cars get new grilles, minor trim changes

DeLuxe convertible added to six- and eight-cylinder Torpedo series

Chief engineer George Delaney works to adapt Pontiac running gear to Hydra-Matic automatic transmission

Wheelbases remain 119 inches for Torpedoes and 122 inches for Streamliners

Straight-eight models out-sell sixes for the first time

Model-year production up 68 percent to 230,600; Pontiac maintains 6th place industry ranking

1

1. The revised grille lost its vertical bars and sported a new indian-head emblem. New teardrop-shaped hood-side trim on all cars no longer identified the engine choice. 2-3. Classified as a Streamliner, the wood-bodied station wagon came with DeLuxe or standard trim. Eight-cylinder wagons sold for $2282 or $2359 with the DeLuxe interior appointments. 4. Exide replacement battery advertising played a familiar tune: pay more for quality. 5-6. Accessories on this Asbury Green Torpedo Eight convertible coupe include a radio, turn signals, fender skirts, and bumper wing guards. The wraparound bumpers introduced in '46 carried over for '47. 7. Due to a lack of leather in the early postwar period, convertibles featured tan bedford cloth with real or imitation leather accents. This car features real leather in green, making it the $1900 DeLuxe model; standard models sold for $1854. 8. Like the 1946 models, '47 Torpedoes had beltline moldings; Streamliners did not.

2

4

3

5

6

7

## 1947 Pontiac Colors

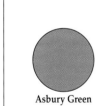      

Asbury Green    Burbank Green    Parma Wine    Smoked Pearl    Mariner Blue    Cairo Cream    Silver Wing Gray

8

# Hudson

With a radically styled new model waiting in the wings, Hudson stood pat for the 1947 season. Only detail changes could be noted, such as the addition of a door lock to the driver's side. As in 1946, buyers could choose from a trio of transmission-related options, but a true automatic transmission wasn't available.

Despite the seller's market that continued to rule the industry, Hudson wasn't growing as fast as some of its competitors. When the model-year production totals were tallied, Hudson had dropped to 11th place with just over 92,000 cars built, but earned a $5.7 million profit.

Hudson produced its three-millionth car this year. It was a Commodore convertible, displayed alongside a 1910 model—from the company's first year in the business—at corporate headquarters. Half a dozen prototype station wagons with wooden bodies were built, but each was earmarked strictly for duty around the factory.

Design changes are slight: new hood medallion, altered front bumpers, and a key lock on the driver's door

Materials shortages and pokey suppliers continue to hamper Hudson production

Hudson purchases a two-thirds interest in Carnegie-Illinois Steel Corporation tin-plate plant, at Shenango, Pennsylvania, to produce its own body steel

Demand increases for eight-cylinder models

Model-year production up 1 percent to 92,038, but Hudson falls two spots to 11th in industry

1

2

3

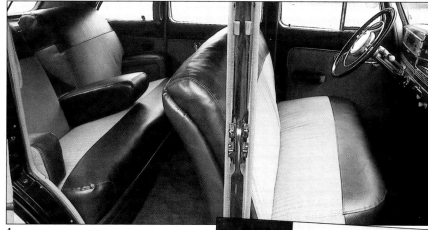

4

5

6

**1.** Like other independent automakers, Hudson swelled with postwar optimism, despite shortages of parts and materials. In September 1947, a Hudson photographer snapped the 3 millionth Hudson, a Commodore Eight convertible, which posed prettily next to the alleged first Hudson, a restored 1910 roadster. Hudson president A.E. Barit is in the Commodore. **2.** The '47 Super Six coupe was virtually identical to the '46 version, except for a freshened front badge and a slightly redesigned front bumper. When built without a back seat, the club coupe seated three rather than five. **3-5.** The Commodore Eight sedan went out the door for $1972; the six-cylinder variant was $1896. Both engines were L-head units. The 254-cid eight was rated at 128 horsepower; the 212-cid six at 102. Inside, buyers found new upholstery choices and a redesigned radio. **6.** Hudson's 1947 catalog emphasized safety, comfort, and sturdy engines. **7-8.** The Super Six brougham convertible, at 3320 pounds, was the heaviest of the Hudson Six models. **9.** Once upon a time, new-car dealerships would come to you if you needed emergency service, hence the Hudson parts-and-service scooter maintained by Roy M. Heath Co. of Kansas. Heath's '47 cab pickup had a ¾-ton payload.

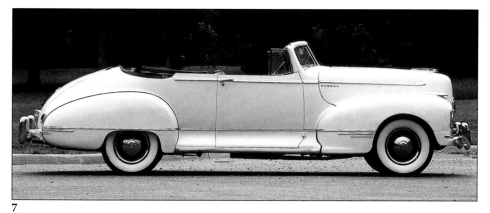

7

8

9

211

# Kaiser-Frazer

The new Kaiser-Frazer Corporation had a pair of brand-new makes ready for sale as early 1947 models. Formed on July 23, 1945, by Henry J. Kaiser and Joseph W. Frazer, the company was the last serious independent challenger to Detroit's Big Three automakers.

Both makes wore slab-sided, modern-looking bodies, designed largely by Howard "Dutch" Darrin with flow-through fenders, little side trim, and blunt hoods. Boasting abundant interior space, Kaisers and Frazers were priced significantly above the low-priced three, well into Buick territory. Frazers were better-equipped, but both boasted strong sales.

Six-cylinder engines evolved from those manufactured by Continental, but most were built by Kaiser-Frazer. Although the Kaiser prototype had front-wheel drive, all production models had more-conventional rear-drive, like every competitor on the market.

By September 1947, more than 15,000 cars per month were rolling off the assembly lines. After losing $19 million in startup-year 1946, Kaiser-Frazer earned a $19 million profit in 1947.

Ramping up in record time, Kaiser-Frazer is second among independents in combined production

Inside, seat width sets new industry standard

Only four-door models offered

Kaiser line consists of Special and Custom models; Frazers are Standard and Manhattan models; both use 123.5-inch wheelbase

Cars use 226-cid L-head six from engine supplier Continental; K-F soon leases Continental factory to increase output

Model-year production: 70,474 for Kaiser, (14th), 68,775 for Frazer (15th)

1

2

3

4

5

6

7

**1-2.** The 1947 Frazers were to be built by what remained of Graham-Paige. When that dissolved, Frazer production fell to Kaiser-Frazer, the parent company that had been founded in the summer of 1945. Frazer ads emphasized value (though with prices of $2295-$2712, these weren't "budget" cars), fabulous ride, capacious interior room, and tidily modern styling by Howard "Dutch" Darrin, who worked from basic designs by Detroit's John Maxwell Associates. **3.** Although Frazer wouldn't have an automatic transmission until 1951, more than 68,000 of the cars were produced for '47. The K-F plant was at Willow Run, Michigan, where Ford had produced B-24 bombers during the war. It was the world's largest building under one roof. **4-5.** The '47 Kaiser Special had a Frazer body; both cars ran with the same 110-bhp, 226.2-cid L-head six. At $2104, the Special cost $191 less than the comparable Frazer Standard. **6.** K-F planned to build two Kaisers for every Frazer, but actual production for '47 was about one-to-one, to satisfy demand. This is a Kaiser Special. **7.** Kaiser interiors were agreeably unpretentious.

1

2

3

4

**1-3.** This one-off Kaiser Special, with interior appointments and custom styling cues by Pinconning, is the only Kaiser two-door that predates 1951. The U-curve back seat and reversible front passenger seat inspired the nickname "Conference Car." **4.** K-F beat the Big Three to the punch with slab-sided flow-through fenders. The uplevel Frazer model was the Manhattan. The relative lack of body ornamentation looks fabulous now, but buyers of the day wanted more glitz, and K-F obliged in later years. Although this handsome Manhattan is one color, many had two-tone bodies. **5.** The $2712 Manhattan price tag brought upscale upholstery of two-tone bedford and other broadcloth, or quality pleated leather. All told, K-F ramped up for postwar production with amazing quickness, and built about 139,000 cars for 1947, good for ninth place overall—a startlingly strong showing that shocked longtime independents Studebaker and Nash.

5

# Nash

Styling modifications were slight for the 1947 Nash line, led by a widened upper grille. Nash earned an $18 million profit this year, after introducing a series of trucks with sedan-type front ends. Most of the trucks were exported, rather than offered for domestic sale.

Nash ranked 10th in model-year production, for a 3-percent share of the passenger-car market in 1947—not bad for an independent automobile manufacturer. Nash acquired new plant sites in two locations: El Segundo, California, and Toronto, Ontario, Canada.

George W. Mason continued to serve as Nash-Kelvinator's president and board chairman. The corporation also turned out appliances. For the only time in the company's history, a Nash was chosen as the pace car for the Indianapolis 500. An Ambassador sedan undertook that duty.

Minor facelift includes wider grilles

Raised center hubcaps introduced

Nash purchases plants in Toronto, Canada, and El Segundo, California, to improve northern and western distribution

Ambassador sedan paces the Indianapolis 500

Model-year production of approximately 101,000 good for 10th in industry

1

1. A Nash Ambassador sedan, the pinnacle of the Nash line for 1947, paced that year's Indianapolis 500 on May 30. It is the only four-door pace car in Indy history. That's Speedway president Wilbur Shaw behind the wheel. Nash grilles were widened for this model year, and the center-raised hubcaps were new. Wheelbase was 121 inches, as in 1942 and '46. 2. Well, it's not exactly aerodynamic, but here's the Ambassador anyway, pushing its 235-cid, 112-horse L-head six and doing its duty, as the Offys and Alfas come up behind.

2

1

2

3

4

1-3. Despite what would soon be dated styling, the Ambassador had an elegant presence that belied its reasonable $1809 price tag. The horizontal grille pieces that wrapped all the way to the front wheel arches followed industry trend. The pleasing horizontal theme was carried over to the dash design, and it's difficult to imagine a more graceful and elegant steering wheel. A sun visor and driving lights were dealer-installed accessories. At 121 inches, the Ambassador's wheelbase was nine inches longer than that of the junior 600 series. 4. The rustic Ambassador Suburban was never intended to be a volume item, but a lure to entice shoppers into Nash showrooms. Extensive handwork forced the price to a hefty $2227. Only 595 were built. 5. At $1415, the 600 brougham two-door was the '47 price leader. 6. This 12-passenger limo was for Nash execs.

5

6

# Packard

Identical in appearance to the Twenty-First Series models of 1946, the '47 Packards again aimed closer to the middle of the market than to well-to-do customers, who were more likely to favor Cadillacs. Packard's Clipper bodies were from Briggs, not manufactured in-house, which led to problems not only with supply but also quality control. Neither obstacle helped Packard maintain an image as a prestige automaker.

Quite an array of accessories was available, including real whitewall tires, which weren't offered in 1946. Introduced during the '41 season, though, the Clipper body was beginning to look dated and in need of more than a facelift. For financial reasons, that was impossible at this point. Instead, stylists tacked on heaps of sheetmetal to create a new Twenty-Second Series convertible, which debuted in late March 1947 as a '48 model. The balance of the 1948 Packard line would follow in the fall.

Packard stands pat with 1946 styling; introduced in 1941, it's starting to become outdated

Standard sedans are dropped from Clipper Eight series

L-head six picks up new block-venting system

New convertible models, registered as '48s, are introduced on March 29, 1947

Suppliers' labor problems force slowdown of Packard production

Model-year production of 51,086 good for 17th in industry

1. As with other automakers in 1946-47, Packard suffered a shortage of parts that was exacerbated by labor disputes at some of its suppliers. On top of that was growing competition from appealing Lincolns and Cadillacs. Packard production for '47, then, was disappointing. Despite the foregoing, few would disagree that the '47 Clipper sedan was an impressive, high-line auto. Note that the silver-gray of the roof is carried onto the bonnet as a restrained yet dramatic stripe. This hood treatment was not common. 2. Inside, gauges and controls were logically placed. The Clipper Six cost $1937; the eight, $2149.

1

2

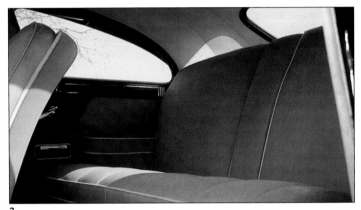

3

**1-3.** The $3140 Custom Clipper club sedan used the same body, engine, and chassis as the $2747 Super Clipper. Upmarket buyers didn't mind, though, as 7480 Custom Super Clippers (four-doors included) went out the door, in contrast to just 4802 of the two- and four-door Supers. Customs like the one seen here were trimmed with plush broadcloth and leather upholstery, special carpeting, and unusually nice faux wood paneling on the dash and inner doors. Two-tone paint combinations became available late in the model year. **4-5.** A Clipper four-door, showing the body contours that, while admittedly handsome, were growing long in the tooth. The symmetrical dash was a refinement of sensible design that predated the war years. Power for the base Clipper came from the prewar 245-cid L-head six, which produced 105 horsepower—not a lot to move a vehicle weighing 3520 pounds. Packard's L-head eights produced 125 and 165 horsepower, but every Cadillac competitor came with a 150-horse V-8. At Lincoln, the only engine was a 125-horsepower V-12. Packard's already tenuous claim to the luxury market was being undermined, year by year. **6.** As in previous years, Clippers found work as taxicabs, giving riders pleasing levels of room and comfort.

4

5

6

218

# Studebaker

Only Studebaker had a truly new automobile for the 1947 season. Jokesters might have had fun asking whether the new, symmetrically shaped model was "coming or going," but it sent Studebaker into the postwar years ahead of the competition.

Offered in both Champion and Commander form, the new Studebaker suggested some of the dream cars that had been envisioned during the war. Simply put, it was years ahead of the competition. Most striking was the Starlight coupe, with its massive wraparound back window. But all Studebakers were low in profile with an abundant glass area and flow-through fenders. Seats were wider, too.

Styling was accomplished mainly at the Loewy Studios. Virgil Exner, previously at Pontiac, was the first director of the 1947 design, but he split from Loewy before its introduction to go freelance. Exner's design was based on earlier Loewy shapes, and chosen over a proposal from Raymond Loewy himself.

In a surprise to the industry, Stude unveils its 1947 models in June 1946

Fresh, unorthodox designs are by Raymond Loewy Studios; wraparound backlights inspire considerable comment

President line is dumped for Land Cruiser sedan

Production split between one- and two-piece windshields

New features: self-adjusting brakes; no-glare instrument panel

Model-year production of 161,496 good for 8th in industry, and 1st among independents

1-2. Studebaker made great strides in 1947 with a redesign that was lower and far more modern than the previous year's offerings. The new bodies were a joint effort of two giants of design, Virgil Exner (*right, in suit, closest to clays*) and Raymond Loewy (*next to Exner*). The two eventually split, but Ex's touch remains evident from the cowl forward.

1

2

3

**1-2.** A Champion Regal DeLuxe convertible with whitewall tires, rocker molding trim, rear stone deflectors, fender side-marker reflectors, and driver-side rearview mirror. The tailpipe extension and driving lights are aftermarket add-ons. Note the "split" backlight. Base price was $1902. **3.** The '47 dash (this one with radio) was predictively modern. **4.** The Starlight coupe was available in the Champion and Commander series. This Champion has rubber stone deflectors. The fabulous wraparound backlight that inspired "Which way is it going?" jokes is very apparent from this angle. **5.** At $2043, the Commander Land Cruiser sedan was the most-expensive closed Stude for the model year. It weighed in at 3340 pounds, and replaced the old President line of 1942. **6.** The three-passenger coupe was available in four iterations spread over both series. **7.** A Studebaker for every use and lifestyle. **8.** Stude helps sell Simoniz. **9.** Here's the panoramic wraparound rear window from inside. **10.** This nonproduction '47 Champion Starlight coupe was customized for designer Raymond Loewy.

4

5

6

1947 Studebaker Champion De Luxe Coupe for three passengers.

1947 Studebaker Commander Regal De Luxe Coupe for five passengers.

1947 Studebaker Champion Regal De Luxe Coupe for five passengers.

1947 Studebaker Commander Regal De Luxe Convertible for five passengers.

1947 Studebaker Champion Regal De Luxe 2-door Sedan for six passengers. This body style also available in the Commander model.

1947 Studebaker Commander De Luxe Coupe for three passengers.

1947 Studebaker Champion De Luxe Convertible for five passengers.

1947 Studebaker Commander Regal De Luxe 4-door Sedan for six passengers.

7

8

9

10

221

# Minor Makes
## AND IMPORTS

Crosley added a new station wagon and expanded convertible production. Reliability was a serious issue. Crosley's COBRA engines were still subject to electrolysis that yielded holes in the cylinders. Willys-Overland added a Jeep pickup, with four-wheel drive optional.

The U.S. car shortage caused some potential customers to look again at the imports, which they might previously have disdained as too small and underpowered. Most of the foreign cars trickling into the U.S. were British. Britain was the second-largest auto-manufacturing country. The MG TC was gaining an audience,

and Jaguar was producing drophead (convertible) coupes as well as sedans. Ford began to send little Anglia sedans and Prefects, with 1930s styling. A few Hillman Minx models turned up, too. Austins began to arrive in November 1947.

Very few examples of the French-built Delahaye ever reached America. With coachbuilt bodies, each one looked different. In Italy, Ferrari was getting underway with its Type 166, but exports would come later. Many early postwar imports reached America in the hands of returning veterans who'd bought them in Europe. Import parts availability and service became new obstacles.

1

2

3

4

5

6

7

8

9

1. A "major" among America's pre- and postwar minor makes, the diminutive Crosley survived for 11 seasons. 2. A Crosley convertible coupe was just $949. The top was cloth laminate. 3. Ads promised that the ragtop could carry "four big passengers." Note the generous use of stamped steel. 4. All Crosleys ran with a 44-cid L-head four rated at 26.5 horsepower. 5. Closed Crosley coupe. 6-7. The 1180-pound Crosley pickup had ¼-ton capacity. It sold for $839. This one has the optional radio. The transmission was a three-speed nonsynchromesh unit. Crosley offered two other light trucks: cab & chassis and chassis. 8. Dated design, but who cares? The fabulous 1947 Delahaye 135MS cabriolet, which could reach 100 mph. 9. Ferrari's 166 Spyder Corsa was powered by a durable 2-liter Colombo V-12 engine, and frequently outlasted larger-displacement cars in competition. The headlamps and fenders were removable. 10. Jaguar's SS drophead coupe ran with a 125-horsepower, 3.5-liter six. 11. Timeless sportster: the MG TC. It rode roughly and top speed was only 80, but the car's agility thrilled Yank drivers. 12. The 1947 VW Type 1 was produced in Germany under British military oversight. 13. A wealth of Willys: the complete '47 line.

10

11

12

13

# 1948

Tucker was the most notable name in the 1948 automotive world—Preston Tucker, to be exact. The maverick entrepreneur created one of the most memorable and forward-thinking automobiles of the postwar period—even if only 51 were actually built. Quite a few independent makes emerged around 1948, including Del Mar, Gregory, Keller, Playboy, and three-wheeled Davis. Few lasted long or attracted more than a handful of customers.

Only Tucker attempted a full-sized six-passenger sedan that might have challenged Detroit. Unfortunately, Tucker promised more than he could deliver in good time, and his Chicago-area company fell under the negative scrutiny of the Securities and Exchange Commission.

Hudson introduced its new "Step-Down" models in October 1947, low in profile and promising the lowest center of gravity of any American automobile. Hudsons quickly earned a reputation for roadability, which eventually translated into stock-car racing victories.

General Motors had some surprises at dealerships in 1948, including the first Cadillacs with tailfins—an idea developed by chief stylist Harley Earl, inspired by a wartime fighter plane. Oldsmobile restyled its luxury 98 series in the modern mode. Pontiac became the third GM make to adopt Hydra-Matic, while Buick introduced Dynaflow.

An assassination attempt on UAW chief Walter Reuther didn't stop the UAW from getting the industry's first cost-of-living escalator in its new labor contract with GM.

Willys launched a new Brooks Stevens-designed Jeepster phaeton with side curtains and a soft top. After making some 361,000 Jeeps during World War II, Willys-Overland sought a comparable splash in the civilian market.

Packard restyled its Clipper, adding enough weight and bulk to prompt derisive comments about its "pregnant elephant" profile. A longer hood covered the most-powerful engine in an American automobile: a 165-bhp straight-eight.

Materials shortages were critical all year long. Steel, in particular, was in short supply. Wage disputes closed many auto plants in the spring.

More than 3.9 million cars were produced during 1948. Chevrolet was number one, followed by Plymouth, Ford, and Dodge. Chrysler Corporation was second only to GM in total sales. Goodrich developed tubeless tires, but they wouldn't appear on production cars until the mid-1950s.

Auto manufacturers donated more than a thousand dual-control cars to high schools for driver education classes. Car-shoppers still weren't haggling over price, as the seller's market continued.

Earl "Madman" Muntz was one of the country's top used-car dealers. "I wanna give 'em away," he moaned in early television commercials, "but Mrs. Muntz won't let me. She's crazy!" Muntz also pushed big-screen TV sets at a time when a 10-inch screen was typical.

Comedian Milton Berle took to TV this year. Affectionately known to millions as "Uncle Miltie," Berle starred in a variety show called *The Texaco Star Theater*. In the early days of television, sponsors commonly incorporated their names into program titles. Other new TV programs included Ted Mack's *Original Amateur Hour* and Ed Sullivan's *Toast of the Town*. Viewers who preferred serious drama might tune in to *Studio One* or the *Television Playhouse*. The Metropolitan Opera was televised for the first time.

Humphrey Bogart starred in two great movies, *Key Largo* and *The Treasure of the Sierra Madre*, the latter winning a best-director Oscar for John Huston. Jane Wyman won an Academy Award

for her portrayal of a deaf-mute in *Johnny Belinda*. Lawrence Olivier was named best actor in *Hamlet*. Paperback books were popular, and radios might be playing *All I Want for Christmas Is My Two Front Teeth*.

Dr. Alfred C. Kinsey interviewed 5300 men for his best-selling book, *Sexual Behavior in the American Male*. His study found that 95 percent of males were sexually active by age 15, but white-collar workers were the least active. Fashions were generally modest in the late 1940s, but some daring American women were looking at the "bikini" swimsuits, named for an island in the Pacific, that trickled into the marketplace.

Real-estate developer Abraham Levitt created one of the first postwar suburban developments, with prefabricated homes, on Long Island in New York. Called Levittown, it would serve as a model for hundreds—perhaps thousands—of tract-housing sites across the country in the coming decade.

Construction quality of the new suburban homes might have been less than deluxe, but they tended to be filled with the latest appliances from Westinghouse, Maytag, and Hoover—plus, as soon as possible, a brand-new automobile in the carport or garage.

In Europe, the Soviet Union began a blockade of West Berlin, Germany. The U.S. soon countered with an 11-month airlift of essential supplies to that war-torn city.

Dwight D. Eisenhower, head of the Allied forces in Europe during the war, was named president of Columbia University. California Congressman Richard M. Nixon was actively involved in hearings with the House Un-American Activities Committee to investigate Alger Hiss, a former State Department official accused of passing secrets to the Soviet Union.

In Europe, the Soviet Union began a blockade of West Berlin, Germany. The U.S. soon countered with an 11-month airlift of essential supplies to that war-torn city.

Displaced persons, often derisively referred to as "D.P.s," were emigrating to the U.S., having seen their homelands disappear during World War II. In June, Congress adopted the Displaced Persons Act to admit 205,000 refugees.

Mauri Rose won the Indianapolis 500 race for the third time. New York City doubled the subway fare to a dime and Babe Ruth died, at 53. A Gallup Poll in August found that most Americans, fed up with rising prices, favored the return of price controls and rationing.

As 1948 ended, one of the biggest upsets in American political history occurred. Harry S. Truman, successor to FDR as President, defeated the front runner, Republican Thomas Dewey of New York. This was the first election to be viewed on national television.

Truman, running under the "Fair Deal" slogan, also had been opposed by Henry Wallace, representing the Progressive Party, and Strom Thurmond of the States Rights Party (or Dixiecrats)—southern Democrats who were displeased with the intentions of the traditional parties. President Truman had ordered an end to segregation in the Army, but the south was still fully segregated, with African-Americans compelled to ride in the back of buses and drink from separate water fountains.

Just as Ford had led resumption of production after the war, in mid-1945, the company was the first of the Big Three to bring all-new models to market. Lincoln and Mercury cars debuted in April 1948. The 1949 Ford was unveiled in June at the Waldorf-Astoria Hotel in New York. Although the company was in financial chaos, it had 2 million orders for '49 Fords by July. Chrysler Corporation, in contrast, gave its 1948 cars an extended life as the year ended, naming remaining examples "First Series" '49s.

# Chrysler Corporation

Like the majority of auto companies as the 1948 model year began, Chrysler was marking time, awaiting the emergence of brand-new 1949 models. In Chrysler's case, the wait would be longer than for most competitors. In fact, leftover cars built during 1948 would be sold starting in December, into the early months of the following year, as "First-Series" 1949 models. Prices were unchanged, until the "real" '49 cars went on sale in March or April of that year.

All four 1948 makes—Chrysler, DeSoto, Dodge, and Plymouth—looked virtually identical to their 1947 predecessors. The big difference was substantial price hikes. Plymouths in 1948 cost as much as $300 more than they had in '47.

Chrysler would drop its six-cylinder Town & Country sedan after 1948, leaving only the wood-bodied eight-cylinder convertible of that name. Wide whitewall tires were available on Town & Countrys, which had initially been offered with simulated "spats."

Chassis modifications snipped about 50 pounds off the weight of a typical Plymouth, which continued to appeal to America's budget-minded shoppers. Around January, the early 1949 Plymouths—which were actually 1948-style cars—switched from 16-inch to 15-inch wheels and tires. Otherwise, they remained the same.

# Chrysler

Again, no styling or mechanical changes

Royal and Windsor continue with a 114-bhp, 251-cid six, while Saratoga, New Yorker, and Crown Imperial retain a 135-bhp, 324-cid eight

Town & Country lineup unchanged, offering a six-cylinder sedan and an eight-cylinder convertible

Model-year production of approximately 130,110 includes First Series '49 models; good for 9th in industry

3

4

5

6

7

8

**1.** While hardly potent by today's standards—or the standards that would be set in the '50s—Chrysler advertised that its eight-cylinder Spitfire engine produced "More horsepower than you can imagine ever using . . . or will ever need." This was one of a series of beautifully illustrated ads featuring various animals to bring home a point about Chrysler's features. **2.** Even the shorter, 121.5-inch-wheelbase six-cylinder Windsor was a stately car in four-door sedan form. Prices started at $2021. **3.** With elongated nose and tail, a New Yorker business coupe looked almost absurdly lengthy for the amount of passenger space, but the hood covered a straight-eight engine and the trunk could hold mounds of luggage. **4-5.** Two-toned both inside and out, this $2163 Windsor Traveler would have made any owner proud. The chrome and wood roof rack was standard. **6.** By far, the most-expensive standard-wheelbase Chrysler was again the Town & Country convertible at $3420. **7.** Derham continued to customize Chryslers, here a Crown Imperial. The roof over the rear seat raised when the door was opened, allowing passengers to enter the car standing up. **8.** Another Derham creation, this time based on a New Yorker club coupe, adding a white leather roof and wicker trim below the side windows. **9.** A production New Yorker club coupe listed for $2385.

9

227

# DeSoto

Essentially carried over from 1946, DeSotos unchanged from '47

DeLuxe and Custom series continue with same body styles, though prices rise considerably

Model-year production of approximately 98,890 includes First Series '49 models; good for 12th in industry

1

2

3

4

5

6

7

1. A DeSoto convertible leads Buick, Cadillac, and Oldsmobile ragtops in a postwar parade. 2. The Suburban rode the same extended 139.5-inch wheelbase as DeSoto's seven-passenger limo, but was aimed at families. At $2631, it was the most-expensive car in the line—but that included the roof rack. The car pictured is wearing modern, narrow-stripe whitewalls. 3. Suburbans were used to transport the Bears baseball team of Eau Claire, Wisconsin. In theory, the starting lineup could fit into a single nine-passenger Suburban. 4. Due to their expansive room, Suburbans were occasionally used as taxis. 5-7. A stylish Custom convertible went for $2296, though that didn't include this car's optional right-side mirror, dual spot lights, fog lamps, and grille guard. 8. This custom club coupe wears similar options, along with an extra-cost external sun visor. Without those accessories, it went for $1874. 9-10. At $1825, a DeLuxe four-door sedan (9) cost $67 less than its Custom sibling (10), the main external difference was the latter's chrome trim around the side windows.

8

9

10

229

# Dodge

Pickup restyled for first time since 1939

Car line continues virtually unchanged save for higher prices

DeLuxe and Custom series keep same body styles and 230-cid, 102-bhp engine

Model-year production of approximately 243,340 includes First Series '49 models; good for 4th in industry

1

**1.** A Custom club coupe cost $1774. The DeLuxe line didn't have a counterpart to this body style. **2.** Also offered only as a Custom was the $2189 convertible. This ad explains the secret to Dodge's popularity is that it delivers "More fun and usefulness per dollar than any other car." **3-5.** Only two of these seven-passenger limos were built from 1946 through mid-1949. The front and rear seats were separated by a glass partition, and two jump seats folded out from the bulkhead beneath it. **6-8.** Pictured top-up is a $2189 Custom convertible. Drop-top dashboards were painted solid colors rather than the woodgrain effect used in closed cars. **9-13.** A lack of chrome side-window trim identifies this as the $1457 DeLuxe four-door sedan, which cost $50 more as a Custom. Note the woodgrain dash paint and third brake light above the license plate. This example is fitted with a "Mopar Deluxe" underdash heater, which had three doors that could be opened to distribute heat. **14.** Pickups received new styling for 1948 that brought them thoroughly up to date. Headlights were incorporated into front fenders that flowed into the doors. The former 218-cid, 95-bhp Plymouth inline six was replaced by the same 230-cid, 102-bhp six used in Dodge cars. **15.** Based on a former military vehicle, the Power Wagon was a one-ton, four-wheel-drive pickup advertised as "The truck the boys wrote home about . . . now in civies." First offered to the public in 1946, it came with a power take-off (PTO) for running stationary equipment such as farm machinery. By 1948, it listed for $2045—a bargain really, considering it was "A rough and ready mixer . . . 'Job Rated' for work no other truck could be expected to do."

*Success Without Limit*

From the day these new Dodge cars made their first appearance the American people have taken them to their heart.

Family members rival one another for the fun of driving them; veteran engineers and experts marvel at them.

What is the secret of their popularity? They deliver more fun and usefulness per dollar than any other car. That's the secret.

*Dodge*

*Smoothest Car "Afloat"*

2

3

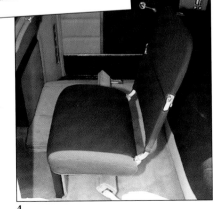

4

5

6

7

8

9

10

11

12

13

14

15

# 1948

# Plymouth

Plymouths are virtual reruns of '48, with no major styling or mechanical changes—just higher prices

DeLuxe and Special DeLuxe series continue with same body styles and 218-cid, 95-bhp engine

Model-year production of approximately 412,540 includes First Series '49 models; good for 2nd in industry

1

2

3

## 1948 Plymouth Colors

Marine Blue

Sumac Red

Chevron Blue

Charlotte Ivory

Airwing Gray

Cruiser Maroon

Balfour Green

Kenwood Green

Battalion Beige

Plymouth Gunmetal

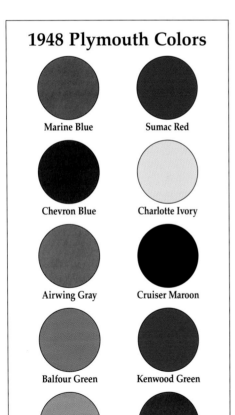

4

5

6

7

1-3. The DeLuxe four-door sedan was Plymouth's basic family car. Priced at $1441, it cost $227 more than the same car in '47. 4. Priced at $1529, the Custom four-door sedan came standard with fancier trim than its DeLuxe counterpart. Most buyers apparently felt the extra flash was worth the extra cash, as it outsold the DeLuxe version by more than four-to-one. 5. Another Custom four-door sedan, this one sporting not only whitewalls, but also the plastic wheel-trim rings originally intended to mimic whitewalls. 6. The least-expensive 1948 Plymouth was the three-passenger DeLuxe business coupe at $1346. It lacked a rear seat but had a huge trunk. 7-10. At nearly the opposite end of the price spectrum was the Special DeLuxe convertible. Save for the low-production wood-sided wagon, it was the most-expensive Plymouth at $1857. Dashboards on convertibles were painted a solid color, while other models had a painted wood-grain pattern. The example pictured is fitted with optional fog lamps, dual spotlights, and front override bar.

8

9

10

233

# Ford Motor Company

"There's a finer Ford in your future," an advertisement proclaimed. Except for the introduction of a new truck line this year, though, Ford vehicles stood pat. Not that it mattered much, because engineers and designers had been busy with a brand-new design. And Ford would be the first of the Big Three automakers to come to market with a truly new postwar passenger car.

Meanwhile, Ford prices rose again. During the 1947 model year, the six-cylinder engine had gained five horsepower and round parking lights were installed. Model-year production dropped, but considering the shortness of the 1948 selling season, that was hardly a tragedy.

Lincoln produced its final V-12 engines this year, for both the regular models and the Continental. Future Lincoln engines would have eight cylinders. This was also the finale for the Continental—at least until 1956, when the Mark II debuted. Corporate management had pondered creating a new postwar Continental at this time, but that prospect was shelved.

Two-door sedans were no longer available with a Mercury badge. Otherwise, no change could be observed in Ford Motor Company's midprice make, which also saw a short model year.

## Ford

Cars are virtually unchanged from '47 awaiting all-new '49s

Sedan delivery dropped

Pickup truck redesigned with new designations

Six-cylinder engine gains five horsepower, now 95

Model year begins on November 1, 1947; runs only through June 1948

Short model run of 247,722 drops Ford to 3rd in industry sales behind Plymouth, and just barely ahead of Dodge

1. Simple poetry described the new Fords in ads, though there was really nothing "new." 2-3. Unlike most other manufacturers, Ford held the line on prices this year. A Super Deluxe V8 Fordor sedan listed for $1440, the same as in '47. It was also offered with a 226-cid, 95-bhp six-cylinder engine for $1372. 4. The rakish Super DeLuxe convertible went for $1740, also the same as in '47. It was only offered with the 239-cid, 100-bhp V-8.

5

6

7

8

9

10

**5.** Priced midway between the Tudor and Fordor sedans was the sedan coupe, shown here in Super DeLuxe V-8 form at $1409. **6.** Another Special DeLuxe sedan coupe, this one in police livery. While both these examples carry Ford's famous flathead V-8, some felt the six was actually quicker, at least at lower speeds. **7.** By this time the Sportsman convertible was falling out of favor, not only due to its high price ($2282), but also because the wood trim required tedious maintenance. Only 28 were built for 1948, and those may have been leftover '47s. Whatever the case, they would be the last of the breed, as the Sportsman didn't return in the redesigned '49 line. **8-9.** The "woody" wagon, however, continued to do fairly well, and the styling theme would continue in modified form for several more years. A V-8 version cost $1972. **10.** Ford's restyled 1948 trucks boasted what would later be considered a classic design. Pictured is an F-1 ½-ton pickup.

# Lincoln

With redesigned '49s on the way, '48s remain unchanged

Like Ford—but unlike the rest of the industry—prices hold at 1947 levels

Last year for the original Continental and for Lincoln's V-12 engine

Benson Ford elected general manager of Lincoln-Mercury Division

Model year begins on November 1, 1947; runs only into April 1948

Shortened run limits model-year production to 7769, dropping Lincoln to 19th in industry

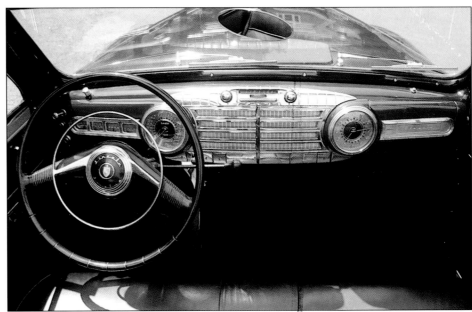

**1-3.** Lincoln's standard convertible cost $3142—right between a Chrysler New Yorker and a Cadillac Series 62. Dashboards carried a symmetrical theme with an abundance of chrome. **4.** Veedol motor oil claimed to make engines run smoother, but it's doubtful it could have improved the liquid hum of a Lincoln V-12. **5-8.** In what would be the final year for the original Continental, Lincoln kept prices at their 1947 levels. In the case of the

5

6

7

8

9

Continental convertible, that meant a lofty $4746. Although always a limited-production specialty car, production of the Continental was less limited than might be expected in this shortened model year. At 452, the convertible actually posted its second-highest volume, bested only by the 1947 total of 738. Dashboards were less chrome-encrusted than the standard Lincoln's. Though they looked very similar and were built on the same 125-inch wheelbase, the Continental convertible had a longer hood and shorter tail than its Lincoln counterpart, along with a squared-off decklid hosting the signature spare tire. The front seatback tilted forward to allow access to a somewhat cramped rear seat. **9-10.** The Continental coupe sold for $4662. Like all Lincolns, the Continental was powered by a 125-bhp 292-cid V-12, which made its last showing in '48. Neither displacement nor power was all that high considering the car's 4100-pound heft, but a Continental was all about prestige, not performance.

10

# 1948

# Mercury

With redesigned models due for '49, the '48s are virtually unchanged

Like other FoMoCo divisions—but unlike the rest of the industry—prices are unchanged

Price-leading two-door sedan is dropped

Benson Ford elected general manager of Lincoln-Mercury Division

Model year begins on November 1, 1947; runs only into March 1948

Shortened run results in model-year production of just 50,268, dropping Mercury to 16th in industry sales

1

2

3

**1-2.** At $2002, a Mercury convertible cost $262 more than its Ford V-8 counterpart. For the difference, Merc buyers got nicer trim inside and out; note the more-intricate grille pattern, dual chrome strips on the fenders, and the bright band between the fancier-looking taillights. Mercurys came standard with the same 100-bhp, 239-cid V-8 that was used on V-8 Fords. **3.** John Cobb held the land speed record in 1948 at 403 mph, a feat this ad claims was aided by Mobiloil lubricants—the same used in Mauri Rose's Indianapolis 500 winner. **4.** Ads promoted Mercury as giving you "*More* of everything: *more* beauty, *more* comfort, *more* liveliness...." Yes, and all for *more* money than a comparable Ford. **5-7.** The most popular of the 1948 Mercs was the $1660 four-door town sedan. One of Mercury's distinguishing features was the dual "nostril" turn-signal lamps that flanked the hood just above the grille. Interiors were subtly two-toned; the seat belts shown on this example were added later. This car also sports accessory

bumper-end guards front and rear. **8.** Lincoln-Mercury Division used this Mercury wagon as a medical transport vehicle. Station wagons sold for $2207.

5

6

7

8

# General Motors

Charles E. ("Engine Charlie") Wilson replaced William Knudsen as head of GM. Dynaflow, Buick's new hydraulic torque-converter transmission that provided automatic operation without gears, was a $244 Roadmaster option. Buick styling was largely unchanged.

Cadillacs wore a traditional egg-crate grille with enlarged openings and a curved two-piece windshield, but the big news was out back. First-ever tailfins were inspired by the Lockheed P-38 fighter plane. GM design chief Bill Mitchell later said fins "gave definition to the rear of the car for the first time." The posh Fleetwood 75 kept old finless styling through 1949.

Chevrolets carried on almost exactly as in 1947.

Oldsmobile called its initial 1948 models "Dynamic," but only details changed. February brought a new "Futuramic" 98 model, simultaneous with the new Cadillac design. Both had been created at Harley Earl's Art & Colour Studio. Despite a slightly shorter wheelbase, the Futuramic Olds looked longer and lower, and public reaction was positive.

Pontiacs got Silver Streak nameplates and Hydra-Matic became optional. Half of the six-cylinder cars had Hydra-Matic, versus 80 percent of eights.

# Buick

Cars get only minor trim changes

Dynaflow automatic transmission introduced as option on Roadmasters

Supers gain 5 horsepower; Roadmasters with Dynaflow gain 6 horsepower

Model-year production down 23 percent to 213,599; Buick falls to 6th in industry

1

2

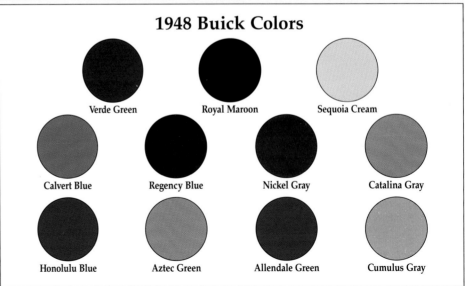

### 1948 Buick Colors

Verde Green

Royal Maroon

Sequoia Cream

Calvert Blue

Regency Blue

Nickel Gray

Catalina Gray

Honolulu Blue

Aztec Green

Allendale Green

Cumulus Gray

3

4

5

7

...as fashioned for a few

6

1. Externally, not much changed for Buick in 1948. The only difference between this '48 Roadmaster Estate Wagon and its '47 counterpart is the script on the front fenders.
2. Buick offered Dynaflow, its first automatic transmission since the failed Safety (semi) Automatic Transmission of 1938. Dynaflow, a $200 option on Roadmasters, used a torque converter developed by Buick during the war for the Hell-Cat tank destroyer. Not as efficient as the Olds and Cadillac Hydra-Matic, it was dubbed "Dyna-slush" by some. The 320-cid inline eights of cars so equipped came with six extra horsepower (150 vs. 144) to make up for the new transmission's tendency to slip. 3. Roadmaster's new interior featured a tenite steering wheel and a two-tone gray instrument panel with silver-gray gauges. A Custom Trim option was offered with cloth upholstery and leather bolsters. 4-5. Buick again sold more convertibles than any other automaker, but ragtop sales were down about 25 percent. The price for the Road-master convertible coupe was up almost $200. 6. 1948 grilles incorporated the Buick crest, which had become wider in 1947. 7. Power windows, driver seat, and top were standard on Roadmaster ragtops.

241

# Cadillac

Complete redesign, inspired by P-38 Lightning airplane, is the first all-new postwar car (along with Oldsmobile) from the Big Three

New "Futuramic" styling includes fins; applies to all cars but Series 75

Dealer apprehension of bold new design soon quelled by popularity

346-cid V-8 engine remains unchanged at 150 horsepower

Series 62 wheelbase decreases 3 inches to 126 as it adopts Series 61 chassis

Late start due to redesign makes model year only nine months long

Model-year production down 15 percent to 52,706 due to abbreviated model year; Cadillac ranks 15th in industry

1

2

1. Cadillac was "The New Standard of the World" in 1948 with the Big Three's first all-new postwar cars (along with Oldsmobile). Model-year production was down, though, because the '48s didn't debut until March. The star of this ad, a Fleetwood Sixty Special, came only as a four-door sedan. Exclusive to the Sixty Special were a simulated vertical airscoop at the leading edge of each rear fender, chrome moldings around each window, and chrome louvers on the rear pillars. 2. Cadillac's redesign was inspired by a trip Harley Earl's design team took to study the Lockheed P-38 Lightning before the war. New cues included a continuous line that ran the length of the car, Cadillac's first tailfins, curved front and rear windows, and two horizontal grille bars (down from five). 3. Cadillacs were the stars of the test track preview at the Milford Proving Grounds. Other GM makes were also on display. 4-5. Series 62 models differed from 61s with stone shields behind the front wheel openings and bright rocker sill moldings. 6. 1948 models had a new interior; the curved dash sported an all-inclusive rainbow-shaped instrument pod. 7. A pair of newer models stand out in the lower right-hand corner of this 1948 Chicago parking lot, namely a Cadillac Series 62 and a Studebaker Champion Starlight coupe. 8. Series 62s had three chrome trim strips below each taillight; the driver-side taillight housed the gas-filler cap.

3

4

5

6

7

8

# Chevrolet

Cars get minor facelift with new grille

Trucks get major redesign; first postwar Chevrolets

President Nicholas Dreystadt dies; W.E. Armstrong takes over for interim and is replaced by T. H. Keating, former general sales manager

Chevrolet Fleetmaster cabriolet paces the Indianapolis 500

A record 211,861 Fleetline Aerosedans sold

Model-year production up 3.7 percent to 696,449; Chevrolet is 1st in industry

1

2

3

4

5

1. Convertible sales were down 28 percent, but the Fleetmaster convertible coupe was still appealing—so much so that it paced the Indianapolis 500. 2. GM built this 1948 Chevy convertible for actor Jimmy Stewart. It wore many Chevy accessories, and the exterior was treated to contrasting paint around the windshield frame and upper body, as well as Buick-like portholes. The steering-wheel hub bore Stewart's signature. 3. Americans were vacationing again and reading a travel magazine called *Holiday*. Chevy developed a series of ads for the new magazine that eventually led to the familiar slogan "See the USA in your Chevrolet." 4-5. Introduced in the summer of 1947, GM's first redesigned postwar vehicles were the 1948 Chevy and GMC pickups. Termed "Advance Design," they had all-new cabs, new sheetmetal, wider beds, and side-mounted cowl vents. 6. Part of the Fleet-line Sportmaster sedan's appeal was its similarity to GM's senior line cars. Sales increased 18 percent over '47, but it was still outsold by the Aerosedan by more than three-to-one. 7-8. Fleetlines were a subset of the Fleetmaster series, all of which had upscale interiors. Differences between the Fleetmasters and Stylemasters included woodgrain door trim, carpeting on the front floormats and rear floor, and available leatherette armrest wear guards. 9. Convertible boots matched the top color. Chrome-plated gravel shields were optional on all models. 10. Spearhead-shaped hood-side trim identified the series of all cars. This Fleetmaster four-door sport sedan features sliding rear quarter windows.

6

7

8

9

10

1

2  3

4

5  6

1. The only Chevy priced over $200 was the Fleetmaster woody wagon at $2013. Wagon production more than doubled to 10,171 units, setting a company record. Wagons would become much more popular in two short years, as GM converted to steel bodies. 2-3. The Fleetline two-door Aerosedan was Chevy's most-popular car, selling more than 210,000 units. This specimen is decked out with all the options, including spotlights, bumper guards, and a sunshade. 4. A 1948 Chevy Fleetline starred in this ad for Hertz's "Drive-Ur-Self" rental service. 5. The five-passenger sport coupe was the only Fleetmaster coupe; Stylemasters had a business coupe as well. 6. The "Advance Design" trucks, including this ½-ton DeLuxe panel delivery, had new styling and Fleetline speedline trim, but rode on prewar running gear.

## 1948 Chevrolet Colors

Liveoak Green | Lake Como Blue | Dove Gray | Silver Gray Green | Battleship Gray | Oxford Maroon | Marsh Brown | Satin Green

# Oldsmobile

98s get Futuramic styling midyear on 2-inch shorter wheelbase; GM's first postwar car (along with Cadillac)

Futuramic styling includes slab-sided, flow-through fenders and a lower, wider appearance

98's 257-cid straight eight increases to 115 horsepower; up 5

98 becomes Oldsmobile's best-seller for the first time

60 and 70 series cars get only new ornament and minor rear-end changes

Final year of production for Oldsmobile straight eights

Model-year production down 11 percent to 172,852; Oldsmobile falls to 8th in industry sales behind Studebaker

1

2

3

4

5

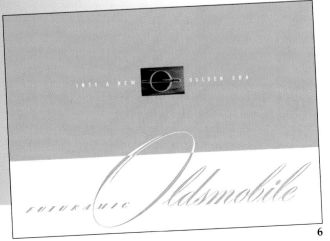

6

**1-2.** "Hydra-Matic" and "Futuramic" were Oldsmobile's catchwords in 1948. Hydra-Matic was old news by now but still a convenience that provided a competitive advantage. The Futuramic 98 Oldsmobiles, introduced midmodel year in February, represented "the dramatic design of the future." **3.** The only 1948 Oldsmobiles with Futuramic styling were the 98 series cars. The front end featured a broader, lower hood; a curved windshield; and a lower, wider appearance. **4-5.** The 98 club sedan sported fastback styling, which was now starting to wane in popularity. All Futuramic 98s had slab-sided, flow-through fenders that marked a great departure from previous designs. The Futuramic 98 proved very popular; 98s became Oldsmobile's best-sellers for the first time. **6.** This 1948 Olds brochure claimed the Futuramic 98 Olds was "specially designed to commemorate the Golden [50th] Anniversary of America's oldest motor car manufacturer."

1

2

3

4

5

6

7

8

9

1-2. The 98 Deluxe convertible coupe helped Olds ragtop sales outdistance Buick convertibles 12,914 to 11,503. Topless Buicks had outsold their Olds counterparts three-to-one in 1947. 3. The 98 club sedan was the least expensive of the senior series cars at $2078. The DeLuxe version (*shown*) cost another $104. 4. DeLuxe features included a deluxe steering wheel, special front and rear floormats, a clock, chrome wheel-trim rings, and a rear center armrest. All 98 dashboards were two-tone. 5. Olds 98 convertibles had power tops, windows, and driver seats. 6. Futuramic 98s came in three body styles: convertible, club sedan, and four-door sedan (*shown*). 7-8. A combination wood and metal Fisher body replaced the Ionia unit on 60 series station wagons for '48. 9. Station wagon interiors remained unchanged from '47, as did the passenger compartments for all 60 and 70 series cars. 10. Two-tone paint schemes, a $12.50 option, were popular for 60 and 70 (*shown*) series cars. 11. For its swan song, the 98's 257-cid inline eight was boosted five horsepower to 115. 12. In their final year, 60 series cars, like this 66 club coupe, eschewed the Special designation for a Dynamic moniker.

10

11

12

# Pontiac

Carryover prewar car designs enter final season; all models share minor facelift that includes revised grille, different taillights, and smooth fendersides

Pontiac introduces its first automatic transmission, Hydra-Matic Drive

DeLuxe trim gets additional brightwork and plusher interior, along with wider availability; it's offered on almost every body style

Inline eight-cylinder engine continues basically unchanged, but power creeps up one horsepower to 104

Model-year production up 2 percent to 235,419; Pontiac climbs to 5th in industry sales

1. Pontiac ads touted new Hydra-Matic Drive four-speed automatic transmission. The $185 option was available linewide, and roughly three-quarters of '48s were so equipped. 2. DeLuxe trim was offered on more models than in the previous year. For '48, it could add sparkle to almost any Pontiac, though some, such as this Torpedo convertible, didn't come in a standard version. 3. The Streamliner DeLuxe four-door sedan started at $1817 with the six, $47 more with the eight. 4. Front brightwork was revised on all models, with a new floating top bar/nameplate. This factory press photo noted that the "deft rearrangement of the grille has added to Pontiac's already impressive width and massiveness." Those were the days.

5

6

7

8

9

10

**5.** Streamliner coupes were available in standard trim, starting at $1677. An additional $89 got you this DeLuxe version, which on all '48s included front-fender trim, full wheel covers, and bright-metal instead of rubber gravel guards. **6.** Almost all models had a faux wood dashboard. DeLuxes, such as this one, also included carpeting, electric clock, and broadcloth seats. **7.** Exterior changes for '48 included round, instead of rectangular, taillights. **8-9.** This was Pontiac's last year for all-wood wagon bodies. Prices started at $2364. **10.** The '48s dispensed with the previous year's three horizontal speedlines on each fender. Thus, standard models, like this Torpedo Eight two-door, had unadorned fendersides.

# Hudson

A year after Studebaker launched a radical postwar car, Hudson had one of its own, displaying startling "Step-Down" styling. The new profile was low and sleek, with a floorpan that sat below the top of the frame, so passengers actually did step down to enter. Occupants were fully surrounded by the chassis girders. Sturdy, semiunibody Monobilt construction meant the body and chassis were welded together.

The Step-Down look evolved from wartime doodles by Frank Spring, and chief engineer Millard Toncray earned credit for the design work. Because Hudsons now had the lowest center of gravity in the industry, they quickly gained renown for great handling and roadworthiness. They also appealed to stock-car racers, who made them successful race cars. A long wheelbase ensured a comfortable ride and roomy interiors. Weight rose by 13 percent, but the six-cylinder engine was new and more powerful. Hudson earned a $13.2 million profit on $274 million in sales, setting a postwar record.

Major, revolutionary redesign as "Step-Down" body style arrives; dubbed "Monobilt" body and frame construction

Low center of gravity, increased head and leg room

Hudson now one of America's safest and most-comfortable cars

262-cid, 121-bhp Super Six L-head engine bows

Hudson purchases six Detroit buildings from Fruehauf Trailer Co., gaining 200,000 square feet of factory floor space

Model-year production up 27 percent to 117,200; Hudson climbs to 10th in industry sales

1

2

3

4

5

6

**1-2.** Stock-car racers and others who referred to the '48 Hudsons as "fabulous" weren't exaggerating. These all-new models were a poke in the eye of the Big Three, and brought Hudson considerable prestige, track dominance, and sales momentum. This Commodore Six four-door sedan exemplifies Hudson's fresh take on "practical" transportation: Room for the whole family, with the added fillip of "Step-Down" design that lowered the floorpan for increased head and leg room; and the splendid handling (and safety) that comes from a dramatically low center of gravity. All of this year's Hudsons rode a 124-inch wheelbase. Closed models had the rakishly lowered rooflines and provocatively narrow glass that Step-Down design allowed. All of that, plus slab-sided styling, made the cars fine examples of the new automotive modernity. The lead designer was Frank Spring. The Commodore Six ran with a sensational, durable new engine, a 262-cid L-head six that produced 121 bhp, and that put many eights to shame. **3-6.** Stylish two-toning highlights this Commodore Eight club coupe, which has the 254-cid L-head eight rated at 128 bhp. This example, an unrestored original, has optional fog lamps, sun visor, and overdrive. Hudson's hydraulic brake system was backed up by a mechanical fail-safe. The flat, upright dash was functional and attractive. **7-9.** A Commodore ragtop; you did indeed step down into a '48 Hudson, right over the frame rails. Owners loved the setup, but did complain that the dropped floor made cleanup difficult.

7

8

9

253

# Kaiser-Frazer

Like the amateur critics who had wondered about the direction in which the new Studebaker was heading, some observers of Kaiser and Frazer sedans were said to ask, "Willit Run?" This play on words suggested a familiarity with the former Ford Willow Run plant in Michigan, where the cars were produced.

Little-changed in appearance in Kaiser-Frazer's second season. Both makes continued to sell well, giving the company a $10 million profit in 1948—down from the first-year figure, but a welcome sum nonetheless. Some analysts, in fact, referred to Kaiser-Frazer as the "postwar wonder car." After 1948, however, Kaiser-Frazer was destined to suffer a rapid decline in sales and earning power.

Minimal changes to '47 design and engineering

Nameplates are redesigned

Skilled expediters travel the country looking for steel, copper wire, and other scarce materials; the idea works, but Kaiser-Frazer pays out big bucks

Kaiser-Frazer posts $10 million profit; company is still an independent phenomenon, but darker days await

Model-year production: Kaiser up 30 percent to 91,851 for 14th in industry; Frazer down 30 percent to 48,071 for 17th

Combined model-year production up marginally to 139,922

1

2

1-2. Kaiser-Frazer's clean styling, which was so dramatic in 1947, now had competition from the '48 Packards and Hudsons. These factory-issued photos show new K-F product at the Willow Run, Michigan, plant. 3-6. The Frazer Manhattan sedan could be had with the standard 226-cid, 100-bhp L-head six, or with an optional six of the same layout and displacement that produced 112 horsepower. Wheelbase was 123.5 inches (as on all of this year's Frazers and Kaisers); the car weighed in at 3375 pounds, and cost $2746. Nearly 18,600 were produced. The hood crest is the Frazer family's. 7. Enormous postwar interest in futurism was freely exploited, even to sell six-year-old whiskey. Neat truck, but what happens to the happy cooks and all that food during panic stops?

3

4

5

6

7

# Nash

Charles Nash died in June 1948, at the age of 84, leaving behind a $43 million estate. Searching for a man suitable for second-in-command, newly named chairman George Mason took on George Romney, later to become governor of Michigan, as Nash-Kelvinator's vice-president. Mason was considered one of the most visionary executives in the industry, forecasting the need for mergers of the independent companies and presiding over the development of a radical new Nash design for '49.

No convertibles had been produced in 1946-47, but Nash remedied that omission this year with a new Ambassador Custom cabriolet. Not until 1965, a decade after Nash had turned into AMC, would the company build another convertible.

Moldings below the beltline were deleted, which gave Nash cars a less streamlined appearance. This would be the last Nash with a separate frame. Three-passenger business coupes weren't nearly as popular as in the past, but Nash added one to its 1948 lineup.

Final Nashes produced with separate body-on-frame construction

Production begins at El Segundo, California, factory

Model line is significantly expanded to meet anticipated postwar demand

George Romney named vice president

Model-year production up 9 percent to 110,000, but Nash falls to 11th in industry

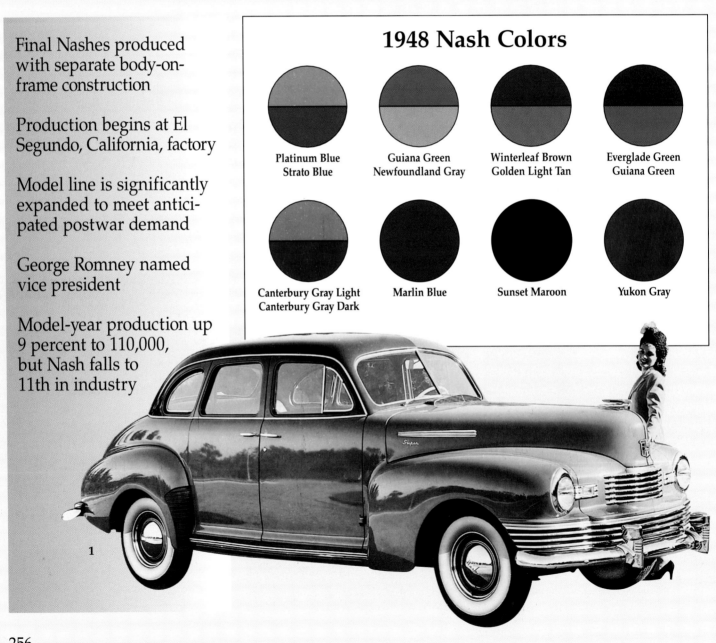

**1948 Nash Colors**

Platinum Blue
Strato Blue

Guiana Green
Newfoundland Gray

Winterleaf Brown
Golden Light Tan

Everglade Green
Guiana Green

Canterbury Gray Light
Canterbury Gray Dark

Marlin Blue

Sunset Maroon

Yukon Gray

1

2

3

4

5

**1.** Nash expanded its model line for 1948, and offered a pleasing variety of body colors, including some nifty two-tones. The 600 Super four-door trunkback sedan cost just $1587. Power came from a 173-cid L-head six that produced 82 horsepower. This year's Nashes were the last with separate frames. All models had a cleaner look, thanks to the removal of chrome strips below the beltlines. **2-3.** The $2047 Ambassador Custom brougham two-door had perky good looks, but the fenders and deco-look horizontal ribbing on the dash were decidedly dated. The standard Ambassador engine was a 235-cid, 112-bhp L-head six. **4-5.** The Ambassador Super brougham two-door cost $189 less than the similar but uplevel Custom brougham. The big six had seven main bearings. **6-7.** Nash fans had but one choice for open-air motoring in '48: the Ambassador Custom cabriolet. At $2345, it was the most-expensive Nash. **8.** Nash built a series of prototype pickups on the Ambassador chassis.

6

7

8

**1 & 3.** The 1948 600-series business coupe, at $1478, was Nash's entry-level model. A total of 925 were built. The back seats of these three-passenger cars were replaced by a useful storage shelf. This example is adorned with sun visor, driving lights, conditioned-air system, side-view mirrors, and glare shield. Most, but not all, '48 Nashes had rectangular parking lights inboard of the headlamps. **2.** Advertising for the 600 series continued to emphasize economy (a claimed 25 mpg), unibody engineering, and ride comfort. **4.** A 600 Custom brougham two-door weighed 3312 pounds, and sold for $2047. **5.** Nash built about 5000 ⅔-ton light-duty trucks for 1948. Most of these were intended for export markets, but a few were taken by Stateside Nash dealers and sold as tow trucks. **6.** "Better living through chemistry," starring the '48 Nash. **7.** A 600 Super four-door trunkback sedan, in Marlin Blue.

# Packard

For financial reasons, Packard had to stick with the Clipper-based body for a few more years. Rather than a mild facelift, designers took a heavier-handed approach for its Twenty-Second series cars.

Packard's 1948 profile was based on the prewar Phantom show car, designed by Ed Macauley. Heavy chunks of metal were tacked onto the structure to create a flowing-fender effect, but they added about 200 pounds to the car and yielded a chubby shape. All over the country, sharp-eyed car fans dubbed the latest Packard a "pregnant elephant." A short, squat grille didn't help matters, as it was less elegant than the tall, narrow grille of the 1946-47 models.

A new 327-cid straight eight went into Super models. The new Station Sedan was almost all-steel, with structural wood bodywork mainly at the tailgate. Six-cylinder Packards were produced primarily as taxis and for export. Despite dubious styling, the 1948 Packards sold well, with nearly 90,000 made in the model year.

Stopgap update gives cars smooth, nearly slab-sided styling

Supers get 327-cid, 145-bhp inline eight-cylinder engine

First postwar convertibles

Beautiful, expensive Station Sedan bows

Six-cylinder engines reserved for taxis and export; 2000 taxis produced

Chairman Alvan Macauley retires after 38 years

Model-year production up 81 percent to 92,251; Packard jumps to 13th in industry

1

2

3

1. Packard's make-or-break, all-new 1948 line was unveiled in August 1947. The magazine ad seen here trumpets eight-cylinder coupes and sedans, and the very attractive but peculiarly nonutilitarian Station Sedan. Observers who had yet to grow accustomed to the new postwar streamlining referred to the '48 Packards as "pregnant elephants." 2-3. Of the '48 line, the convertible bowed first, and made a positive impression on the general public. Super Eight ragtops, like those seen here, sold for $3250. Model-year convertible production totaled 7763 units.

1

2

1-4. Except for Packard's six-cylinder taxis (some 2000 of them, in standard and limo styles), the '48 lineup ran with L-head eight-cylinder engines. Packard made eights in 288, 327, and 356 cid; these were rated at 130, 145, and 160 horsepower, respectively. The $3750 Custom Eight sedan seen here has the biggest engine, and rides the line's midsize, 127-inch wheelbase. Only Custom Eights had eggcrate grilles and the uniquely dramatic cormorant hood ornament. Sheetmetal ahead of the firewall was exclusive to the model; likewise the fender skirts, double-bar rocker panel molding, and "stacked" front-bumper design. 5. Ads for the convertibles emphasized the solidity imparted by the cars' chassis, which weighed 100 pounds more than that of the comparable Packard sedan. 6-9. The wooden body work (maple panels framed with birch) of the Station Sedan was structural only at the smallish tailgate. Wood at the door panels and window frames was inlaid. 10. The Custom Eight limo weighed a staggering 4880 pounds. It seated seven, and sold for $4868.

3

4

5

6

7

8

9

10

# Studebaker

Still attracting attention on the road and in dealer showrooms, the modern-looking Studebakers gave the company a record $18 million profit this year. Hudson had a sleek new model on the market, but the major automakers weren't quite ready with their postwar designs, giving the independents a valuable lead.

Plant capacity was doubled over the prewar level, to meet anticipated demand. Construction of a new Studebaker factory began in Hamilton, Ontario, Canada, which would eventually be the last remaining production facility for the make when it went out of business in 1966.

Prices rose a bit, and Studebakers got a few trim changes; mainly, a winged hood medallion on all models. Material shortages were less bothersome than in 1947. Paul G. Hoffman left in April to direct the Marshall Plan from Washington, D.C. Harold S. Vance took over as company president and board chairman. Studebaker truck output was particularly strong, with a record 67,981 sold.

Minor front-end changes distinguish 1948 Studes from '47s; more substantial bumper guards are the most noticeable

500,000th postwar Stude is built during the model year

New nameplates clearly identify series

Upholstery material is upgraded

Model-year production up 15 percent to 184,993; Studebaker climbs to 7th in industry sales race

1. Changes for '48 were cosmetic: simplified bumper guards and more chrome across the top of the grille. Prices were hiked about $200. The convertible in this striking ad is a $2431 Commander Regal DeLuxe, identifiable by the strakes on the wing vent. 2-5. The Commander Land Cruiser was the only model on a 123-inch wheelbase; other wheelbases were 112 (Champion) and 119 (Commander) inches. The Cruiser seated five and sold for $2265. Studebaker's well-publicized 500,000th postwar car was a Land Cruiser. 6-8. At $2431, the Commander ragtop was the most-expensive '48 Stude. Commander dashes had a rounded gauge housing; it was rectangular on Champions. 9. A Commander ragtop with a Champion three-passenger coupe (*top*) and a Champion Starlight coupe.

## 1948 Studebaker Colors

Boulevard Gray

Melody Blue

Parkway Green

Iroquois Blue

Peacock Green

Rodeo Tan

Varsity Maroon Metallic

Silver Gray Metallic

2

3

4

5

6

7

8

9

# Tucker

Nothing like it could be seen on any road—in 1948 or anytime thereafter. Not only was it sizable inside, but the Tucker Torpedo was surprisingly futuristic, including a fully independent suspension, disc brakes, a pop-out windshield, and a rear-mounted engine. Standing only 49 inches tall, the Tucker even had a third headlight that rotated in unison with the steering wheel.

A preselector gearbox worked with the six-cylinder engine, which could yield a 120-mph top speed. Six exhaust outlets suggested performance might be satisfying, which it was, in part thanks to the car's low center of gravity.

Sadly, Preston Tucker was indicted on 31 counts of fraud by the Securities and Exchange Commission. As moviegoers in the 1990s learned from the Tucker biopic, he was charged with having built no running automobiles. In fact, 51 were produced, a number of which were driven to the courthouse where Tucker was tried. Most of those ill-fated Tuckers still exist, too.

Maverick inventor/salesman Preston Tucker bucks the odds with his futuristic Tucker Torpedo

Rear-engine stunner is powered by a 335-cid, 166-bhp flat-six helicopter engine

Body/frame has step-down design

Well-publicized safety features abound

Performance outstrips that of any comparable U.S. production car

Model-year production limited to 51 (including prototype) as Preston Tucker is indicted of fraud and the startup company ceases operations

1

2

3

4

5

6

7

8

**1.** The intriguing Tucker Torpedo managed only 51 examples (including one prototype). Its potential seemed great, but simple business mismanagement killed it. Developer Preston Tucker (*left*), at a 1947 event, with radio personality Art Baker (*with mic*); son, Noble Tucker; and press agent Charles T. Pearson. **2.** Here, the prototype, which wowed auto show crowds. **3-5.** The Tucker's backswept roof, aggressive front and rear grilles, and tall suicide doors still look great. Because the floorpan was just nine inches above the ground, the Tucker was a "step-down," *a la* the '48 Hudsons. **6.** Interior padding and a steel-braced "Safety Chamber" helped protect occupants. **7.** The cyclopean center head-lamp turned with the steering wheel. **8.** Following a flirtation with a rear-mounted 589-cid flat six, Tucker chose a rear-mounted 335-cid "Talisman" Bell Helicopter flat six built by Air-Cooled Motors. The engine could run at maximum horsepower (166) for 150 hours!

# Willys

Willys-Overland continued to make steel station wagons, but the new Jeepster phaeton occupied center stage. Introduced in April 1948, the four-cylinder Jeepster had been designed during the war by Brooks Stevens, borrowing styling ideas from the basic military Jeep.

Sporty-looking Jeepsters had a big open compartment behind the cowl and a mechanically operated soft top. Up front, they looked much like the wagons and pickups, but with a revised grille. Produced only with rear-wheel drive on the wagon's frame (with an added X-member), the Jeepster was better-equipped than a wagon. The phaeton designation was no joke, as roll-up windows were not installed. Instead, Jeepsters had side curtains, like phaetons in the old days.

Also new this year was a six-cylinder Station Sedan—essentially a luxury version of the station wagon with a larger body and wider seats. "Basket-weave" trim gave the new model a distinctive appearance, but underneath it was essentially a Willys station wagon.

L-head six Station Sedan debuts

Wood-look paint on metal-bodied Station Sedan continues

Jeepster "phaeton convertible" debuts; has mechanically operated top

Model-year production: 22,309, plus 63,170 Jeeps

1-2. Willys' all-steel Station Sedan added a new, more-powerful L-head six model (72 horsepower) with wider seats and, for the first time, four-wheel drive. This uplevel wagon sold for $1890, $245 more than the four-cylinder model. The horizontally split liftgate allowed easy stowage. All seats, except the driver's, were removable.
3-5. The other new offering for '48 was the Jeepster phaeton convertible, a combination of utility and fun that ran with a 134-cid L-head four producing 63 horsepower. The Jeepster had a mechanically operated top, and was designed by Brooks Stevens.
6. Jeepster's interior was austere but not unhandsome, with simple gauges. 7. The split grille was a pleasing, carlike touch.

3

4

5

6

7

# Minor Makes
## AND IMPORTS

Entrepreneurs were creating some intriguing new makes, but few lasted more than a couple of years. About 17 three-wheeled Davis cars were built, and perhaps 90 Playboy minicars (which had a folding steel top). The Towne Shopper was a mostly aluminum two-seater.

Crosley continued as the most prominent minor make. Of the 28,000 cars sold this year, 23,000 were station wagons, which made little Crosley the world's foremost wagon builder. Plant capacity expanded by 40 percent. A delivery sedan joined the 1948 lineup.

Imports continued to flow slowly into the market. High-end motorcars were typically imported by small dealerships that took special interest in foreign cars. Like their American counterparts, British automakers were working on new-for-1949 models. Jaguar continued to issue prewar-style models, and HRG built roadsters that rivaled the MG TC. Aston Martin made its first cars, dubbed DB1. Sydney Allard was turning out street/competition cars in Britain. Gracefully styled, the Italian-built Cisitalia was rarer than a Ferrari in America.

7

8

9

10

11

**1 & 3.** Combined Crosley sales for '48 across four models hit an impressive 29,084. Prices ranged from $799 to $929. **2 & 4.** The Davis Motor Co. of Van Nuys, California, built 17 Davis Divans from 1947 to '49. The little streamliner was a single-seat three-wheeler with room for four. The enterprise collapsed when the company's owner was convicted of fraud. **5-6.** The Towne Shopper was manufactured by International Motor Car of San Diego. Power came from a rear-mounted, 10.5-bhp Onan two-cylinder engine that produced 50 mpg and 50 mph. **7.** To drive the '48 J2 Allard was no easy feat. It had a stiff ride, a long stretch to the gear lever, a long clutch stroke, copious engine heat, and a straight-legged driving position. Performance, however, was a treat, coming from a 239-cid side-valve Ford V-8. **8.** A 66-bhp Fiat inline four powered the Pinin Farina-styled Cisitalia 202 Gran Sport. **9.** Ferrari's first roadgoing chassis, the 166, carried numerous body types; this is the Barchetta roadster. A 122-cid V-12 cranked out 110-150 bhp (due to different carb setups). **10.** Britain's HRG did well in competition, but struck many shoppers as old-fashioned. **11.** 1948 was the final year for Jaguar's Mark IV saloon, which did the 0-60 sprint in 16.8 seconds.

Postwar prosperity was well underway as 1949 began, and car shortages were easing. Manufacturers, at last, had all-new cars with which to tempt customers, and sales records to be broken. As the "seller's market" faded away, automobile manufacturers would begin searching for new ways to hike the sales totals.

By 1949, nearly all the automakers had introduced all-new models or had them ready—though a few emerged a little late in the season. The typical 1949 model was lower, wider, with faired-in front fenders that tapered into the bodyside. Just about every model—including Ford, finally—had an independent front suspension.

Ford adopted a boxy, slab-sided look for all of its 1949 models. The cars were lighter and lower, and they retained the familiar flathead V-8 engine. Ford got a jump on the competition, too, introducing its '49 models early—in June 1948.

Lincoln and Mercury models were especially curvaceous and shapely, with no hint of the prior design evident. Two-door models, in particular, looked sleek and eager. Lincoln abandoned its V-12 engine in favor of a big flathead V-8. Ford Motor Company saw production top the million mark for the first time since 1930.

Chevrolets, Pontiacs, and smaller Oldsmobiles were more curvy in profile. Buicks had a look all their own, for one year only. Not only did they sport "portholes" ahead of the front doors, but a new Riviera "hardtop convertible" body style joined the ranks. The pillarless design was meant to look like a convertible, but provide the harsh-weather comfort of a closed automobile. Cadillac offered a similar hardtop called

the Coupe de Ville, while Oldsmobile called its version the Holiday. Hardtop coupes typically had a contrasting color for the roof.

Cadillac and Oldsmobile turned to significant underhood changes, unveiling the first postwar overhead-valve V-8 engines. Cadillac's version was bigger and more powerful than the Olds Rocket V-8, but both were revolutionary and their design would soon be adopted by all other U.S. automakers.

Nash redesigned its cars, giving them what came to be called an "inverted bathtub" shape. All had a curvy fastback rear end and partially covered front and rear wheels. Inside, a Uniscope pod above the steering column held all the instruments.

Chrysler Corporation issued carryover 1948 models, calling them "First Series" '49s. The real 1949 cars, dubbed the "Second Series," were brand-new but more square in profile than most of the competition. Chrysler products were also taller than most, partly due to the fact that company president K. T. Keller liked to wear a hat—and believed there should be room in a car for a man with a hat. Dodge launched a single-seat Wayfarer roadster with detachable windows, but few were made. Plymouth turned out an all-steel Suburban station wagon, DeSoto fielded a nine-passenger wagon, and Chrysler products adopted an ignition-key starter.

Frazer also had something unique with its new Manhattan: the first four-door convertible since prewar days. Kaiser introduced what it called the Virginian four-door hardtop, as well as a Traveler utility sedan that lacked a left-side rear door but included a two-section hinged back hatch.

In June, Regulation W, which limited consumer auto financing to 24 months, came to an end. The defunct Tucker company was ordered to return its leased Chicago plant to the War Assets Administration. Steel and coal strikes took place in the fall.

With so many new models on the market, the auto industry set a production record by turning out 5,119,466 cars in 1949.

Total vehicle output topped 6.2 million, breaking a 20-year record, and the future looked even stronger for sales.

"Transportation Unlimited," the first GM car show since 1940, opened in New York City. On a less-pleasant note, National City Lines, an organization formed by General Motors and other corporations that had been buying up urban streetcar lines, was found guilty of antitrust violations. Executives of the involved companies wound up paying trivial fines.

Nearly 10 million television sets now sat in American living rooms in the new suburban houses. Families were buying 100,000 each week. Early advocates of television touted its potential as an educational tool, and programs like *Ding Dong School*, with Dr. Frances Horwich, attracted preschoolers. Quiz shows were also popular.

Much of TV programming was on quite another level, however, including soap operas, roller derby, and professional wrestling—the latter peopled with such colorful characters as "Gorgeous George." Russell Lynes, editor of *Harper's* magazine, declared that people fell into three intellectual categories: highbrow, lowbrow, and middlebrow—according to their tastes.

Plenty of Americans still listened to their favorite radio programs—whether *Duffy's Tavern* or *My Friend Irma*, Jack Benny or Fred Allen. *Dragnet* began on radio, but would soon switch to TV. Innovative comedian Sid Caesar went on TV with the *Admiral Broadway Review*. Three competing color-TV systems were presented to the Federal Communications Commission for consideration, but color was far in the future.

People were reading Nelson Algren's novel of drug addiction, *The Man with the Golden Arm*. George Orwell published *1984*. James Cagney starred in the gangster film *White Heat*. Broderick Crawford got an Academy Award for his portrayal of down-home politico Willie Stark in *All the King's Men*.

A jet bomber crossed the U.S. in three hours and 46 minutes. Another bomber managed a nonstop flight around the world, refueling four times in midair.

Joe DiMaggio earned $90,000 this year—the highest salary in baseball. *Death of a Salesman*, Arthur Miller's play about the troubles of burned-out salesman Willy Loman, opened on Broadway with Lee J. Cobb playing the lead role. It won a Pulitzer Prize. Mary Martin starred in the classic musical *South Pacific*.

Dinah Shore sang *Baby, It's Cold Outside*, Perry Como crooned *Bali Ha'i*, and Hank Williams hit the airwaves with *I'm So Lonesome I Could Cry*. Also heard on records and radio: *Diamonds Are a Girl's Best Friend* and *Rudolph the Red-Nosed Reindeer*. RCA introduced the 45-rpm record, a day after Columbia showed the first 33⅓-rpm disc.

Walt Kelly's *Pogo* made its first appearance in a comic strip. Pyramid Clubs saw a short-lived, but significant, revival, tempting modest-income people who thought they could amass a fortune without any real effort.

China fell to the communists in August. A month later, it was learned that Russia had the atomic bomb. The "Cold War" was escalating and the fear of an A-bomb attack would permeate the 1950s. At the same time, though, America was well on its way to an increasingly affluent society that centered on Suburbia—and on the automobile.

# Chrysler Corporation

When they finally went on sale in early spring 1949, Chrysler products looked less sleek than the competition. Pursuing utility over beauty, K.T. Keller still wanted "three-box" styling with ample headroom, in contrast to the lower rooflines favored by rivals. So, the 1949 cars were boxy, upright, and conservative. Virgil Exner was hired, but his impact would come later.

A wood-trimmed Town & Country convertible debuted, but no T&C wagon was included in the silver-anniversary Chrysler lineup. Instead, steel-bodied wagons arrived. Chryslers wore ornate, massive eggcrate grilles and humped vertical taillights. Sales suffered against the flashier makes of '49, though marketers expressed a fondness for gimmicky system names, including a Safety-Level Ride and Hydra-Lizer shocks.

Fluid Drive worked with Tip-Toe hydraulic shift in DeSotos, which kept a six-cylinder engine. A bust of Hernando DeSoto decorated each hood and glowed at night. In addition to a wood-bodied wagon, DeSoto's line included an all-steel Carry-All, with a fold-down back seat.

Dodge introduced a low-cost Wayfarer series that included a novel roadster with side curtains and no back seat. Like its more-costly mates, Plymouth promised comfort, space, and good visibility. A short-wheelbase series debuted, including a three-passenger coupe and an all-steel Suburban wagon.

# Chrysler

"First Series" '49s are carryover '48s

"Second Series" '49s are redesigned with flush front fenders, but styling is considered conservative

Sixes are on a 125.5-inch wheelbase; Eights ride a 131.5-inch span

Engines carry over, but six gets more power

Short model year for "real" '49s limits production to 124,218; Chrysler is 12th in industry

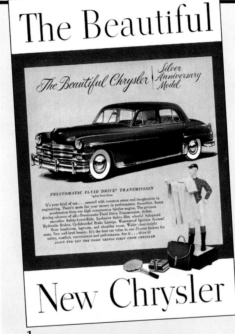

1. Chrysler's 25th anniversary was duly noted in ads for the company's totally redesigned "Second-Series" '49 models. Safety was stressed with such features as Safety-Level Ride, Safety-Rim wheels, and Safeguard Hydraulic Brakes. 2. And if that wasn't enough, interiors boasted the industry's first padded dashboard, with the padding extending into the doors. Gauges were now housed in a large, semicircular pod in front of the steering wheel, while a fluted bright-metal band stretched across the dash enclosing the radio controls, clock, glovebox, and the company's first starter/ignition key switch. Heater controls hung below the dashboard in a separate panel. 3. Though the Town & Country series contained only a convertible for '49, this prototype hardtop was also built. It would see limited production in 1950 as the Town & Country Newport, which would prove to be the final hurrah for these beautiful cars.

1

2

3

4

5

6

1. A 1949 family photo reveals the boxy lines and similar styling themes shared by the corporate cousins. Shown left to right are a Chrysler New Yorker, DeSoto Custom, Dodge Coronet, and Plymouth Special DeLuxe, all four-door sedans. Against their likewise redesigned competition, the cars were tall and conservative. 2. Price of entry to a new Chrysler rose to the $2114 asked for this Royal club coupe, the least-expensive car in the line. 3. Windsor remained the top-line six, this sedan going for $2329. 4-6. A snazzy New Yorker convertible was $3206. Note the fully wrapped rear bumper; it was trimmed back for '50.

1

2

3

4

5

1. A New Yorker four-door sedan now tipped the scales at well over two tons and cost $2726. **2.** Derham continued to modify Chrysler products, here placing a fabric top on a New Yorker sedan. **3.** Unique rear deck and taillights were constructed specifically for the Town & Country—it's surprising Chrysler would go to those lengths for a car selling in such low volume. But since it was basically a New Yorker otherwise, the 20-percent price premium charged for a Town & Country (now selling for $3970) may have made it worth the trouble. Wood trim was just an outline this year, the underlying panels being body-colored steel. **4-5.** Although only 1400 Crown Imperials were produced from 1946 through 1948, the stately model returned for '49 in the new design, still riding a 145.5-inch wheelbase. Fewer than 100 were built, with prices starting at $5229.

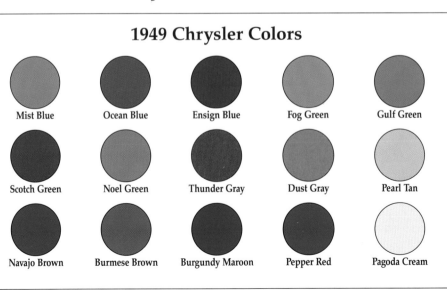

## 1949 Chrysler Colors

Mist Blue | Ocean Blue | Ensign Blue | Fog Green | Gulf Green
Scotch Green | Noel Green | Thunder Gray | Dust Gray | Pearl Tan
Navajo Brown | Burmese Brown | Burgundy Maroon | Pepper Red | Pagoda Cream

# DeSoto

"First Series" '49s are carryover '48s

"Second Series" '49s are completely redesigned, but with conservative styling

First station wagon debuts, as does Carry-All four-door sedan with folding rear seat

DeLuxe and Custom return on four-inch-longer (125.5-inch) wheelbase

Six-cylinder engine still 237 cid, but gains three horsepower to 112

Short model year for "real" '49s limits production to 94,201; DeSoto is 14th in industry

1. DeSoto's new interior still sported "woodgrain" paint, but the dashboard was no longer of symmetrical design. 2. The only convertible was again in the upscale Custom line; it was now priced at $2578. 3-4. DeSoto's first true station wagon appeared in the lower-line DeLuxe series at $2959. It had a concealed outside spare tire, and the center section of the rear bumper dropped down so the tire could clear it when the tailgate was lowered. The body was all-steel with wood trim. 5. New to the DeLuxe series was the $2191 Carry-All sedan. As noted in this ad, the rear seat could be folded to form a long, flat load floor. 6. Other ads touted DeSoto's new "wide, low look," despite the fact they were taller and narrower than most of their newly redesigned competitors.

1

2

3

1-2. The redesign meant the front fenders were now flush with the body and the rear fenders were much narrower. DeSotos also had wider bodies for '49, providing greater shoulder room. That allowed passengers more-spacious accommodations while cruising in a snappy Custom convertible. The example shown has the optional fog lamps and bumper override bars. 3. A Custom club coupe listed for $2156. Surprisingly, this model was the second-most-popular DeSoto in the postwar years, outselling everything but the Custom four-door sedan. 4. Goodyear's claim to fame for its Super cushion tires was that a larger footprint allowed lower tire pressures, so "Your car flows along almost as smoothly and comfortably as though it were running on a thick, luxurious carpet"—which some would say is how '40s cars felt anyway.

4

276

# Dodge

Carryover '48s become "First Series" '49s

Completely redesigned "Second Series" '49s are conservative compared to most rivals

New models: Low-priced Wayfarers ride a shorter 115-inch wheelbase, Meadowbrook and Coronets use a longer 123.5-inch span

Short model year limits production to 256,857; Dodge is 8th in industry

1

2

3

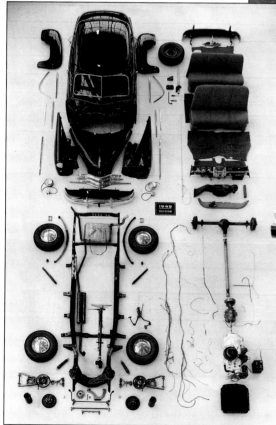

4

5

**1.** Whereas the redesigned '49 models of most competitors were "longer, lower, and wider," Dodge ads tried to justify its cars' conservative styling by explaining that being higher on the inside, and shorter and narrower on the outside made them roomier and easier to park. Furthermore, the "New Get-Away" engine was claimed to provide "New flashing performance"—this from the same 230-cid six as before, but with exactly one more horsepower. **2-3.** The new top-line model was the Coronet, shown here in $1927 sedan form. Note that the rear doors were now hinged at the front. **4.** A brand-new Dodge, some assembly required. **5.** Dodge wagons had all-steel bodies for the first time, though they were trimmed with wood. This Coronet wagon went for $2865.

1

2

3

4

5

**1.** The price leaders of the new Dodge lineup were the Wayfarers. The series offered a business coupe, two-door sedan, and two-seat roadster, all built on a 115-inch wheelbase—4.5 inches shorter than the '48 Dodge, and 8.5-inches shorter than the company's other '49 models. The most-alluring car of the Wayfarer series was the nifty little $1727 roadster, the least-expensive open car offered by the Big Three. It was originally built in the true English roadster style, having snap-in side windows instead of a convertible's roll-up windows. It also had a manually operated top at a time when most convertible tops were powered. **2-3.** The roadster's rudimentary design didn't last long, however, as it became a proper convertible at midyear with the addition of roll-up side windows and vent panes. The spartan interior had a body-colored dashboard (vs. woodgrain paint on other models), vinyl upholstery, and rubber floormats, all in an effort to keep prices down. **4.** The least-expensive Dodge was the Wayfarer business coupe at $1611. But that was still $24 more than the previous year's DeLuxe business coupe, which was quite a bit larger. **5.** By far the most popular of the Wayfarer series was the $1738 two-door sedan, the only Wayfarer with a rear seat. It was also the most expensive, though it undercut Dodge's cheapest full-size car, the Meadowbrook four-door sedan, by $110.

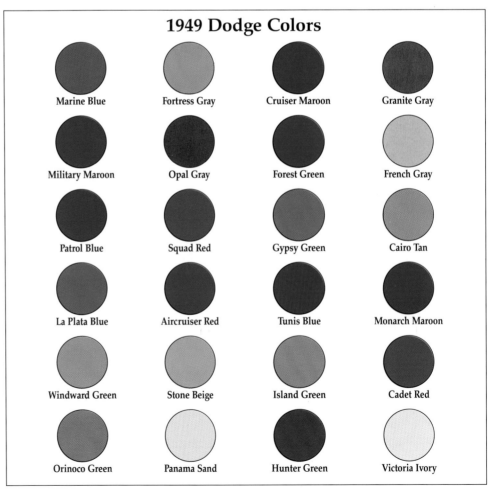

## 1949 Dodge Colors

| | | | |
|---|---|---|---|
| Marine Blue | Fortress Gray | Cruiser Maroon | Granite Gray |
| Military Maroon | Opal Gray | Forest Green | French Gray |
| Patrol Blue | Squad Red | Gypsy Green | Cairo Tan |
| La Plata Blue | Aircruiser Red | Tunis Blue | Monarch Maroon |
| Windward Green | Stone Beige | Island Green | Cadet Red |
| Orinoco Green | Panama Sand | Hunter Green | Victoria Ivory |

# Plymouth

"First Series" '49s are actually carryover '48s built after December 1, 1948

Completely redesigned "Second Series" '49s arrive in March 1949, with conservative styling

Flush front fenders and narrow rear fenders blend into wider bodies

All-steel wagon debuts

DeLuxe and Special DeLuxe series continue on two wheelbases: 111 inches and 118.5 inches

Familiar 218-cid six returns with two more horsepower, now 97

Despite conservative look and short model year, Plymouth holds onto 3rd place in industry with production of 520,385 cars

1

2

3

4

5

6

1-2. Although it's properly a 1949 model, this "First Series" DeLuxe club coupe is really a carryover '48. Built on a 117-inch wheelbase, it cost $1409. 3. The "Second Series" '49 lineup included a wood-sided Special DeLuxe wagon, Plymouth's most-expensive offering at $2372. All Special DeLuxe models rode a 118.5-inch wheelbase. 4. Lacking any wood trim was the two-door, all-steel Suburban wagon. Offered only in the DeLuxe series on the shorter 111-inch wheelbase, it listed for $1840, and outsold the four-door "woody" wagon nearly six-to-one. 5. An ad for Plymouth's full-size woody wagon points out its eight-passenger capacity, removable seats, and new body construction with steel floor and roof. 6. Other ads touted that Plymouth had hit "a new high in automotive value."

1

2

3

1-3. The $1629 Special DeLuxe four-door sedan was, by far, the most-popular car in the '49 line, topping the quarter-million mark in sales. This example lacks the whitewall tires usually seen (but not standard) on Special DeLuxe models, but does have the optional exterior sun visor and bumper-override bars. Dashboards featured round gauges, again surrounded by woodgrain paint. The DeLuxe club coupe and four-door sedan rode the same 118.5-inch wheelbase as the Special DeLuxe models, but lacked some of their chrome trim. The

4

5

ribbed bumpers used on '49 Plymouths later became popular with customizers. **4-6.** A convertible was again offered only in the Special DeLuxe series. Priced at $1982, it proved far more popular than ever before, selling nearly as many units in '49 as had been sold in the previous four years of postwar production. Dashboards were painted solid colors instead of the closed models' wood-grain, and seats were upholstered in vinyl rather than cloth. A power top was standard, and rear quarter windows appeared for the first time.

6

# Ford Motor Company

Styling for the 1949 Ford had begun early in 1946. Development costs approached $120 million, and the cars went on sale in mid-1948. Ford had solicited ideas from freelance designers, as well as from its in-house studio. George Walker, assisted by Richard Caleal, developed an integral-fender design. Final work, including the spinner-style grille, was accomplished with the assistance of Robert Bourke and Bob Koto, both borrowed from the Loewy Studios.

Hot rodders loved the '49 Ford, with its easy-to-modify flathead V-8 and available overdrive transmission. Customizers also liked the look, finding plenty of ways to alter it to their tastes.

Lincoln adapted an idea from customizers for its 1949 model: recessed, or "frenched," headlights. Dignified in profile, conservative in demeanor, yet abundantly curved, Lincolns came in basic or Cosmopolitan guise, the latter sporting a one-piece curved windshield. Instead of the familiar V-12, a flathead V-8 provided the power.

James Dean established the new Mercury coupe as a car to remember in *Rebel Without a Cause*. Smoothly curved, low and quick, the new Merc looked especially sharp in two-door form. The same body was used on smaller Lincolns. Model-year output set an all-time record, with 301,319 built.

# Ford

Modern styling with flow-through fenders earns credit for saving Ford Motor Company

Solid front axle finally replaced by independent suspension rear has longitudinal leafs

Models now called "Standard" and "Custom V8," both on 114-inch wheelbase

Six-cylinder and V-8 return with same power ratings

New design and long model year combine for 1.1 million sales, netting first place in industry

1

2

1. The body drop mated sleek new sheetmetal with an equally new ladder-type frame, though the old X-type frame was still used under convertibles and station wagons due to its greater strength. An independent A-arm front suspension with coil springs replaced the old tubular axle on a transverse leaf. In back, the rear axle was now mounted on longitudinal leaf springs instead of a transverse leaf. However, engine choices remained a 95-horsepower six or a 100-horse V-8. 2. Ford was betting the farm on the new '49s, so exercises such as this cold-weather test were vital. The gamble paid off: The new cars sold like hotcakes, saving the company from financial ruin.

**1.** Proclaiming it "The Car of the Year!"ads for the '49 Ford extolled virtues such as "Mid ship" ride, larger brakes, greater luggage space, wider seats, and better visibility. **2-3.** Prices were understandably up, with this Custom V-8 convertible listing for $1886. Dashboards were less ornate than before, being practically devoid of chrome trim **4.** Another convertible celebrates the one-millionth Ford built for 1949. Production would go on to reach 1,118,308, enough to catapult the company into first place in industry sales—though an 18-month model year helped. **5-6.** Customs far outsold the Standard models. The only exterior difference was a pair of "Custom" badges for the front fenders, so most of the extra $86 or so went for fancier interior trim. This Custom Fordor sedan cost $1559. **7.** Ford's most popular '49 was the Custom V-8 Tudor sedan, which started at $1511.

1

2

3

**1.** Ads promoted the new two-door wagon "With its heart of steel and the new Ford feel" as perfect for families. All models, including convertibles and wagons, could be ordered with either the six-cylinder or V-8 engine. **2-3.** Unlike previous Ford wagons, the new '49 had an all-steel body overlaid with molded plywood paneling—none of the wood was structural. It was only offered in the Custom series at $2119, making it Ford's most-expensive car. **4.** Now *that* guy loves his new Ford. When flood waters surrounded his house, an enterprising Canadian fashioned a sling for his car and hoisted it off the ground with a block-and-tackle suspended from a rather unsubstantial-looking tree limb. Perhaps he didn't realize a '49 Ford sedan weighed a bit over 3000 pounds. **5.** This Custom Tudor sedan sports several popular period accessories, including optional whitewall tires, front sun visor, fender skirts, and backup lamps. **6.** Body-colored wheels and lack of red striping on the grille distinguish a '49 F-1 pickup from a '48. **7.** "The Great Gildersleeve," a radio comedian, offered a new Ford to the person who came up with the best name for this little girl. The promotion was sponsored by Parkay "Oleo-margarine." **8.** A familiar sight to many youngsters growing up in the '50s was a Ford-based Good Humor truck. **9.** A Ford police car may have been a familiar sight to many ice-cream lovers' older brothers. **10.** A young Ricardo Montelban jacks up a '49 Ford in what was probably a Hollywood promotional shot.

4

5

6

7

8

9

10

285

# Lincoln

Redesigned envelope bodies have flow-through fenders and are shared with Mercury

Unitized structure gives way to body-on-frame

Independent front suspension with coil springs replaces beam axle; rear has longitudinal leafs

Wheelbase cut four inches to 121 on base model; uplevel Cosmopolitan stays at 125

Continental dropped

337-cid, 152-bhp V-8 replaces V-12; automatic transmission optional

New design and long model year produce 73,507 sales; Lincoln is 17th in industry

1

2

3

4

5

6

7

8

9

10

11

1. The base four-door sedan rode a shorter 121-inch wheelbase, but still weighed over two tons. It was priced at $2575, not much more than in '48. 2. Replacing Lincoln's venerable 125-horsepower, 292-cid flathead V-12 was a 152-horse, 337-cid flathead V-8 used the previous year in big Ford trucks. 3. Lincoln's least-expensive car, the base coupe, sold for $2527. Note the longitudinal chrome trim strip, which identified the base models. 4. The "senior" Cosmopolitan rode a 125-inch wheelbase and featured heavy chrome "eyelids" over the front wheel wells. This coupe sold for $3186. 5. A four-door Cosmopolitan sport sedan sold for $3238. Don't let the "sport" nomenclature fool you; it tipped the scales at more than 4200 pounds. 6. All four-door sedans retained the rear-hinged "suicide" back doors of their predecessors. 7. Ads called the new Lincoln Cosmopolitan "The most luxuriously comfortable car of all," extolling virtues such as the standard power windows and one-piece windshield. 8. The $3238 Cosmopolitan town sedan sported an unpopular fastback roofline, and it was discontinued before the year was out. 9. By far the priciest Lincoln was the $3948 Cosmopolitan convertible. 10. More affordable was the $3116 base convertible. 11. A Lincoln Cosmopolitan sport sedan was chosen as the basis for a stretched Presidential limousine. Note the Continental kit, duplicate "eyebrow" over the rear wheel well, and clear rear roof section mounted over the stacked convertible top.

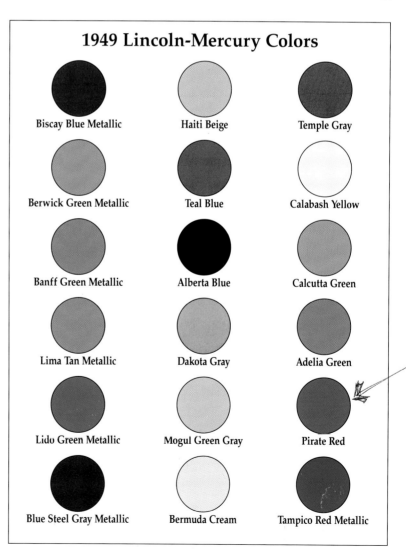

## 1949 Lincoln-Mercury Colors

| | | |
|---|---|---|
| Biscay Blue Metallic | Haiti Beige | Temple Gray |
| Berwick Green Metallic | Teal Blue | Calabash Yellow |
| Banff Green Metallic | Alberta Blue | Calcutta Green |
| Lima Tan Metallic | Dakota Gray | Adelia Green |
| Lido Green Metallic | Mogul Green Gray | Pirate Red |
| Blue Steel Gray Metallic | Bermuda Cream | Tampico Red Metallic |

# 1949

# Mercury

New envelope bodyshells shared with lower-line Lincolns save for wagon, which is shared with Ford

Coil-spring independent front suspension replaces beam axle; rear has longitudinal leafs

Wheelbase stays at 118 inches

V-8 grows from 239 to 255 cid, gains 10 horsepower to 110

New design and long model year move Mercury from 16th to 6th in industry on sales of 301,319

1

2

3

4

5

6

7

8

9

10

11

**1.** The factory was hopping as more than 301,000 Mercs came off the line in the long model year; the company had previously never topped 100,000 units. **2.** Benson Ford, Henry Ford II's brother and general manager of Lincoln-Mercury Division, looks pleased with this styling study of the '49 Merc. Note, however, that the model is rendered in a six-window fastback design that never materialized. **3. 6.** Mercury ads stated "Owners claim this long, low, handsome new Mercury is the best-looking car they've ever owned." **4-6.** The least-expensive Mercury was the $1979 club coupe. It would go on to become a favorite with hot-rodders. **7-9.** A new two-door wagon body style was shared with Ford. It was an all-steel structure with molded plywood paneling used to create that "woody" look. Interiors featured wood paneling on the doors and woodgrain paint on the dashboard. **10-11.** The only four-door in the line was the sport sedan, which sold for $2031. This one carries the optional front sun visor and rear fender skirts. **12.** Safety consciousness was growing: A boy on his bike and a roller-skating girl are the poster children for this sign that encourages drivers to "Watch out for Kids."

12

# General Motors

Buicks got a profile all their own for 1949—sleek and graceful—though the lower-priced Special kept the 1948 design. Harley Earl's Art & Colour Studio adapted aircraft-inspired "fuselage" styling, which saw the first use of Buick's trademark portholes. Buick offered one of the first pillarless hardtop coupes, named Riviera.

High-compression, overhead-valve V-8 engines went into Cadillacs and Oldsmobiles. Cadillac's V-8 weighed 188 pounds less than the previous L-head engine. A Cadillac could hit 60 mph in 13 seconds. Luxurious 75-series models got the new engine, but stuck with old-fashioned styling for one more year. The most striking body was the Coupe de Ville, a pillarless hardtop akin to Buick's Riviera and Oldsmobile's Holiday.

Chevrolet and Pontiac adopted two-piece curved windshields in their shapely new notchback and fastback bodies. Pontiacs offered six- or eight-cylinder engines. Cleanly styled, with flow-through fenders, Chevrolets were among the best-looking cars of the year.

Oldsmobiles got a smaller new V-8 than Cadillac, this one nicknamed "Rocket." Tucking the V-8 into a smaller 88-series body produced a swift machine. Stock-car racers devoured those 88s, which scored big at NASCAR events.

General Motors paid its 436,000 stockholders $190 million in dividends at year's end—the biggest ever to date in U.S. business.

# Buick

Super and Roadmaster completely redesigned on shorter wheelbases; Specials redone midyear

Roadmaster Riviera introduced with stylish hardtop

Dynaflow offered on Supers; Super's 248-cid inline 8 boosted to 120 bhp for Dynaflow cars

Roadmaster's 320-cid inline 8 now 150 bhp across the board

Model-year production of 324,276 up 52 percent; Buick regains 4th place in industry

Around about Autumn

Buick ROADMASTER with Dynaflow Drive

1

1. Buick claimed to be "The Buy in Big Cars." This ad shows buying a Buick was more than just a car purchase; it was a lifestyle choice. 2. Although Buick fell to third in convertible output, the Super convertible outpaced 1948 production by more than 3000 units. 3-4. The new Roadmaster Riviera, with its pillarless hardtop, became a style leader as soon as it hit showroom floors late in the model year. Early models had straight side trim as seen on Buick's other models; later cars received the sweep-spear side trim shown here. Riviera production for 1949 was only 4343 units, but that would grow drastically in the next two years. 5. All Buicks sported a new asymmetrical dash with controls below the right-hand instruments. 6. Starting in mid-July, the Riviera's sweep-spear trim was available on Roadmaster convertibles at extra cost. Roadmaster ragtop prices jumped $313 to $3150.

2

3

4

5

6

1

2

3

**1.** Buick's first redesign since before World War II shortened Roadmaster's wheelbase three inches to 126. "VentiPorts," more commonly known as portholes, made their debut with the '49s; Roadmasters had four and Supers and Specials had three. Buick claimed the holes helped cool the engine; actually, they did for the first few months, but thereafter they were plugged. Portholes found their roots on styling chief Ned Nickles' '48 Roadmaster. He installed amber lights behind his and wired them to the distributor so they would flash on and off. Division chief Harlow Curtice liked the look, and had them added to the '49s minus the lights. **2.** The second-most-popular Buick was the Super two-door sedanet. Dynaflow automatic transmission was now available on Supers; Supers so equipped came with five more horsepower. **3-4.** The new station wagon body used far less wood than in previous years. Estate wagons came in Super (*shown*) or Roadmaster form. Overall, wagon sales were down, partially due to price; the Super wagon cost $3178, almost $600 more than the next closest Super, the convertible.

4

# Cadillac

Minor facelift includes new grille, hood, trim

Revolutionary new 331-cid, overhead-valve, short-stroke, high-compression V-8 introduced; makes 160 horsepower

Series 62 Coupe de Ville introduced with stylish hardtop

One-millionth Cadillac built November 25, 1949

Model-year production up 76 percent to 92,554 for new record; Cadillac up to 15th place in industry

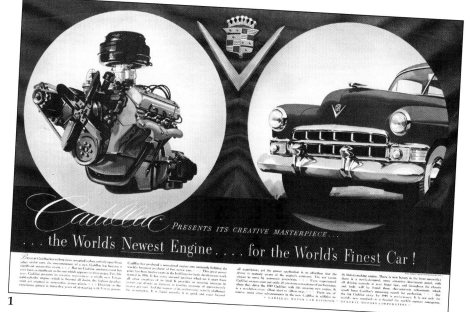

1

2

3

4

5

1. Cadillac knew it had a story on its hands with its 331-cid V-8, as this 1949 ad shows. A new piston design allowed for a shorter stroke in a smaller package. Compression was up to 7.5:1 and it would climb in the coming years as higher-octane gasoline was made available. The new engine put out 160 bhp, up 10 from 1948, and gas mileage increased 20 percent. 2. Cadillac's best-seller in a record year was the Series 62 four-door sedan. Stone shields behind the front wheel wells and chrome rocker moldings differentiated 62s from Series 61s. 3. The three chrome strips below the taillights of '48 Series 62s were gone in '49. Here, the $2966 Series 62 two-door fastback club coupe. 4. Cadillac produced a pamphlet devoted to its new engine, noting the more than one-million miles of testing it had endured. 5. The Series 75 models returned for one more year in their 1941 configuration. The redesign would have to wait until 1950, but at least the '49s got the new Cadillac V-8. Prices started at $4750.

1

2

3

4

5

7

8

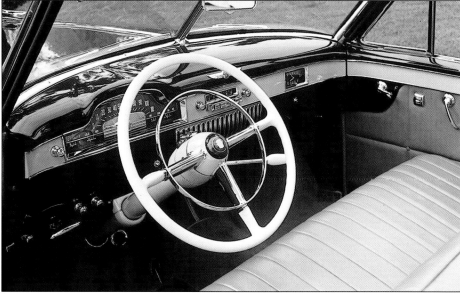

6

1. Cadillac's 1949 grille was wider and lower than the previous version, now featuring one horizontal bar and five vertical bars, down from two and seven, respectively. 2. A late-year release, the Series 62 Coupe de Ville hardtop earned accolades for its styling. At $3497, the price of admission was high, though; it cost only $26 less than the convertible. 3. The idea for GM's hardtops (Buick and Olds had them, too) is said to have originated with the wife of a GM executive. She liked the open feel of a convertible but didn't want the wind to mess her hair. The hardtop was designed to combine convertible sportiness with coupe practicality. 4. Cadillac's 1948 dashboard had only a one-year run. The '49 unit was redesigned with a hooded, more-conventional look. 5. Development of Cadillac's overhead valve V-8 started way back in 1936. The resulting engine was 200 pounds lighter, five inches shorter and four inches lower than the previous L-head V-8. 6. The 1949 Cadillac brochure claimed that the the '49 was "The most beautiful Cadillac ever built." 7-8. Convertible sales jumped to 8000 units, a 47-percent increase. 9. Power windows and a power driver seat were standard on convertibles and optional on other models.

9

# Chevrolet

First postwar car redesign sports slab-sided styling; cars available in bustleback and fastback designs

Fleetline name designates fastback design in both series; Styleline designates bustlebacks

Stylemaster series renamed Special; Fleetmaster becomes DeLuxe

Cars don't change mechanically, but wheelbase down one inch to 115

Steel-bodied station wagon debuts; woody wagon still available until midyear

Model-year production up 45 percent to 1,010,013; Chevrolet sets new company record but falls to 2nd in industry sales behind Ford

1

2

3

4

5

6

7

8

9

10

1. New Chevrolets prepare to sail from Detroit to Cleveland aboard the steamer *T.J. McCarthy.* 2. Fleetline no longer designated Chevy's top series; instead it meant fastback styling. This Fleetline DeLuxe four-door sedan is decked out with headlamp shades, windshield visor, wheel-trim rings, and wide whitewalls. 3. Chevrolets were popular with the American public because they mimicked higher line GM style at a lower price. As this ad shows, Chevy was aware of its competitive advantage. 4. Styleline denoted bustleback or notchback styling, and the series were renamed (base) Special and (high line) DeLuxe. The Styleline DeLuxe sport coupe stickered for $1508. Two-tones were optional on Stylelines, but weren't offered on Fleetlines. 5. Chevrolet only offered convertibles as DeLuxe Styleline models; prices started at $1857. 6. Symmetry was history on '49 Chevy dashboards as the instruments were clustered into a single circular unit. 7. Chevy's last woody, the Styleline DeLuxe station wagon, used less wood than previous models. A full steel-bodied wagon replaced the woody midyear. 8-9. The Styleline DeLuxe four-door sedan (*left*) outsold its Fleetline counterpart (*right*) by more than 10,000 units, the first signs of a trend toward notchback popularity. The new cars had 30-percent-more windshield glass area, and passenger accommodations were moved forward so nobody would sit above the rear axle. 10. Chevy pickups were unchanged after 1948's redesign. Painted bumpers were standard; chrome was optional.

# Oldsmobile

All cars adopt Futuramic styling

Olds introduces 303-cid Rocket V-8, a revolutionary short-stroke, high-compression, overhead-valve engine that makes 135 horsepower

Six-cylinder engine increased to 257 cid and 105 horsepower

Model lineup pared to 76, 88, and 98

76 and 88 ride 119.5-inch wheelbase; 98 still 125

Holiday hardtop coupe added to 98 lineup

76 series gets fastback styling

Steel-bodied station wagon debuts; woody wagon still available until midyear

88 convertible paces Indianapolis 500

Oldsmobiles win six of nine NASCAR Grand National races

Model-year production of 288,310 up 67 percent; Oldsmobile reclaims 7th place in industry sales

1

2

3

**1.** Though only a few months old, a few trim changes were made to the 98s. As shown on this 98 DeLuxe club sedan, Olds removed the door and front fender-side trim strips, added rear fender-top trim, deleted the "8" designation from the decklid, and placed "Futuramic" lettering on the forward portion of the rocker-panel trim. **2.** Interior appointments of the 98 series' DeLuxe package included two-tone upholstery, a rear-seat armrest, deluxe instrument cluster, aluminum sill plates, deluxe floormats front and rear, an electric clock, and a deluxe steering wheel. **3-4.** The Olds Rocket V-8 (along with Cadillac's new V-8) changed the way the industry thought about engines. With a 90-degree

4

5

6

7

overhead-valve design, a short stroke, and a high compression ratio, the new 303-cid engine put out 135 horsepower. It was designed to take advantage of the higher-octane fuels that were on the way, and had the potential for much larger bores yielding even more power. **5-6.** Olds, like Cadillac and Buick, offered a hardtop coupe late in the year named Holiday. The price was $2973, same as the 98 convertible. **7.** All 98 ragtops came with Deluxe appointments. **8.** Oldsmobile's best-seller, the 98 four-door sedan, combined for sales of 57,821 in standard and Deluxe trim.

8

1

2

3

4

5

6

7

1. All-steel bodies replaced the steel and wood bodies on station wagons late in the year. Wagons were offered in the 76 and 88 series. This 76 woody wagon sold for $2895, almost $750 more than the next-closest 76 series car. 2-3. All station wagons featured DeLuxe appointments and leather interiors. Cargo capacity was 80 cubic feet with the rear seat folded down. 4. Series 76 models, like this club coupe, lacked "Futuramic" lettering on the rocker-panel molding. 5. Olds offered two types of four-door sedans in the 76 and 88 series, a fastback (*shown*) and a notchback. The "88" on this car's rear quarter panel appeared on the front quarter of some models. 6-7. Olds supplied two Rocket 88 pace cars for the '49 Indy 500, one white, the other maroon. Both had large chrome rockets on the front fenders that were designed to produce a smoke trail during the pace lap. That idea was discarded, but the rockets remained. Wilbur Shaw paced the race in the white car. 8. Years of strong car sales, a burgeoning economy, more paved highways, and city growth created what would become a staple of Los Angeles life—traffic jams.

8

# Pontiac

Line is completely redesigned, with flow-through-fender styling similar to that of new-for-'48 Cadillacs

Pontiac's two-wheelbase arrangement is dropped in favor of 120-inch wheelbase for all models

Sedan delivery offered—the division's first truck since the 1920s

Notchback body styles switch names from Torpedo to Chieftain; fastbacks continue as Streamliners

Price of optional Hydra-Matic automatic transmission is reduced $26 to $159; roughly three-quarters of '49 Pontiac buyers choose it

Model-year production up 29 percent to 304,819; Pontiac maintains 5th-place industry ranking

1

2

3

4

1. Smiles abound for Pontiac's first truly new car since 1942. All models rode a 120-inch wheelbase, which split the difference between the previous 119- and 122-inch designs. Chieftain notchbacks and Streamliner fastbacks were offered, in standard and DeLuxe versions. Shown here is the Chieftain four-door sedan in standard trim. 2. Convertibles were part of the Chieftain series and, as before, were available in DeLuxe trim only. They started at $2138 with the six. 3. For roughly $95 extra, most models came in a DeLuxe version, as shown on this Chieftain four-door. The uplevel package included more exterior brightwork and a better interior. 4. Pontiac brochures boasted the "Finest of new features in the smartest of cars." Listed among new extras was "Travelux Ride." Puffery aside, the cars did incorporate significant ideas aimed at improved ride comfort. Most notable was a more-forward-mounted engine, which allowed passengers to sit ahead of the rear axle.

1

3

2

4

## 1949 Pontiac Colors

Starlight Blue

Sheffield Gray

Rio Red

Blue Lake Blue

Wellington Green

Parma Wine

Nankeen Cream

Sage Green

Coventry Gray

Mayan Gold

5

1-2. A Chieftain four-door sedan shows the '49's lower profile, due in part to the switch from 16- to 15-inch wheels. 3-4. Streamliner four-door sedans started at $1740 with the six, $1808 with the eight. 5. A small amount of wood was still used in Pontiac wagons, but unlike previous designs, most of the '49's doors and all of its roof were steel. Later in the model year, steel panels covered with simulated wood replaced this last remaining cabinetwork. 6. Pillarless Pontiacs were still a year away, but the "Special Catalina Coupe" (*left*) gave an early peek. This would materialize for 1950 as the Catalina hardtop. The showcase and chandelier next to it attempt to lend some drama to the inline-eight engine, but it was unchanged from '48, as was the six. 7. The Chieftain coupe sedan started at $1710. This one sports DeLuxe trim, along with an accessory sun visor. 8. Pontiac had last dabbled with trucks in 1928 and decided to give it another try, offering a sedan delivery for '49. Alas, history repeated itself, and it found only 2488 buyers.

6

7

8

# Hudson

It was billed as "the modern design for '49." Except for the addition of a Super Eight Brougham, though, little was new in the Step-Down's second season. Prices started out identical to the 1948 figures, but were then cut a bit as availability of some raw materials improved. Profits dropped to $10.1 million, due in part to a loss in parts/accessory income. Model-year production rose sharply, topping 159,000 units.

Hudson's spring sales campaign promised a "Revelation Ride" in the latest Step-Down. As part of its 40th anniversary, in April, Hudson sponsored a national radio broadcast to promote the brand, opened by Michigan Governor G. Mennen Williams. Company president A.E. Barit held a press conference in June to discuss the potential of the Super Six engine. Should 100-octane fuel become available, he claimed, the six-cylinder engine could withstand a compression ratio up to 12.5:1.

Body styling is unaltered

Company is hit by a strike, supplier strikes, and a heat wave

L-head Super Six is made more efficient; 7.12:1 compression ratio is optional

Hudson announces its commitment to L-head sixes and eights, rather than overhead-valve engines

Brougham model is added to Super Eight series

Model-year production up 36 percent to 159,100 as Hudson climbs to 9th in industry sales

1

2

3

4

1. Hudson spent a fortune to redesign its entire line for 1948, so it's no surprise that the company stood pat for '49. What changes there were could be found inside the cars: leather-grained trim on armrests and other surfaces, a nonglare dashtop, and other pleasing touches. 2. Hudson celebrated its 40th anniversary in 1949, and made hay with a little publicity. Here, A.E. Barit and other Hudson execs sit in a new Commodore Custom Brougham convertible ($3041), while lesser mortals occupy an '09 model. 3. The entire line, like this Super Six sedan, stuck with the previous year's 124-inch wheelbase. Note that window cranks and armrests were recessed into the door panels, to increase interior room. 4-5. At $2952, the Commodore Six convertible was expensive, which helps to explain why only an estimated 655 were produced. The inline six remained unchanged linewide: 262 cid, 121 bhp. Inside, ragtops gained the front-seatback storage pouches that had previously been available only on closed Hudsons. 6-7. This Super Six business coupe has plenty of add-ons: spotlight, side-view mirrors, rear bumper guard, and venetian blinds. An unadorned example would have sold for $2053. 8-9. This one-off, custom-bodied Commodore Eight by Derham featured a padded roof, an interior glass partition, and a reduced backlight.

5

6

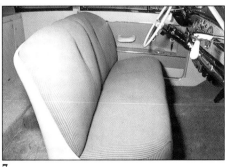

7

8

9

# Kaiser-Frazer

After two years in their original form, both makes were restyled in 1949 by a team under Bob Cadwalloder. Two completely new body styles appeared. One was a four-door convertible, marketed first as a Frazer Manhattan and later as a member of the Kaiser DeLuxe series.

If that wasn't startling enough, the company also launched a Frazer Manhattan four-door hardtop—years ahead of the major automakers—fitted with a cloth-covered roof. Another new-

comer was the Kaiser Traveler utility sedan, with a fold-down back seat and hatchback rear—and a left rear door that was welded shut.

Because the Big Three auto companies now had truly new postwar models on sale, no 1949 Kaiser-Frazer product sold well. In fact, Kaiser-Frazer had to borrow from the Reconstruction Finance Corporation to stay afloat—and to develop the forthcoming compact Henry J sedan. Edgar Kaiser was named president this year.

Restyle includes wider, more-massive grille and large, horizontal taillights

Upmarket Special DeLuxe is added

A utility sedan, the Special Traveler, is introduced

A DeLuxe convertible is added to Kaiser and Frazer lines

Redesigned dash becomes ornate, with giant speedo

Kaiser outsells Frazer by almost four-to-one

Model-year production: Kaiser down 13 percent to 79,947 for 16th in industry; Frazer down 56 percent to 21,223 for 18th

Combined model-year production down 28 percent

1

2

1. On August 29, 1948, Henry Kaiser and Joe Frazer (*right*) came to Willow Run to observe their first '49, a Kaiser, roll off the K-F line. 2. Willow Run's "body bank." 3. A $10 million cosmetic redesign made the '49 Kaisers, like this luxurious, $2995 DeLuxe (formerly the Custom series) Virginian hardtop sedan, appear wider and lower, though the cars were the same height as in 1948. The trick was added body overhang, and a full-width horizontal grille. Taillights also grew. 4-5. Kaiser's sole '49 convertible was the four-door DeLuxe Virginian, which, at $3195, saw production of barely more than 50. The glovebox clock was standard on DeLuxe models. 6. Kaiser DeLuxe four-door sedan. 7. Kaiser's $2088 Special-series Traveler utility sedan was as plain as its name suggests, but more than 22,000 were made. 8-10. Kaiser-Frazer never made a true wagon, but the Traveler and DeLuxe-series Vagabond utility sedan (*shown*) were as close as it ever got. 11. A DeLuxe four-door sedan was marketed as a taxi in limited numbers. 12. A Vagabond, with pop-up tent!

3

4

5

6

7

8

9

10

11

12

**1.** Frazer production for 1949 totaled about 24,900, hardly better than a quarter of the year's Kaiser output. Overall, Frazer sales dropped by about 40 percent from '48. The eggcrate grille; rectangular parking lights; and large, dual-lens vertical taillights were new. The hood badging rode lower than in '48. All '49 Frazers had the more powerful (112 bhp) of K-F's 226-cid inline sixes. **2.** An interestingly impressionistic ad for the Frazer Manhattan describes the sedan as "the pride of Willow Run." **3-4.** Frazer's Manhattan convertible sedan, with standard fender skirts, didn't arrive in showrooms until January 1949. Only about 70 of the $3295 ragtop were built. A hood ornament was a first-time Frazer option this year. **5-7.** The Frazer Manhattan four-door sedan, like all '49s, had new chrome beneath the door handles and double chrome strips at the rocker panels. This car's electric clock, radio and antenna, twin spotlights, fog lamps, whitewalls, hood ornament, and two-tone paint were factory options.

# Nash

A 1949 Nash ad promised "cockpit control" and "airplane-type seats," its headline screaming "Now—Everybody Wants It!" Just about everyone was stunned by Nash's new look.

First Studebaker, then Hudson, and now Nash—three radical designs from three independent companies. None of the Big Three automakers had anything as sensational-looking, even with their brand-new postwar models now on sale. Whether the new Nash Airflyte, whose unique fastback profile soon earned the derisive appellation "bathtub Nash," qualified as beautiful is another question.

All four wheels were enclosed in the unibody design, which came only in sedan form. People wondered how a flat tire could be changed, but it wasn't that much of a problem. Two six-cylinder engines were available, but coupes and convertibles were extinct. Sales reached a record 142,592, for a $26 million profit (though that figure included earnings from the company's Kelvinator appliance division).

Complete redesign introduces genuinely aerodynamic "Airflyte" styling

First postwar Nash two-door bows

One-piece curved windshield standard on all models

All-new "Uniscope" instrument panel is introduced

Twin convertible beds standard on two-door sedans

Model-year production up 23 percent to 135,328 as Nash climbs to 10th in industry sales

1

2

1-2. Indie automakers were forced to take enormous risks to remain competitive, and their gambles paid off surprisingly often, as with Nash's radical '49 Airflyte. The new car had unibody construction, functional streamlining (just 113 pounds of drag at 60 mph), a one-piece curved windshield, a novel "Uniscope" gauge pod, and flow-through "Weather-Eye" ventilation. The remarkable "bathtub" styling was mainly the work of Holden "Bob" Koto, with an assist from Ted Pietsch. Airflyte came in two series: 600 and uplevel Ambassador.

# 1949 Nash

1

3

4

5

6

**1949
Nash
Colors**

Ashland Green Light
Nile Green Light

Steel Blue Dark
Horizon Blue Medium

Seal Brown Dark
Fawn Brown Medium

Blue Black
Nash Ivory

Yukon Gray Dark
Peru Gray Light

310

2

7

1-4. Airflyte styling inspired debate in 1949, and still sparks lively argument today. To many eyes, the design seems simply the logical extension of the bathtub look that had been successfully exploited by Packard and Hudson. The Airflytes certainly had buyer appeal, with sales of 130,000 units, which was sufficient to put Nash in a lofty tenth-place position for 1949. This Ambassador Super four-door sedan has optional side-view mirrors, hood ornament, tailpipe extension, radio and antenna, and rayon-twill seat panels. Full-recline front seatbacks were standard. Ambassador's 121-inch wheelbase was nine inches longer than that of the similar 600 because of an elongated front end. 5. Nash's assembly line; note the chalk notation on the fenderwell of the lead sedan, which identifies it as a Custom submodel. 6. Here, a "bathtub" caravan, about to head out to happy Nash dealers. 7. Those standard fold-down front seats were popular with family men—and single fellas, too. 8. Ambassador Brougham two-door. 9. The turn radius of all Nashes, including this Ambassador two-door sedan, was compromised by the "archless" front wheel openings.

8

9

| | | | | |
|---|---|---|---|---|
| Guiana Green Medium Everglade Green Dark | Seal Brown Dark Nile Green Light | Marlin Blue | Sunset Maroon Light | Arlington Gray Light |

# Packard

Packard celebrated its half-century of production in 1949, issuing a line of "Golden Anniversary" cars midyear that got enough of a facelift to become the Twenty-Third series. Except for a back window that was 33 percent larger, few details were significantly different from 1948. A new "Goddess of Speed" mascot went on the hood. Inside, oval clutch and brake pedals were installed.

The new models didn't go on sale until May 1949. Sales of the "still-pregnant" Packards remained strong into 1949, before starting a precipitous decline. Revenue was lost when Packard's government contract to build jet engines expired.

To mark the anniversary, Nash painted 2000 cars in a custom gold color and gathered them at the company's Proving Grounds in Utica, Michigan. An Ultramatic automatic transmission became standard in Custom Eight Packards late in the year, then in lesser models as well.

First Series '49s are visually identical to '48s

Second Series '49s get chrome beltline and oval taillights; considered Packard's Twenty-Third series models

Packard celebrates its 50th Anniversary; 2000 gold cars are commissioned for publicity purposes

Ultramatic two-speed automatic transmission is introduced on Second-Series cars

Super Eight wheelbase now 127 inches, up 7

President George Christopher resigns in October; is replaced by Hugh Ferry

Model-year production up 26 percent to 116,248; Packard holds at 13th in industry sales

1

2

3

5

4

6

7

**1-2.** Packard introduced its 50th-anniversary line in two increments. First-Series models were unchanged from 1948. Midyear Second-Series cars sported chromed front-bumper centers, "PACKARD" block lettering, narrow chrome sidespears, larger rear windows, and oval taillight housings. The news, however, was Ultramatic Drive, the only automatic transmission developed by an independent without outside help. This Super Eight four-door sedan is from the First Series. It rides a 120-inch wheelbase; other wheelbases were 127, 141, and 148. Horsepower of the 288- and 327-cid inline eights rose by five, to 135 and 150. Super Eights started at $2827. Whitewalls and a radio with antenna were extra-cost options. **3.** Tender care from the friendly guys at Texaco. **4.** As this ad shows, Packard was still trying to change its image from a luxury brand to a midprice make. **5-6.** The Super Eight Victoria convertible was the only '49 Packard ragtop with a horizontal, rather than eggcrate, grille. Price was $3250; production, 1237. **7-8.** The $2383 DeLuxe Eight four-door sedan arrived midyear.

8

# 1949

# Studebaker

Even the most striking designs can start to turn stale after a year or two. Except for a revised grille, Studebakers looked about the same as in 1947-48. The Commander's engine was enlarged, and the spare tire sat vertically in the trunk to yield more cargo space.

Studebaker now had two serious rivals—Hudson and Nash—in addition to fresh models from the Big Three automobile manufacturers. Management contracted with Borg-Warner for a new automatic transmission, to be readied for Studebaker's 1950 models.

Tom McCahill, the caustic auto critic from *Mechanix Illustrated* magazine, had kind words about Studebakers. "If there's any place where pride in workmanship still exists in the auto industry," he wrote, "it's in the Studebaker plant." Actually, Studebaker suffered its first formal strike early in January, as 16,000 workers walked out to protest a series of firings. But the stoppage was short-lived. Profits set a record at $27.5 million.

All models have wrap-around bumpers, front and rear

Upholstery and body-color choices are expanded

Studebaker wagon, with body by Cantrell, debuts

Anticipating design change-over for 1950, Stude limits model-year production to 129,298; down 30 percent as Studebaker falls to 11th in industry sales

1

2

3

4

5

6

7

1. Studebaker's top-line Commander series wasn't really a luxury car, but it did field a larger engine for the first time since 1938, a 246-cid inline six with 100 horsepower (up from 226/94). 2. The '49 lineup carried on as it had since 1947, with two series: base Champion and uplevel Commander. Clockwise from top left: Commander Regal DeLuxe Starlight coupe, three-passenger Champion DeLuxe coupe, Commander Regal DeLuxe ragtop, Champion Regal DeLuxe two-door sedan, Commander Regal DeLuxe four-door sedan, and Commander Regal DeLuxe Land Cruiser. 3. Wraparound front and rear bumpers, as seen on this Champion Starlight coupe, were now standard on all Studebakers. 4-6. The $1731 Champion Regal DeLuxe coupe cost hundreds more than comparable Fords and Chevys, but was a solid car that could be nicely optioned; this one has twin spotlights, whitewalls, radio, electric clock, and Hill Holder. 7. This 1949 DuPont antifreeze ad is drawn in the style of popular cartoonist Jimmy "They'll Do It Every Time" Hatlo. 8. Borg-Warner's new automatic transmission was endorsed by Indy champ Wilbur Shaw.

8

# Willys

Willys-Overland launched a new four-wheel-drive version of its all-steel wagon—the first vehicle to combine 4WD and the utility-wagon body style. In fact, this Jeep wagon could be considered the grandfather of today's ubiquitous sport-utility vehicles.

Jeepsters lost some equipment in their second year. Whitewall tires, overdrive, and even the unique grille treatment became optional rather than standard fare. For shoppers who bemoaned the previous model's lack of power, a six-cylin-

der engine was newly available.

Parts shortages hurt Willys production periodically throughout the year, due largely to strikes at supplier companies. What kept sales down the most, though, was a dwindling supply of interested buyers. Consumers had a lot more to choose from in 1949, including some appealing new steel-bodied station wagons from major automakers. Despite the addition of new models, total Willys-Overland sales dropped to 82,865 units as buyers looked elsewhere.

Four-wheel-drive wagon debuts midyear—first SUV

Six-cylinder Jeepster debuts

Two new engines: 134-cid F-head four, and 149-cid L-head six, both 72 bhp

W-O purchases forge and stamping plant to decrease reliance on outside suppliers

Model-year production: 32,928, plus 31,595 Jeeps and 18,342 commercial vehicles

**1.** Rear power takeoff, a $90.87 option, allowed the hardy Jeep CJ 2A to operate a variety of farm machinery. Other buyers were attracted by the vehicle's spartan, bohemian air. With the windshield in the "up" position, for instance, the passenger-side wiper blade had to be operated manually. **2-3.** Starting midyear, the Willys wagon could be had on a new 104.5-inch wheelbase; the two-door design, though, limited practicality. **4.** Willys introduced its first F-head engine—a 72-bhp, 134-cid four—and offered it in the '49 Jeepster. A Jeepster with a 149-cid, 72-bhp inline six became available as well. Four-cylinder Jeepster production was 2307; 653 sixes were made. These phaeton-only cars were priced at $1495 with the four and $1530 with the six.

# Minor Makes
## AND IMPORTS

Restyled with integral fenders and a smooth hood, Crosleys were much better cars in 1949. For one thing, an engine with a cast-iron block replaced the problematic COBRA. A Hotshot roadster debuted, and Crosleys gained disc brakes, which unfortunately proved troublesome, deteriorating when exposed to road salt.

Europe continued to emphasize small, low-cost automobiles. In 1949, more than 12,000 imported cars were sold in the U.S. The first two Volkswagen Beetles reached America from Germany. Britain began to send over the new Morris Minors and Triumph 2000s, as well as the sleek Jaguar XK-120. France was exporting the tiny Renault 4CV.

Kurtis-Kraft, a California race-car maker, announced a new sports car. Most new and recent American makes were even less-known. Not many people today remember the Imp or Del Mar, the Delcar wagon, or the fenderless Cubster. The two-passenger Hoppenstand lasted two seasons, as did the little wood-bodied Pup.

1

2

3

**1.** A massive chassis, a twincam six (160 gross horsepower), and a modern envelope body with integral fenders were new for Jaguar in '49. The swoopy lines were the work of Jag founder Sir William Lyons. **2.** The Mark V was Jaguar's first new postwar saloon. It ran with a pair of sixes —163 cid (105 bhp) and 213 cid (125 bhp)—and was a capable rally competitor. **3.** The Morris Minor saloon was uniquely emblematic of the "democratic" side of postwar British car production. This one, running with a 919cc four, could reach 62 mph. **4.** Triumph's 1800 Series offered saloon and convertible models for '49. It was faintly bulky, and slow, to boot. **5.** With the VW factory in Germany completely repaired, 43,633 split-window Beetles were made for 1949, up from 19,244 a year earlier.

4

5

1

1. Crosley introduced a sports car, the Hot Shot (*right*) for '49, and fresh styling on existing models, distinguished by new front sheetmetal that included a freshly contoured hood, complete with medallion. Wheel-arch contours were reshaped, and wraparound bumpers, following current automotive styling, were added. 2. Following success as a builder of Indy cars, Frank Curtis entered the sports-car market with the Kurtis 500, a fiberglass-bodied cutie that could be had with almost any engine the buyer wished; most were fitted with a modified Ford V-8 of 239 cubes and 110 bhp. The 500 could be purchased as a kit, or finished. Thirty-six were built during 1949-50. 3. The Cubster came with a racing chassis and an optional body. 4. Just 102 inches overall, the boxy Delcar, from Troy, New York, had room for six. 5. Fewer than 10 of the Del Mar subcompact were built. Bodies were aluminum, steel, and plastic. 6. The fiberglass Imp was 475 pounds and went 35 mph. 7. The curvy Hoppenstand was aluminum-bodied. 8. The Pup came as roadster and a slab-sided coupe (*shown*), both wood-bodied.

2

3

4

5

6

7

8

# Index